The Essen
Lenten Handbook

The Essential Lenten Handbook

A DAILY COMPANION

A REDEMPTORIST PASTORAL PUBLICATION

Liguori
LIGUORI, MISSOURI

Compiled by Thomas M. Santa, C.Ss.R.
Published by Liguori Publications
Liguori, Missouri
http://www.liguori.org

The compiler and publisher gratefully acknowledge permission to reprint/ reproduce copyrighted works granted by the publishers/sources listed on pages 287–288.

Library of Congress Cataloging-in-Publication Data

Santa, Thomas M.
    The essential lenten handbook : a daily companion / compiled by Thomas M. Santa, C.Ss.R.—1st ed.
        p.   cm. — (A Redemptorist pastoral publication)
    ISBN 0-7648-0567-3 (pbk.)
    1. Lent. 2. Lent—Prayer-books and devotions—English. 3. Catholic Church—Prayer-books and devotions—English. I. Santa, Thomas M., 1952– II. Series.
BX2170.L4 E77   2000
263'.92—dc21   99–041170

Copyright 2000 by Liguori Publications
Printed in the United States of America
04 03 02 01 00   5 4 3 2

Acknowledgments

This book would not have been possible without the contributions of the members of the Redemptorist Pastoral Publication team and the publications staff at Liguori Publications. Each contributed to this collection in his or her own special way. Father Paul Coury and Brother Dan Korn need to be singled out for praise, since each of them contributed to this handbook the fruits of their own reflections and prayer. It is my hope that this book is useful to all who travel on their spiritual journeys. Perhaps, as a result of this effort, your celebration of the Easter feast will be a time of blessing for you and for the members of your family.

Contents

Contents

Contents

Section Five: Modern Practices and Prayers for Lent 101

Section Six: Daily Meditations for Lent 135

Contents

How to Use This Book

L *ent. Forty days before Easter. Ashes. Penance. Fasting. Giving up something that is enjoyable. Completion of the Easter Duty. Penance services. Parish missions. Stations of the Cross. Purple vestments. Palm Sunday. Passion of the Lord. Good Friday.*

Each of the symbols, experiences, and expectations listed above somehow comprises the popular understanding of that time of the year identified as Lent. For some people, each concept is necessary for a full experience of Lent, and for still others a selection from the "liturgical menu" provided for observance of the season is enough. Whether it is the "full course" or perhaps only an "appetizer," it seems that some sort of effort and participation is called for when Lent comes around.

What may be most important, and perhaps the different images listed above may serve as a reminder, is that there is something different about the period of time known as the season of Lent. There is no other time period in the liturgical year that so completely focuses the attention of people on the great religious themes and traditions of Western Christian practice. It is certainly an appropriate focus despite popular and secular promotions that have otherwise focused on Christmas and the shopping season associated with that feast, for it is Easter that is truly the primary feast of Christianity.

Acknowledging the importance of the season is one thing, responding appropriately is yet another. Perhaps it is one of the signs of the times that we live in, a time filled with all sorts of demands on personal time and activity, or perhaps it is just the human condition, but for whatever reason we often seem unprepared when Ash Wednesday is suddenly upon us. In some years, when Easter is celebrated as late as the third week of April, Ash Wednesday does not occur until the first week of March. However, in other years, because Easter is a movable feast day (not celebrated on the same date every year as is Christmas, for example), we can find ourselves in the Lenten season as early as the first week of February. The Christmas tree has been barely packed away, and the charge-card bills have yet to be paid!

This handbook is conceived as an essential reference for the season of Lent, and for the reader's spiritual preparation for the feast of Easter. Every effort has been made to collect in one resource prayers, practices, and customs, in short, all that may be needed to provide you with the opportunity to journey with the Lord from Ash Wednesday to Holy Thursday, the beginning of the Easter Triduum. You will have your choice of prayers and devotions that in the best sense of the word are understood as traditional, many of which are prayers that are hundreds of years old. In addition, you will be introduced to prayers and devotions that are modern, contemporary expressions of ancient themes and truths.

Central to this collection is a series of daily meditations, based on the changing liturgical cycle, which provide an opportunity to journey through the season with Scripture and the Word. The meditations are a contemporary reflection, weaving together story, anecdote, and practical wisdom, in order to provide a springboard for private prayer and meditation.

Because this collection is a representative sampling of that which is old and that which is new, suggestions for the possible use of the handbook may be helpful. What follows are two "maps" that may be useful for charting your own personal Lenten spiritual journey and one "map" for a family journey guided by a family leader.

The Traditional Model In this plan, an emphasis is placed on using the resources provided that are time-tested and true. The presumption of the traditional plan is that repetition is useful and productive in the spiritual journey.

First thing in the morning pray the assigned prayer for the particular day of the week, from Section Four, "Traditional Prayers Appropriate for Lent." Each day include the praying of the Our Father, the Hail Mary, and the verse and response provided at the conclusion of the prayer designated for that particular day of the week. At some time during the day, perhaps in the afternoon when you are able to get a few moments of quiet, choose from Section Two, "Traditional Practices of Lent," one of the meditations provided by Saint Alphonsus Liguori. Each evening, before you retire for the night, pray from Section Four, a prayer to commemorate the seven last words of Jesus. One prayer may be prayed each day. In addition, pray an act of faith, hope, and love, and the traditional Confiteor, also from Section Four. When the appropriate time is presented, use the examination of conscience from Section Two in preparation for your celebration of the sacrament of reconciliation.

The Contemporary Model In this plan, an emphasis is placed on the resources provided that may be categorized as "modern." The presumption of the contemporary plan is that the meditation on the Word of God, chosen from the liturgical calendar, is the necessary starting point for your spiritual journey.

First thing in the morning, read the assigned scripture passages and meditation provided from Section Six, "Daily Meditations for Lent." The emphasis for your time of prayer should be on the regularity of the time chosen, the place you choose to pray, and the position you choose (that is, kneeling, sitting, or so on) and, finally, the amount of time reserved for prayer. In this model, the discipline necessary for the spiritual journey may be discovered in the commitment made to the morning meditation. Everything else that you choose to do, such as reading additional selections provided in this book or adopting the habit of reading from another spiritual book in the afternoon, is chosen for the purpose of supporting or enriching the morning meditation. In the evening, before retiring, five to seven minutes of silent reflection on the day and perhaps the recitation of the litany of forgiveness from Section Five, "Modern Practices and Prayers for Lent," is highly recommended.

The Family Model   In this plan, an emphasis is placed on the resources provided that may be used by the family as a unit. The presumption of this plan is that certain members of the family may well choose to follow the traditional, the contemporary, or some other plan for Lent, but there is also a commitment to share the spiritual journey with the rest of the family.

Essential to the plan is a family meeting, held before Ash Wednesday and the beginning of Lent, at which all members of the family have an opportunity to commit to the plan. It is important that there be a family commitment; the spiritual journey needs to be freely chosen by all, it cannot be imposed.

At the family meeting, the leader of the group, who is chosen for this task, asks the individual members of the family to commit to common expressions of Lenten penance and a common period of prayer. The Lenten penances can be as simple as determining that no deserts and no snack foods will be available or something a little bit more profound, such as a commitment to "quiet time" in the house at agreed upon periods during the day. During the designated quiet time, everyone agrees not to use the phone, the television, the stereo, the computer, or so on. The purpose of quiet time is to give one another the necessary time to perhaps read, meditate, or just simply rest quietly in the Lord. In addition to the common expression of penance, there is a commitment to a common period of prayer. Two recommendations for this prayer time may be found in Section Five, "Modern Practices and Prayers for Lent" (A Family-Centered Way of the Cross and Lenten Family Graces).

These suggestions for the possible use of this book do not exhaust all of the possibilities or, for that matter, they do not even begin to use all of the resources provided herein. The purpose of the suggestions is to simply provide a starting point, a place where your own creativity can be grounded.

SECTION ONE

The Meaning of Lent

E ven to the most casual observer of the Catholic experience, there seems to be an awareness of this forty-day period before the feast of Easter. Lent, which comes from the Anglo-Saxon word *lencten*, meaning "spring," is a time that seems marked with particular rituals. The most obvious ritual is the reception of ashes on Ash Wednesday, but certainly Lenten rituals are not limited to the reception of ashes. Discussion around the water cooler might reveal that a person has "given up chocolate" or "given up dessert" as a Lenten practice. Still others may reveal that not only have they given something up they have also added something to their normal Catholic practice. "I go to the Stations of the Cross on Wednesday night so I will have to pass on the invitation," someone says. All the other Wednesdays during the year are available for socializing, but for some reason the Wednesdays of Lent have been reserved for other things.

What is Lent? What is the purpose of each of these peculiar rituals? Do they have something to say to each of us who live in the modern age or are they rituals and practices left over from an era that can almost be remembered as "once upon a time"?

1. Short History of Lent

What is acceptable, common, and even expected in the Catholic expression of Lent has not always been so acceptable, common, or even expected. It may come as a surprise to learn that in the first three centuries of the Christian experience preparation for the Easter feast was usually for a period of one or two days, perhaps a week at the most. There was even a tradition, explained by Saint Irenaeus of Lyons, which speaks about the *forty-hour* preparation for Easter. This is not exactly the season of Lent as it is routinely practiced today.

The first reference to a period of forty days occurs in the fifth canon or teaching of the First Council of Nicaea in 325 A.D. Some scholars disagree with the assertion that this notation was a reference to Lent and prefer to hold that it is in fact referring to another unknown practice. Whatever the case, certainly by the end of the fourth century, the forty-day Lenten period was established and accepted.

Once established, Lent quickly became associated with the sacrament of baptism, since Easter was the great baptismal feast. Those who were preparing to be baptized participated in the season of Lent in preparation for the reception of the sacrament of baptism. Eventually, those who were already baptized considered it important to join the catechumens (candidates preparing for baptism) in their preparations for Easter. The custom and practice of Lent soon took hold in much the same form that we recognize it today.

2. Lent's Central Emphasis on Baptism

The baptismal emphasis is prominent and obvious today in most Catholic parishes throughout the season of Lent. The present liturgical practice features a significant role for the Rite of Christian Initiation of Adults (RCIA). The dismissal of the candidates at the completion of the Liturgy of the Word and before the Liturgy of the Eucharist during the ordinary Sunday celebration is a common and accepted practice. During Lent, this practice is enhanced through the celebration of certain rites in preparation for baptism which will take place during the Easter Vigil (Holy Saturday). During Lent, the catechumens celebrate the Rite of Election (enrollment of names of those to be baptized) on the First Sunday of Lent and then celebrate the *scrutinies* (a spiritual prayer, sometimes called an exorcism, that is intended to purify and strengthen the elect) on the third, fourth, and fifth Sundays of Lent.

(a) The Rite of Election is usually celebrated within the Mass of the First Sunday of Lent after the homily. In this rite, the catechumens are asked if they intend to celebrate the sacraments of initiation at the Easter Vigil. If they indicate that they do intend to seek baptism, confirmation, and the Eucharist, their names are enrolled and from that moment on they are identified as the "elect."

(b) The first scrutiny, or purification, is a prayer that asks for the necessary grace for the elect to experience the fullness of the power of the word of God, freeing them from the power of evil and helping them to recognize any evil within themselves. Sometime after the celebration of this first scrutiny, the elect are presented with a copy of the profession of faith (creed) which they are expected to memorize. This is not the first time that they have seen the creed, but it is rather a formal presentation of a treasure that the Church holds dear and which the Church now shares with the elect.

(c) The second scrutiny asks for the necessary grace for the elect to enjoy the light that comes from knowing the truth of the Word of God. A specific petition is included that asks for the necessary freedom to resist temptation for all those "who struggle under the yoke of the Father of Lies."

(d) The third and final scrutiny asks for the necessary grace to rescue the elect from death and lead them to the light of the resurrection. A specific petition is included that asks for the necessary grace to free the elect from "the power of the evil spirit that brings death." Sometime after the celebration of this scrutiny, the elect are presented with a copy of the Lord's Prayer.

The Rite of Election and the three scrutinies lead the elect on a journey directly to the celebration of the sacraments of initiation at the Easter Vigil on Holy Saturday. For the elect and for those who accompanied them on their Lenten journey, there is a clear path from the ashes of Ash Wednesday to the new life celebrated at Easter.

3. Lent Understood As a Journey

Lent is often portrayed as a journey, from one point in time to another point in time. The concept of journey is obvious for those who participate in the Rite of Christian Initiation of Adults, as outlined above, but it is not limited to the elect. For all Catholics, Lent is a journey that is measured from Ash Wednesday through Easter Sunday in the common understanding, but, more accurately, Lent is measured from Ash Wednesday to the beginning of the period of time known as the Triduum. The Triduum after the Mass on Holy Thursday, celebrates Good Friday, and concludes with the Easter Vigil on Holy Saturday. Lent officially ends with the proclamation of the *Exscultet*, "Rejoice O Heavenly Powers," during the vigil Mass of Holy Saturday. However the journey is measured, it is not only the period of time that is important but also the essential experiences of the journey that are necessary for full understanding and appreciation of what is celebrated.

The understanding of the season of Lent as a journey is also essential to the understanding of spiritual growth. Lent as journey presumes movement from one state of being to another state. For example, some people may find themselves troubled and anxious at the beginning of Lent as a result of a life choice or an unanswered question, and, at the end of Lent, they may fully expect a sense of conversion, a sense of peace, or perhaps simply understanding and acceptance. In this sense, Lent is a movement from one point of view to another or, perhaps, from one interpretation of life to a different interpretation.

Scripture, psalms, prayers, rituals, practices, and penance are the components of the Lenten journey. Each component, tried and tested by years of tradition, is one of the "engines" that drives the season and which brings the weary traveler to the joys of Easter.

4. Traditional Hymns of Lent

Much of the experience and expectations of the season of Lent may be discovered in the hymns that are commonly sung during the season. The words assigned to traditional and well-known melodies serve as one means of bringing many persons to a place within themselves that is seen as preparation for the journey. Two such hymns, *Again We Keep This Solemn Fast,* attributed to Saint Gregory the Great (540–604) and a much later hymn, *Lord, Who Throughout These Forty Days,* by Claudia Hernaman (1838–1898) serve as illustrations. The first stanzas of each of these hymns is given below.

> Again we keep this solemn fast,
> A gift of faith from ages past,
> This Lent which binds us lovingly
> To faith and hope and charity.
>
> Lord, who throughout these forty days
> For us did fast and pray.
> Teach us to overcome our sins
> And close by you to stay.

5. Penitential Nature of Lent

The popular understanding of Lent is that it is a penitential period of time during which people attempt to become more sensitive to the role of sin in their lives. Lenten sermons will speak of personal sin, coming to an awareness of the sins of others and the effect such sin might have, and, finally, the sin that can be found within our larger society and culture. Awareness of sin, however, is balanced by an emphasis on the love and acceptance that God still has for humanity, despite the sinful condition in which we still find ourselves.

Awareness of sin and the need for penance is emphasized through the practice of meditation on the Passion of the Lord, his suffering, and his death. There is also a traditional concern for the reception of the sacrament of reconciliation during Lent, although this is a relatively new development. Originally, the sacrament of reconciliation was celebrated before Lent began, the penance imposed on Ash Wednesday, and the penance given was performed during the entire forty-day period. The penitent could not receive holy Eucharist until Easter Sunday.

One of the most traditional Lenten penances was the voluntary practice of not eating any eggs or milk during Lent. The money not spent on the purchase of dairy products was collected and donated to the Church. A church tower at the Rouen cathedral in Germany is known as the "butter tower," because it was built from these proceeds. The common practice of Easter eggs is also directly related to this practice; at the end of Lent that which was prohibited was given as a gift to celebrate the end of the season.

6. Call to Penitential Living

"Jesus came to Galilee proclaiming the good news of God, saying, 'The time is fulfilled, and the kingdom of God has come near; repent, and believe the good news'" (Mk 1:15 [RSV/C]). This call to conversion announces the solemn opening of Lent. Participants are marked with ashes, and the words of blessing are prayed, "Repent, and believe the good news." This ritual act is understood as personal acceptance of the desire to take on the life of penance for the sake of the Gospel. For forty days, the example of Jesus in the desert fasting and praying is imitated. It is time to center attention on conversion. During Lent, the expectation is to examine our lives and, through the practice of prayer, fasting, and works of charity, seek to conform our lives to Christ. It is a call to conversion. For some, it will be a turning from sin to grace. For others, it will be a gracious turning toward the mystery of God in Christ.

7. Tradition of Prayer, Fasting, and Acts of Charity

The Old Testament and the New Testament present many examples of these three practices. The liturgical readings of Ash Wednesday and the forty days of Lent read like a handbook on the importance of taming the "ego." However, the Church is always vigilant in admonitions about penance. Fasting must not lose sight of its goal, which is to open eyes and hearts to see the darkness of sin and evil and the grace to ask for forgiveness of sins and faults.

Prayer

In his desert experience of forty days, Jesus combines prayer with fasting. From his example, we know that prayer and fasting work together in bringing a person to an awareness of the deeper mysteries of life. Prayer in the biblical practice connected with fasting is understood as "vigil," keeping watch over the senses. During Lent, a person may become more alert in prayer and adopt practices that increase the time dedicated to prayer. When a person's prayer quality improves because of the time dedicated to the task, it is possible to experience the spiritual life with renewed rigor. The things of the "spirit" become alive. Prayer calls a person to deny self, which leads to a deepening capacity for prayer.

Fasting

Fasting is a traditional form of penance. Fasting is traditionally understood as a way of purifying a person, making him or her open to the work of the Spirit. Fasting limits the quantity of food or drink. This is an ancient practice that can be found in many religious cultures. Fasting has also received acceptance as an alternative medical remedy and sometimes recommended as a way of purifying the body.

However, the Christian tradition uses the discipline of fasting as a way to focus a person's attention on the spiritual life. When the results of fasting are experienced (a hunger and desire for that which is denied), those fasting are then reminded of the reason why they are adopting this practice.

Christian fasting is always for something other; it is never understood as the end itself. A Christian fasts for the poor, for peace and nonviolence, or to be in solidarity with those oppressed. Lenten fasting helps people to center their living on imitating Jesus. Fasting is one expression of the desire to share in the redemptive love of Christ. Those who fast hope that fasting might make them more loving and compassionate.

Acts of Charity

The Christian community from its beginning considered almsgiving and works of charity as basic elements in living the Christian life. The letter of the apostle James instructs all "to care for orphans and widows in their distress" (Jas 1:27 [RSV/C]). Early in the life of the Church, works of charity were associated with living an ascetical life. While the desert monks and nuns left the busyness of the urban life for a life of prayer and penance, they continued to return to the city to practice charity. Traditional Lenten penitential living must also express works of charity. Prayer and fasting should move a person to stretch beyond personal needs and give the fruits of prayer and fasting in the service of others.

8. Tradition of Fast and Abstinence

Ashes might be the most easily recognizable sign of the Lenten season, but certainly the tradition of fast and abstinence is also commonly associated with Lent. In today's practice, the expectations for fasting and abstinence seem to be of great concern only on Ash Wednesday, Good Friday, and all of the other Fridays of Lent, though it has not been that long ago when all Catholics fasted each and every day during the Lenten season.

We have early evidence of the Christian custom of fasting in a second-century collection of writings called the *Revelations to the Shepherd of Hermas* (Liguori, MO: Liguori/Triumph, 1998). In this document, some of the earliest directives for fasting can be recovered: "The day on which you shall fast you will take only bread and water. The food that you denied yourself you are to give to a widow or orphan or any person in need."

There is also an important dialogue in the *Revelations* that provides significant insight and teaching. It goes like this:

"What are you doing here?" the shepherd asked. "I am fasting, sir."

"And why are you fasting?" "I am fasting, sir, because it is my custom to fast at this time."

"You do not know how to fast," the shepherd said, "and so this fast is utterly useless and is not a fast at all. Let me teach you about true fasting, which is acceptable and pleasing to the Lord. If you fast simply by giving up food, or abstaining from certain foods, the Lord is completely indifferent to your efforts. The only fast which he wants is for you to abstain from all evil acts, to give up every form of evil desire, and let your heart become pure. So the person who once was malicious and schemed against others, but gives up all malice and scheming, is making a true fast. The person who once was jealous and wanted the possessions of others but gives up jealousy and is content with what the Lord provides is making a true fast. Come down from your high mountain and make your fast among people."

Depending on the time and the place, the rules and regulations for fasting and abstinence were more or less strict. In some periods of Church history, the concern for what could and what could not be consumed became seemingly more important than the reason for the regulation. At the same time, there also seemed to be an operative pastoral concern to make sure that the Lenten practice did not come to be too burdensome.

9. Purpose of Penitential Living

The practices of fasting, prayer, and works of charity are understood to comprise the exercise of asceticism, a word taken from the Greek *askesis*, which means "exercise" or "training." The practice of asceticism was considered a special training exercise to help achieve deeper union with Christ. Through the centuries, asceticism was sometimes overemphasized. Similar to many religious practices, without careful direction a person's zeal can sometimes prove to be more of a hindrance than a help.

The Church reformed the practice of asceticism in 1966 with the apostolic letter of Pope Paul VI entitled, Apostolic Constitution on Penance (*Poenitemini*). The Holy Father called each person of faith to understand ascetical practices as a call to conversion, "that is to say, a condemnation of and detachment from sin and a striving toward God." The apostolic letter is rooted in the Scripture call to "be converted and believe in the Gospel." This call is for all who follow Christ to announce the kingdom of God by actions. Acts of penance give witness to the kingdom of God by the life of conversion lived. People of conversion are Christians who witness the *Maranatha*, "Our Lord has come." "You must stand ready, because the Son of Man is coming at an hour when you do not expect" (Mt 24:44).

10. Admonitions on Penitential Living

In the practice of penitential living, the call of Christ is expressed in the Gospel of Matthew: "Beware of practicing your piety before others in order to be seen by them; for then you have no reward from your Father in heaven" (6:1 [RSV/C]).

The admonitions for penitential living are rooted in Scripture and easily discovered in the biblical books of Joel and the prophet Isaiah:

"Even now," says the Lord, "return to me with your whole heart, with fasting, weeping, and mourning; rend your hearts and not your garments, and return to the Lord, your God."

Joel 2:12–13

Is this the manner of fasting I wish, of keeping a day of penance: that a man bow his head like a reed, and lie in sackcloth and ashes? Do you call this a fast, a day acceptable to the Lord? This, rather is the fasting that I wish: releasing those bound unjustly, untying the thongs of the yoke; setting free the oppressed, breaking every yoke; sharing your bread with the hungry, sheltering the oppressed and the homeless; clothing the naked when you see them, and not turning your back on your own.

Isaiah 58:5–7

The penitential way of life is chosen so that conversion may blossom within. A life of conversion is not a negative expression of Christian life but rather a positive reflection of the Gospel. Pope Paul VI teaches in his Apostolic Constitution on Penance, "Following the Master, Christians must renounce themselves, take up their cross and participate in the sufferings of Christ. Thus transformed into the image of Christ's death, they are made capable of meditation on the glory of the resurrection."

11. Fruits of Penitential Living

Penitential living is understood as a path to holiness. When people enter into the season of Lent with prayer, fasting, and works of charity, they conform themselves to Christ. As Saint Paul says, "It is no longer I who live, but it is Christ who lives in me." For forty days the person on the spiritual journey demonstrates a willingness to experience discipline for the love of Christ.

Purgation

This Lenten discipline consists in the denial of the ordinary pleasures of living. Through prayer, fasting, and works of charity, people seek to purge themselves of selfishness so that the love of Christ might be increased. By willing acceptance of the sacrifices that come from penitential living, a person can advance toward the goal of seeking to imitate the crucified Christ.

One belief about this type of Lenten self-denial is that it imitates, in the body of the person making the spiritual journey, the dying of Jesus for the salvation of the world. Like the monks and nuns of the desert, those seeking purgation are willing to journey into the inner desert of the soul by prayer, fasting, and works of charity. This purging of the body for the sake of the kingdom of God is a call to holiness and a demonstration of commitment to the spiritual path.

Illumination

The penitential practices of Lent are not discipline for the sake of discipline. Penance and prayer are related. The purpose of the Lenten fast is to strengthen the inner self to be more aware of the things of the kingdom. Those who fast pray that their fasting might lead to conversion, a desire not only to convert from something but also a conversion toward something. The primary purpose and desire of penitential living is to draw closer to God. A person fasts and prays for enlightenment about the things of God. It is a practice that acknowledges that lives can become clouded with so many distractions and anxiety that block the light of God.

Prayer and fasting, understood as a response to the call and inspiration of the Holy Spirit, will urge a person toward works of charity for others. The discipline of Lent can strip people of selfishness so that they can see and hear the cry of the poor around them. The good works of mercy and compassion allow a person to come to awareness, an illumination of a gospel truth, the presence of Christ hidden in the lives of the poor. Penitential living forms a person into the light of Christ in a world of darkness and despair.

Union With Christ

"We are one body in this one Lord," says Saint Paul. The practice of the Christian life should lead a person to a life of union with Christ. Christians believe that baptism has rooted them into the paschal mystery, the suffering, death, and Resurrection of Christ. The dying and rising up of Christ continues in every baptized person as they daily pick up their personal crosses to follow the Lord. Discipleship is the Christian call. "If you would be my disciple pick up your cross and follow me," says the Lord Jesus.

The purpose of penitential living is to help a person to follow the Lord. A person denies self so that he or she might live more fully in the love of Christ. When a person is purged from self, the possibility exists that the light of Christ may shine more fully in him or her. In the light of this presence, a person is then invited into an intimate relationship with Jesus. Penance is the response to the call to be open and accepting of the love of Christ. Penitential living offers a person an invitation through prayer, fasting, and works of charity to live in close union with Jesus Christ.

12. Church Teaching on Fast and Abstinence

The *Code of Canon Law*, in Canons 1249–1253, clearly outlines the penitential understanding of the meaning of fast and abstinence, especially during the season of Lent. The *Code*, as only a code of law can do, explains that the need for penance is not a human idea or invention, but rather a human response to divine law. It is not an option, but rather the responsibility of a believing Christian to do penance. The *Code* then proceeds to distinguish between fast and abstinence by explaining that abstinence from meat or from some other food determined by the conference of bishops of a particular jurisdiction is required on all Fridays of the year, Ash Wednesday, and the Friday of the Passion and death of the Lord. This requirement begins with all those who have completed their fourteenth year and continues to the beginning of the sixtieth year. The *Code* ends by reminding parents that even if their children are not yet bound by the law they should, nevertheless, teach their children about the "authentic sense of penance." The exact meaning of what "fasting" might mean is not explained by the *Code* but is rather presumed as something that is understood by all Christians.

For Catholics who reached the age of consent and reason before the Second Vatican Council there may well be a sense of surprise and wonder that there is not more emphasis and explanation in the *Code*. Gone are the prescriptions that determined that the primary meal of the day was not to exceed the sum of the morning and evening refreshment. Such attention to detail led to the unusual practice in some circles of special Lenten scales that were used to weigh the food that was to be consumed in order to ensure that the rule was accurately followed. Many older Catholics can share stories about weighing saltine crackers and using them as a unit of measurement to either add to or subtract from the food that was about to be consumed!

13. Seven Penitential Psalms

The seven penitential psalms, as enumerated in the *Vulgate*, or Latin Bible of Saint Jerome, are 6, 31, 37, 50, 101, 129, and 142; modern Bibles list them as 6, 32, 38, 51, 102, 130, and 143. The penitential psalms are found in the Old Testament or, as it is sometimes identified, the Hebrew Scriptures, in the Book of Psalms. These psalms are traditionally understood as prayers that express sentiments of repentance and sorrow for sin.

Since the sixth century, these psalms have been classified as "suitable for penance." Cassiodorus (a Roman monk, 490–583) interpreted them allegorically and taught that they were indicative of the seven means available for obtaining forgiveness: baptism, martyrdom, almsgiving, a forgiving spirit, conversion of the sinner, love, and penance. During the Middle Ages, at the direction of Pope Innocent III, they were commonly recited on the Fridays of Lent. Pope Pius X (1903–1914) added them to the Divine Office (now called the Liturgy of the Hours) for recitation during Lent. They are still widely used in the liturgy, especially Psalm 130 (129), the *De Profundis,* and Psalm 51 (50), the *Miserere.*

Another traditional understanding of the penitential psalms are that they are representative of the lament of Jesus in his Passion and death. The traditional encouragement for the praying of the penitential psalms is often discovered in the voices of the saints who discovered within these psalms the experience of the voice of Jesus praying. In Psalm 38 (37), for example, the "voice" of the Lord seems very present: "My wounds stink and fester within me....Stooped and bowed down, I go about mourning all day."

Psalm 6

Psalm 6 is a prayer of the afflicted, a prayer of a sick person and a traditional intercessory prayer that asks for the grace to be freed from the sickness of sin and affirms the intention to have nothing to do with evil.

> O LORD, in your anger do not reprove;
> > nor punish me in your fury.
> Have mercy on me, O LORD,
> > for I have no strength left.
> O LORD, heal me, for my bones are in torment.
> My soul also is gently troubled.
> How long, O LORD, how long? How long will you be?
>
> Come back to me, O LORD, save my life;
> > rescue me for the sake of your love.
> For no one remembers you in the grave;
> > who will praise you in the world of the dead?
>
> I am weary with moaning;
> > I weep every night, drenching my bed with tears.
> My eyes have grown dim from troubles;
> > I have weakened because of my foes.
>
> Away from me, you evildoers,
> > for the LORD has heard my plaintive voice.
> The LORD has heard my plea;
> > the LORD will grant all that I pray for.
> Let my enemies fall back in shame,
> > all of a sudden—the whole bunch of them!

Psalm 32 (31)

Psalm 32 (31) is representative of the relief that is often felt after the confession of sin. Buried sin ruins the conscience. Confession is understood as a type of liberation. A person's well-being, in the truest meaning of the word, depends on the quality of his or her relationship with God: what sin has destroyed will only be restored by trust in God who pardons the humble and the repentant.

> Blessed is the one whose sin is forgiven,
>> whose iniquity is wiped away.
> Blessed are those in whom the LORD sees no guilt
>> and in whose spirit is found no deceit.
> When I kept my sin secret, my body wasted away,
>> I was moaning all day long.
> Your hand day and night lay heavy upon me;
>> draining my strength, parching my heart
>> as in the heat of a summer drought.
> Then I made known to you my sin
>> and uncovered before you my fault,
>> saying to myself,
> "To the Lord I will now confess my wrong."
> And you, you forgave my sin, you removed my guilt.
> So let the faithful ones pray to you in time of distress;
>> waters may overflow, the flood will not reach them.
> You are my refuge; you protect me from distress
>> and surround me with songs of deliverance.
> I will teach you, I will show you the way to follow.
>> I will watch over you and give you counsel.
> Do not be like the horse or the mule—
>> senseless and led by bit and bridle.
> Many woes befall the wicked,
>> But the LORD's mercy enfolds those who trust in him.
> Rejoice in the LORD, and be glad, you who are upright:
>> sing and shout for joy, you who are clean of heart.

Psalm 38 (37)

Psalm 38 (37) teaches that the greater the sin, the greater must be the trust in God. Oftentimes, people relate sickness to sinfulness. It is not unusual for people to assume that what they may be suffering is connected to their choices and their actions. Another common reaction that is experienced, perhaps because of the presence of guilt, is the assumption that "things will go wrong" because of sin. This psalm reflects such feelings and assumptions. Another traditional interpretation is that it is reflective of the agony of Jesus in his Passion.

O Lord, rebuke me not in your rage,
    punish me not in your fury.
Your arrows have struck me;
    your hand has come down heavily upon me.

Your anger has spared no part of my body,
    my sin gives no peace to my bones.
For my transgressions overwhelm me;
    they weigh me down like an unbearable load.

My wounds stink and fester within me,
    the outcome of my sinful folly.
Stooped and bowed down,
    I go about mourning all day.

My loins burn, my flesh is diseased, my body,
    worn out and utterly crushed;
    I groan in pain and anguish of heart.
All my longing O Lord is known to you;
    my sighing is not hidden from you.
My heart pounds as my strength ebbs;
    even the light has deserted my eyes.

My friends avoid me because of my wounds;
    my neighbors stay far off.
Those who seek my life lay snares for me;
    those who wish me harm speak of my ruin
    and plot against me all day long.

But like a deaf-mute,
    I neither hear nor open my mouth.
I am like one whose ears hear not
    and whose mouth has no answer.

For I put my trust in you, O LORD;
    you will answer for me, LORD God.
I pray, "Don't let them gloat over me,
    nor take advantage of my helplessness when my foot slips."

For I am about to fall, my pain is ever with me.
    I confess my transgression, I repent of my sin.
Many are my foes; many are those who hate me for no reason,
Those who pay me evil for good and harass me
    because I seek good.
Forsake me not, O LORD, stay not far from me, O my God.
Come quickly to help me, O LORD, my savior!

Psalm 51 (50)

Psalm 51 (50), the *Miserere*, laments the sinful condition of humanity and admits the presence of personal sin in the life of the penitent. The psalm imagines the sinner standing humbly before the
throne of God, expecting to be forgiven and expecting that a new
heart and a new spirit will be freely given. The proof offered to God
that the sinner is truly penitent is the broken spirit of the penitent,
freely laid before the throne of God; the expectant response is the
gift from God to the sinner of a pure heart.

Have mercy on me, O God, in your love.
   In your great compassion blot out my sin.
Wash me thoroughly of my guilt; cleanse me of evil.
For I acknowledge my wrong doings
   and have my sins ever in mind.
Against you alone have I sinned;
   what is evil in your sight I have done.
You are right when you pass sentence and blameless
   in your judgement.
For I have been guilt-ridden from birth,
   a sinner from my mother's womb.

I know you desire truth in the heart,
   teach me wisdom in my inmost being.
Cleanse me with hyssop and I shall be clean, wash me,
   I shall be whiter than snow.
Fill me with joy and gladness;
   let the bones you have crushed rejoice.
Turn your face away from my sins and blot out all my offenses.

Create in me, O God, a pure heart;
   give me a new and steadfast spirit.
Do not cast me out of your presence
   nor take your Holy Spirit away from me.
Give me again the joy of your salvation
   and sustain me with a willing spirit.

Then I will show wrongdoers your ways
   and sinner will return to you.
Deliver me, O God, from the guilt of blood,
   and of your justice I shall sing aloud.

O LORD, open my lips, and I will declare your praise.
You take no pleasure in sacrifice;
>were I to give a burnt offering
You would not delight in it.
O God, my sacrifice is a broken spirit;
>a contrite heart you will not despise.
Shower Zion with your favor; rebuild the walls of Jerusalem.
Then you will delight in fitting sacrifices,
>in burnt offerings, and bulls offered on your altar.

Psalm 101 (100)

Psalm 101 (100) is an examination of conscience, originally prayed, at least according to tradition, by King David. This examination leads a person to a way of life that is reflective of perfection and the desire to do only God's will each and every day. At the same time, the psalm leaves the penitent with a question (it is probably this question that suggests the authorship of King David) that needs to be answered by God; "When I do all of these things, then will you come to me?"

I will sing of your love and justice,
>to you, O LORD, I will sing praise.
I will walk the way of integrity—O LORD,
>when will you come to me?
>With a blameless heart I will walk within my house.
I will not set before my eyes anything that is base.
>I hate the deeds of faithless people;
>I will have no part in them.
I will banish all wicked hearts, and evil I will not know.
He who deals with others treacherously,
>I will silence. He who talks and acts arrogantly,
>I will not endure.

I will choose from the faithful of the land
    those who may dwell with me;
    only the upright shall be my servant.
No double-dealer shall live in my house;
    no on who utters falsehood shall stand before my eyes.
Each morning I will clear the land and silence all the wicked;
I will uproot all the evildoers from the city of the LORD.

Psalm 130 (129)

Psalm 130 (129) is a prayer that speaks of suffering that seems to have been always present. The psalmist cannot remember a time when there has not been oppression, however, even more important, despite the pain and the suffering, there has always been an expectant hope. The image that is powerfully suggested is the image of a watchman who, although surrounded by darkness that seems to be complete and eternal, never gives up hope that the dawn of a new day will soon come upon all who wait.

Out of the depths I cry to you, O LORD,
O LORD, hear my voice!
    Let your ears pay attention to the voice of my supplication.

If you should mark our evil, O LORD, who could stand?
But with you is forgiveness, and for that you are revered.

I waited for the LORD, my soul waits,
    and I put my hope in his word.
My soul expects the LORD more than watchmen the dawn.

O Israel, hope in the LORD, for with him is unfailing love
    and with him full deliverance.
He will deliver Israel from all its sins.

Psalm 143 (142)

The last penitential psalm, Psalm 143 (142) is a cry for mercy from a person who has been beaten down and oppressed. The psalmist pictures the penitent like a piece of farmland that has experienced drought for an extended period and now longs for a drop of cool and refreshing water to restore some life to the earth. The psalm hints that the penitent is weak and needs a response very quickly or he will be lost. Not so lost and forsaken, however, that he does not have the energy to pray that all of his enemies are destroyed!

O Lord, hear my prayer, listen to my cry for mercy;
    answer me, you who are righteous and faithful.
Do not bring your servant to judgement,
    for no mortal is just in your sight.

The enemy has pursued me,
    crushing my life to the ground,
    sending me to darkness with those long dead.
And so my spirit fails me, my heart is full of fear.

I remember the days of long ago;
    I mediate on what you have done
    and consider the work of your hand.
I stretch out my hands to you,
    and thirst for you like a parched land.

O Lord, answer me quickly:
    my spirit is faint with yearning.
Do not hide your face from me;
    save me from going down to the pit.

Let the dawn bring me word of your love,
　　for in you alone I put my trust.
Show me the way I should walk,
　　for to you I life up my soul.

Rescue me from my enemies,
　　O LORD, for to you I flee for refuge.
Teach me to do your will, for you are my God.
　　Let your spirit lead me on a safe path.
Preserve me, O LORD, for your name's sake;
　　free me from distress, in your justice.
You who are merciful, crush my enemies and
　　destroy all my foes,
For I am your servant.

SECTION TWO

Traditional Practices of Lent

O f the many pious practices that have developed in two-thousand years of Christianity, there are a certain number that are associated with the season of Lent, although they are not limited to this season of the liturgical year. For example, even though some representations of the Stations of the Cross hang in all Catholic Churches, it is during Lent when the praying of the Stations of the Cross enters the liturgical calendar of the parish church. This is not to say that the devotion is not practiced throughout the year in private but rather that during Lent it receives a prominent and public observance.

In addition to the Stations of the Cross, certain other pious devotions and practices also receive some prominence. Commonly, there is an emphasis on celebrating the sacrament of reconciliation, both in private and in communal celebrations, an emphasis on taking time to make visits to the Blessed Sacrament or, in some instances, the practice of Adoration of the Blessed Sacrament, and an emphasis on some sort of special daily meditation and prayer.

1. History and Origins of the Stations of the Cross

The Stations of the Cross, also commonly referred to as the Way of the Cross, is a familiar devotion in the Catholic tradition of piety. As practiced today, the Stations of the Cross are representative of fourteen particular events experienced by Jesus as he walked to Calvary.

Early pilgrims to the city of Jerusalem in the first centuries of Christianity would often retrace the steps of Jesus, stopping along the way at appropriate and predetermined places, to contemplate the meaning of the Passion and death of the Lord. An early tradition, as related in a vision to Saint Brigid, suggests that the places where the pilgrims visited were the exact places the Blessed Mother visited after the Ascension of the Lord. What can be determined for certain is that each of the stations is at least representative of the places visited and marked by the veterans of the Crusades in the twelfth and thirteenth centuries.

The modern devotion and practice can be reliably traced to the promotional efforts of the Franciscans, beginning in 1342, the year they were given custody of the Holy Land, as a way to promote devotion and piety. The practice grew and eventually became a regular feature in monasteries and convents, and eventually parish churches throughout the world.

Today there are fourteen stations, but that has not always been the case. At various times, there have been as little as four or five and as many as twenty. In earlier collections, stations might have included the house of Dives and the houses of Herod and Simon the Pharisee. In some collections, there may have been as many as seven falls commemorated and some included the scene known as *Ecce Homo,* or "Behold, the man," the words with which Pilate presented Jesus to his accusers. However, by the seventeenth century, the content of the Stations of the Cross, as we know it, seems to have been set by popular custom.

Some theologians and liturgists have suggested that the Way of the Cross is incomplete and that a fifteenth station is needed. The new station suggested is a station that provides the opportunity for meditation upon the Resurrection of the Lord. This suggestion has been implemented on some occasions but is still debated.

2. Saint Alphonsus Liguori's Stations of the Cross

Saint Alphonsus was a man who was in love with Jesus, the Most Holy Redeemer. In the meditations that follow, we are offered an insight into the mind of a saint and the emotion and passion that formed his devotion. For Alphonsus, the Stations of the Cross provided the opportunity to meditate on the true meaning of the Redeemer's love: a love for the will of his Father and a love for the people whom he was called to redeem.

This arrangement of Saint Alphonsus' Way of the Cross has been prepared for congregational use. It presumes a dialogue between leader and assembly. However, it is still just as practical for individual devotion.

Preparatory Prayer
(To be said kneeling before the altar)

Leader and Assembly: My Lord Jesus Christ, * you have made this journey to die for me with unspeakable love, * and I have again and again ungratefully abandoned you. * But now I love you with all my heart, * and because I love you, I am sorry for having sinned. * Pardon me, my God, and allow me to go with you on this journey. * You accepted your Cross because of your great love for me; * I desire, my beloved Redeemer, to die for love of you. * My Jesus, I will live and die always united to you. *(Stand)*

Hymn: At the Cross Her Station Keeping
All sing:
At the cross her station keeping,
Stood the mournful Mother weeping,
Close to Jesus to the last.

Through her heart, his sorrow sharing,
All his bitter anguish bearing,
Now at length the sword had passed.

The First Station
Pilate Condemns Jesus to Die

Leader: We adore you, O Christ, and we praise you. *(Genuflect)*
Assembly: Because by your holy Cross you have redeemed the world. *(Stand)*

Consider Jesus, scourged and crowned with thorns, being unjustly condemned to die on the Cross. *(Kneel)*

My adorable Jesus, * it was not Pilate; * no, it was my sins that condemned you to die. * By the merits of this sorrowful journey, * help my soul on its journey to eternity. * I love you, my beloved Jesus; * I love you more than myself, * and I repent with all my heart of ever having offended you. * Never allow me to be separated from you again. * Grant that I may love you always, and then do with me as you will. *(Stand)*

The Second Station
Jesus Accepts His Cross

Leader: We adore you, O Christ, and we praise you. *(Genuflect)*
Assembly: Because by your holy Cross you have redeemed the world. *(Stand)*

Consider Jesus making this journey with the Cross on his shoulders, thinking of us and offering to his Father, in our behalf, the death he was about to undergo. *(Kneel)*

My beloved Jesus, * I embrace all the sufferings you have destined for me until death. * I implore you, by all you suffered in carrying your cross, * to help me carry mine with perfect patience and resignation. * I love you, Jesus my love, * and I repent of ever having offended you. * Never allow me to separate myself from you again. * Grant that I may love you always, and then do with me as you will. *(Stand)*

The Third Station
Jesus Falls the First Time

Leader: We adore you, O Christ, and we praise you. *(Genuflect)*
Assembly: Because by your holy Cross you have redeemed the world.
(Stand)

Consider the first fall of Jesus. His flesh had been torn by the scourges,
his head, crowned with thorns, and he had lost a great quantity of
blood. He had been so weakened he could scarcely walk, and yet he
had to carry that great load upon his shoulders. The soldiers struck
him cruelly, and so he fell several times. *(Kneel)*

My beloved Jesus, * it was not the weight of the Cross * but the
weight of my sins which made you suffer all that pain. * By the merits of this fall, * keep me from the misfortune of falling into mortal
sin. * I love you, O Jesus, with all my heart, * and I repent of ever
having offended you. * Never allow me to offend you again. * Grant
that I may love you always, and then do with me as you will. *(Stand)*

The Fourth Station
Jesus Meets His Afflicted Mother

Leader: We adore you, O Christ, and we praise you. *(Genuflect)*
Assembly: Because by your holy Cross you have redeemed the world.
(Stand)

Consider the meeting of the Son and the Mother which took place
on this journey. Jesus and Mary looked at each other, and their looks
became as so many arrows to wound those hearts which loved each
other so tenderly. *(Kneel)*

My most loving Jesus, * by the sorrow which you suffered in this
meeting, * grant me the grace of a truly devoted love for your most
holy Mother. * And you, my Queen, who were overwhelmed with

33

sorrow, * obtain for me by your prayers * a tender and lasting remembrance of the Passion of your divine Son. * I love you, Jesus my love, * and I repent of ever having offended you. * Never allow me to offend you again. * Grant that I may love you always, and then do with me as you will. *(Stand)*

All sing:
Is there one who would not weep,
Whelmed in miseries so deep,
Christ's dear Mother to behold?

Can the human heart refrain
From partaking in her pain,
In that mother's pain untold?

The Fifth Station
Simon Helps Carry the Cross

Leader: We adore you, O Christ, and we praise you. *(Genuflect)*
Assembly: Because by your holy Cross you have redeemed the world. *(Stand)*

Consider how weary Jesus was. At each step, he was at the point of death. Fearing that he would die on the way, when they wished him to die the shameful death of the Cross, the soldiers forced Simon of Cyrene to help carry the Cross behind our Lord. *(Kneel)*

My most sweet Jesus, * I will not refuse the Cross as Simon did. * I accept it; I embrace it. * I accept in particular the death that you have destined for me, * with all the pains that may accompany it. * I unite it to your death; I offer it to you. * You have died for love of me; * I will die for love of you and to please you. * Help me by your grace. * I love you, Jesus my love, * and I repent of ever having offended you. * Never allow me to offend you again. * Grant that I may love you always, and then do with me as you will. *(Stand)*

The Sixth Station
Veronica Offers Her Veil to Jesus

Leader: We adore you, O Christ, and we praise you. *(Genuflect)*
Assembly: Because by your holy Cross you have redeemed the world. *(Stand)*

Consider the compassion of the holy woman, Veronica. Seeing Jesus all afflicted, with his face bathed in sweat and blood, she presented him with her veil. Jesus took the veil, wiped his face, and left upon the cloth the imprint of his adorable countenance. *(Kneel)*

My most beloved Jesus, * your face was beautiful before you started this journey, * but now it has lost all its beauty, * as wounds and blood have disfigured it. * At one time, my soul was beautiful as well * when it received your abundant grace in baptism, * but I have since disfigured it by my sins. * You alone, my Redeemer, can restore it to its former beauty. * Do this by the merits of your Passion, * and then do with me as you will. *(Stand)*

The Seventh Station
Jesus Falls the Second Time

Leader: We adore you, O Christ, and we praise you. *(Genuflect)*
Assembly: Because by your holy Cross you have redeemed the world. *(Stand)*

Consider the second fall of Jesus under his Cross. This fall renews the pain in all the wounds of the head and body of our afflicted Lord. *(Kneel)*

My most gentle Jesus, * how many times you have forgiven me, * and how many times I have fallen again and offended you! * By the merits of this second fall, * give me the grace to persevere in your love until death. * Grant that, in all my temptations, I may call upon

35

you in prayer. * I love you, Jesus my love, with all my heart, * and I repent of ever having offended you. * Grant that I may love you always, and then do with me as you will. *(Stand)*

All sing:
Holy Mother, pierce me through,
In my heart each wound renew
Of my Savior crucified.

Let me share with you his pain,
Who for all our sins was slain,
Who for me in torments died.

The Eighth Station
Jesus Speaks to the Women

Leader: We adore you, O Christ, and we praise you. *(Genuflect)*
Assembly: Because by your holy Cross you have redeemed the world. *(Stand)*

Consider the women of Jerusalem. They wept with compassion at the pitiful sight of Jesus walking alone, bathed in his own blood. Jesus said to them, "Weep not so much for me, but rather for your children." *(Kneel)*

My Jesus, laden with sorrows, * I weep for the sins which I have committed against you, * not only because of the pains they have deserved * but still more because of the displeasure they have caused you * who have loved me with an infinite love. * It is your love, more than the fear of hell, * which causes me to weep for my sins. * My Jesus, I love you more than myself, * and I repent of ever having offended you. * Never allow me to offend you again. * Grant that I may love you always, and then do with me as you will. *(Stand)*

The Ninth Station
Jesus Falls the Third Time

Leader: We adore you, O Christ, and we praise you. *(Genuflect)*
Assembly: Because by your holy Cross you have redeemed the world. *(Stand)*

Consider the third fall of Jesus. His weakness was extreme, and the cruelty of his executioners was excessive: they tried to quicken his steps when he hardly had enough strength to move. *(Kneel)*

My outraged Jesus, * by the weakness you suffered in going to Calvary, * give me the strength to conquer all my desire for human respect * and all my evil passions which have led me to despise your friendship. * I love you, Jesus my love, with all my heart, * and I repent of ever having offended you. * Never allow me to offend you again. * Grant that I may love you always, and then do with me as you will. *(Stand)*

The Tenth Station
Jesus Is Stripped of His Garments

Leader: We adore you, O Christ, and we praise you. *(Genuflect)*
Assembly: Because by your holy Cross you have redeemed the world. *(Stand)*

Consider the violence with which the executioners stripped Jesus of his clothes. The inner garments were blood-clotted with his torn flesh, and the soldiers tore them off so roughly that the skin came with them. Show compassion for your Savior so cruelly treated, and say to him: *(Kneel)*

My innocent Jesus, * by the torment that you suffered in being stripped of your garments, * help me to strip myself of all unnecessary attachment to earthly things, * that I may give all my love to you who are so worthy of my love. * I love you, O Jesus, with all my heart, * and I repent of ever having offended you. * Never allow me to offend you again. * Grant that I may love you always, and then do with me as you will. *(Stand)*

All sing:

Virgin of all virgins blest!
Listen to my fond request:
Let me share your grief divine.

Let me to my latest breath,
In my body bear the death
Of that dying Son of yours.

The Eleventh Station
Jesus Is Nailed to the Cross

Leader: We adore you, O Christ, and we praise you. *(Genuflect)*
Assembly: Because by your holy Cross you have redeemed the world. *(Stand)*

Consider Jesus thrown upon the Cross. He stretches out his arms and offers to his eternal Father the sacrifice of his life for our salvation. The executioners fasten him with nails and then, raising the Cross, leave him to die in anguish. *(Kneel)*

My crucified Jesus, * nail my heart to the Cross, * that it may always remain there to love you and never leave you again. * I love you more than myself, * and I repent of ever having offended you. * Never allow me to offend you again. * Grant that I may love you always, and then do with me as you will. *(Stand)*

The Twelfth Station
Jesus Dies Upon the Cross

Leader: We adore you, O Christ, and we praise you. *(Genuflect)*
Assembly: Because by your holy Cross you have redeemed the world. *(Stand)*

Consider that, after three hours' agony on the Cross, Jesus is at length consumed with anguish, and abandoning himself to the weight of his body, he bows his head and dies. *(Kneel)*

My crucified Jesus, * devoutly do I kiss the Cross on which you have died for love of me. * I have merited by my sins to die a terrible death, * but your death is my hope. * By your death, * give me the grace to die embracing your feet and burning with love for you. * I yield my soul into your hands. * I love you with all my heart, * and I repent of ever having offended you. * Grant that I may love you always, and then do with me as you will. *(Stand)*

The Thirteenth Station
Jesus Is Taken Down From the Cross

Leader: We adore you, O Christ, and we praise you. *(Genuflect)*
Assembly: Because by your holy Cross you have redeemed the world. *(Stand)*

Consider that, after our Lord had died, two of his disciples, Joseph and Nicodemus, took him down from the Cross and placed him in the waiting arms of his afflicted Mother. She received him with unspeakable tenderness and pressed him close to her breaking heart. *(Kneel)*

O Mother of Sorrows, * for the love of your son, * accept me as your servant, and pray to God for me. * And you, my Redeemer, who has died for me, * allow me to love you, * for I desire only you and nothing more. * I love you, Jesus my love, * and I repent of ever having offended you. * Never allow me to offend you again. * Grant that I may love you always, and then do with me as you will. *(Stand)*

The Fourteenth Station
Jesus Is Placed in the Tomb

Leader: We adore you, O Christ, and we praise you. *(Genuflect)*
Assembly: Because by your holy Cross you have redeemed the world. *(Stand)*

Consider the disciples carrying the body of Jesus to the place of burial. After his holy Mother arranges his body in the tomb with her own hands, they pull back the stone and depart. *(Kneel)*

My buried Jesus, * I kiss the stone that entombs you. * Yet I know that you rose glorious on the third day. * I pray that by your Resurrection, you will make me rise glorious on the last day, * to be united with you, so to praise and love you forever. * I love you, Jesus my love, * and I repent of ever having offended you. * Grant that I may love you always, and then do with me as you will. *(Stand)*

All sing:
Christ, when you shall call me hence,
Be your Mother my defense,
Be your cross my victory.

While my body here decays,
May my soul your goodness praise,
Safe in heav'n eternally.

3. Saint Alphonsus Liguori's Lenten Meditations

Saint Alphonsus published the meditations that follow in 1767. They are part of a much longer work entitled *The Way of Salvation and of Perfection*. Although the meditations can be enjoyed and appreciated as they are presented, it was the intention of Saint Alphonsus that they be used within the context of meditation. For many people the idea of meditation can be threatening, but it does not have to be. For example, the method of meditation proposed by Saint Alphonsus is easily learned and practiced. You do not need to be an expert at praying to profit from this kind of meditative practice. All that is required is a willingness to communicate with the Lord.

The proposed method of meditation consists of three parts: preparation, consideration, and conclusion.

In the preparation we remind ourselves of the presence of God, we pray for humility, and we pray for inspiration. We say, "My God, I believe that you are present, and I adore you. O my God, I am sorry for having offended you. Eternal Father, for the love of Jesus and Mary, grant me inspiration in this meditation, that I may profit by it." Then pray a Hail Mary to the Virgin Mother and a Glory to the Father, in honor of your guardian angel.

The second step is what Saint Alphonsus calls the "consideration." This step includes reading a reflection for the day, such as something from Scripture or a spiritual reading book and then some time spent recalling the Passion of Christ. It must be understood that the fruit of prayer does not consist in meditating but rather in producing (a) affections [prayers of praise], for example, affections of humility, confidence, love, sorrow, offering, and resignation to the will of God: (b) in making petitions, especially in imploring God to grant us perseverance and his holy love; (c) in making resolution to avoid some particular sin and practicing some particular virtue.

Finally, in the third step, the conclusion, we pray, "I thank you

41

God, for the insight that you have given me. I intend to keep the resolutions that I have made and I ask for the necessary grace from you to fulfill them." Never forget to recommend to God the poor souls in purgatory and all poor sinners. Never, regardless of how you might feel, no matter how cold or how weary you may be, omit your daily meditation.

The Death of Jesus Christ

How is it possible for us to believe that Jesus was willing to die for us? Yet we must believe it, because faith teaches it. The Council of Nicaea commands us to confess: "I believe in one Lord, Jesus Christ, the only Son of God, who for us and for our salvation was crucified for us, suffered, died, and was buried."

And if it is true, O God of love, that you died for the love of your people, can there be anyone who believes this and does not love you, so loving a God? But, O God, of those who are guilty of such ingratitude, I am one! Not only have I not loved you, my Redeemer, but I have many times, for the sake of gratifying my miserable and depraved inclinations, renounced your grace and your love.

Lord and my God, you died for me; how could I, knowing this, so often have disowned you and turned my back on you? But you, my Savior, did come from heaven to save what was lost. My ingratitude, therefore, does not deprive me of the hope of pardon. Yes, O Jesus! I hope that you will pardon me from all the offenses which I have committed against you, through the death which you suffered for me on Mount Calvary. Oh that I could die of grief and of love as often as I think of the offenses that I have committed against the love which you have shown to me. Make known to me, O Lord, what I must do from this day on to make amends for my ingratitude. Keep in my mind a continual remembrance of the bitter death you suffered for me, that I may love you and never more offend you.

God, then, has died for me; shall I be able to love anything else but God? No, my Jesus, I will love no one but you. You have loved me too much. You can do no more to compel me to love you. By my sins I have obliged you to cast me away from your face, but you did not abandon me forever. You think of me with tender affection and you invite me to love you, and I will no longer resist. I love you, my only good. I love you, my God, who are worthy of infinite love. I love you, my God, who has died for me. However, I do not love you enough; increase my love! Grant that I may turn away from all things, and forget all else, so that I may learn to please you and to love you, my Redeemer, my love, and my all. O Mary, my hope, recommend me to your divine Son!

The Sacred Wounds of Jesus

Saint Bonaventure says that the wounds of Jesus wound the hardest hearts and inflame the coldest souls. How can we believe that Jesus permitted himself to be beaten, scourged, crowned with thorns, and finally put to death for the love of us, and not love him? Saint Francis of Assisi frequently lamented the ingratitude of people as he walked through Italy, saying, "Love is not loved, Love is not loved."

Behold, my Jesus, I am one of those who are ungrateful, who have lived in this world so many years and who have not loved you. Shall I, my Redeemer, remain ungrateful forever? No, I will love you until death and will give myself completely to you. Mercifully accept me and help me.

The Church, when it shows us Jesus Christ crucified, exclaims, "His whole figure breathes forth love, his head bowed down, his arms extended, his side opened." The Church cries out, "Behold your God, who has died for your love; see how his arms are extended to embrace you, his head bowed down to give you the kiss of peace, his side opened to give you access to his heart. If only you could love him!"

Assuredly, I will love you, my treasure, my love, my all. Whom shall I love, if I will not love God who died for me? Pardon me, O

Jesus, and draw my whole heart to yourself so that I may not desire, nor seek, nor yearn for any other beside you. O Mary, my mother, help me to love Jesus!

The Love of Jesus Crucified

Our loving Redeemer may well declare that he came upon the earth to enkindle divine love and that he desired nothing else but to see this sacred fire burning in our hearts, "I have come to bring fire upon the earth and how I wish it were already kindled" (Lk 12:49). And, in fact, how many happy souls have been so inflamed with the thoughts of a crucified God as to leave all other things and give themselves entirely to this holy love. What more could Jesus have done to induce us to love him than to die in torment upon a cross to prove how much he loved us? With good reason did Saint Francis Paola, when he contemplated Jesus crucified, exclaim in ecstasy, "O love, love, love."

But, alas, most people live lives that are forgetful of so loving a God. If the vilest human being, or if a slave had done for me what Jesus Christ has done and suffered for me, how would I be able to live without loving that one? O God, who is he that hangs upon the cross? That cross, those thorns, those nails, exclaim, and with a still louder voice, those wounds cry out and demand our love.

"May I die," said Saint Francis of Assisi, "for the love of your love, O Jesus, who has died for the love of my love." To make an adequate return for the love of God in dying for us would require another God to die for Jesus. It would be little, it would be nothing, were each of us to give a thousand lives in return for the love of Jesus Christ. Jesus is satisfied with the gift of our hearts, but he is not completely satisfied until we give them entirely to him. For this purpose, says the apostle Paul, did Jesus die that he might have the entire dominion of our hearts: "Christ experienced death and life to be Lord both of the living and of the dead" (Rom 14:9).

My beloved Redeemer, how can I ever forget you? How can I love anything else, after having seen you die in torment on an infamous cross in reparation for my sins? How can I remember that my sins have reduced you to this and not die with grief at the remembrance of the offenses that I have committed against you? Jesus, help me. I desire nothing but you. Help me and love me. O Mary, my hope, assist me by your prayers.

The Love of the Father in Giving Us His Son

God's love was so great for us that, after having loaded us with gifts and graces, God gifted us with his own Son: "Yes, God so loved the world that he gave us his only Son" (Jn 3:16). For us poor miserable worms of the earth, the eternal Father sent his beloved Son into the world to live a poor and despised life. Jesus suffered the most ignominious and bitter death that any mortal on earth had ever suffered, an accumulation of internal as well as external torments. These torments caused Jesus to exclaim, "My God, my God, why have you forsaken me?" (Mt 27:46).

O eternal God, only a God of infinite love could have bestowed upon us a gift of such infinite value. I love you, O infinite goodness! I love you, O infinite love!

"If he did not spare his own Son, but gave him up for us all, how will he not give us all things with him?" (Rom 8:32). God eternal, consider that this divine Son, whom you have doomed to death, is innocent and has been obedient to you in all things. You love him as you love yourself, then how can you condemn him to death for the expiation of our sins? To this question, the eternal Father replies, "It was precisely because he was my Son, because he was innocent, because he was obedient to me in all things that it was my will that he should sacrifice his life, so that you might know the greatness of that love which we both hold for you."

May all creatures forever praise you, O God, for the excess of your gifts which have caused your own Son to sacrifice himself so that your servants may be redeemed. For the love of your Son, have pity on me, and save me. Let my salvation be to love you forever, both in this world and in the next. O Mary, unite me more and more to my dearest Savior.

The Moment of Death

Imagine yourself, dear friend, dead, and your soul entering into eternity. If you had just now departed from this world, what would you wish that you had not chosen as you face eternal life? Now consider what such wishes would accomplish at this moment, if you had not spent the days of your mortal life in serving God?

If you would now prevent that which you have time to prevent, use your imagination and imagine yourself in your grave, or upon your deathbed. Imagine yourself to be dying, on the point of breathing your last, and listen to the regretful voice of your conscience, and do not delay in silencing it by repentance. Delay not, for you have no time to lose.

My God, enlighten me, make known to me the way in which I should walk, and I will obey you in all things.

Saint Camillus de Lellis, looking at the graves of the dead, often remarked, "If those who are buried here could return to life again, what they do differently in order to become saints. I, who have time at my disposal, what do I do for God?" In this way, Saint Camillus animated himself to become more and more closely united with his Lord. Know then, dear friend, that the time which God in his mercy now grants you is a gift of the greatest value. Do not wait for time to work for your salvation until you are in eternity, or until the arrival of that awful moment when it will be said to you, "Depart Christian soul, out of this world." Move fast, for there is no more time for you to work: what is done is done.

O Jesus, remember that I am the lost sheep for whom you have laid down your life. I beg you, help your servant whom you have redeemed by your precious blood. Give me light and grace to do now that which I will one day wish that I had done at the hour of my death. Blessed Virgin Mary, deprive me not of your powerful protection.

The Remorse of the Reprobate

The condemned soul is tormented with three kinds of remorse. The first type of remorse is the kind that comes from realizing what a mere trifle the soul has incurred for everlasting misery. How long does the pleasure of sin last? Only for a moment. To the people at the point of death, how long does their past life appear? A mere moment. To the people in hell, how might the fifty or sixty years of their life journey upon the earth appear, when, in the gulf of eternity, they are able to understand that after a hundred or a thousand million years, they are only beginning eternity? "Alas," they exclaim, "for a few moments of indulgence in poisonous pleasures, I must forever suffer, lament, and despair in the fiery furnace of hell, abandoned by all, for as long as God is God."

O my God! I give you thanks for your great mercy. I implore you to continue to have mercy on me.

The second kind of remorse comes from the reflection of the condemned on the little which they needed to do in order to be saved, but they chose not to do, and that now there is no remedy. "Alas," they might say, "if I had frequently confessed my sins, given myself to prayer, restored ill-gotten property, pardoned my enemies, and avoided the dangerous occasion of sin, I would not have been lost." How often does this thought torment the wretched soul, even more than the fire and all the other torments of hell, that it might have been happy forever, but now must be miserable for all eternity.

O Jesus! It is now the time of mercy, mercifully pardon me. I love you, my only good, and I am exceedingly sorry for having ever despised you.

The third and most bitter kind of remorse arises from the consciousness of the wretched souls of the great happiness that they forfeited by their choices and decisions. These souls remember that God offered abundant means of gaining heaven, that Jesus died for their salvation, and that they were permitted to be born in the bosom of the true Church. These souls recall numberless graces and reflect that all have been rendered useless and ineffective through their own fault. "I am lost," the soul exclaims, "and neither the merits of Jesus Christ, nor the intercession of the Mother of God, nor the prayers of the saints are of any use to me, for every gleam of hope is vanished from me forever."

Oh, that I had died, my God, rather than to have ever offended you. Receive me now into your favor. I love you, and I will love you forever. Mary, most gracious advocate of sinners, intercede for me.

Concluding Prayer

This prayer should be said after each meditation.

PRAYER TO JESUS CHRIST TO OBTAIN HIS HOLY LOVE

My crucified love, my dear Jesus. I believe in you, and confess you to be the Redeemer, the true Son of God. I adore you from the abyss of my nothingness, and I thank you for the death you suffered for me, so that I might obtain the life of divine grace. My beloved Redeemer, to you I owe all of my salvation. Through you I have escaped hell and received pardon for my sins. But I am so ungrateful that, instead of loving you, I have repeated my offenses against you. I deserve to be condemned, so as not to be able to love you any more. Yet, my Jesus, punish me in any other way, but not in this. If I have not loved you in times past, I love you now, and I desire nothing but to love you with all my heart. Without your help I can do nothing. Since you have commanded me to love, give me also that strength to fulfill this sweet and loving commandment.

My Lord Jesus, you have promised to grant all that we ask of you. I ask, first of all, pardon for all of my sins, and I repent, above all things, because I have offended you, O infinite goodness. I ask for holy perseverance in your grace until my death. But above all, I ask for the gift of your holy love. Ah, my Jesus, my hope, my love, my all, inflame me with the love which you came to light upon this earth! For this end, make me always live in conformity with your holy will. Enlighten me, so that I may understand more and more how worthy you are of love, and that I may know the immense love you have for me, especially in giving your life for me. Grant, then, that I may love you with all my heart and may love you always and never cease to beg of you the grace to love you in this life, so that I may one day come to love you in all eternity.

O Mother of beautiful love, my advocate and my refuge, Mary, who are of all creatures the most beautiful, the most loving, and the most beloved of God, and whose only desire it is to see God loved: By the love that you have for Jesus Christ, pray for me, and obtain for me the grace to love him always with all my heart. This I ask for and hope from you. Amen.

4. Lenten Reconciliation Service

A traditional practice during Lent is the individual confession and absolution of sins within the context of the sacrament of reconciliation. For many people confession is a very private matter and they choose to celebrate the sacrament within the regularly scheduled times for confession in their local parish church. However, for others, the celebration of reconciliation is more meaningful if it is celebrated with the community. Responding to this need most Catholic parishes schedule at least one common reconciliation service for those who prefer this practice.

The service that follows is one example of a community celebration of reconciliation. Although it is intended for use by a community gathered together, it may also be used by an individual person preparing for the celebration of the sacrament. For individual use, all parts of the service are prayed by the individual person; for the communal celebration, the different parts are designated to accurately represent the communal nature of the celebration.

Theme: This is the definition of sin: The misuse of powers given by God for doing good. (Saint Basil the Great)

Call to Worship
Joel 2:13

Rend your hearts and not your clothing. Return to the Lord, your God, for he is gracious and merciful, slow to anger, and abounding in steadfast love, and relents from punishing. *(Please stand.)*

Greeting

Lent is a time for us to listen to the call of repentance. We are called to turn away from sin and to believe in the Gospel. We center our attention on the Passion of Jesus Christ and bring our sinfulness to the foot of the cross, crying out: "Have mercy on us, have mercy, O Lord!"

Opening Prayer

God of mercy and compassion, hear us as we call upon you for mercy. Jesus Christ, by his Passion, death, and Resurrection has won for us the forgiveness of our sins. We call out to you and beg you to send your mercy and pardon on your people gathered to confess their sins. We ask this through Christ our Lord. Amen.

Liturgy of the Word

The congregation is seated for the following readings.

FIRST READING

Joel 2:12–17

RESPONSORIAL PSALM

Psalm 51:3–10

SECOND READING

Hebrews 3:12–15

GOSPEL

Luke 15:1–7

Examination of Conscience

(Please kneel or remain seated.)

Priest: Let us pray. Lord Jesus, open my mind and heart to your Holy Spirit. Show me where I am failing to love your heavenly Father. Show me where I am failing to love you as my Savior, failing to seek you and yield to you as my Lord. Show me where I am failing to love the Holy Spirit, failing to be open and to be led by Wisdom and Love.

(The reader for the examination should be chosen before the service so he or she can prepare. The petitions should be read slowly, with a pause for reflection between each.)

Leader: For the times I have failed to see the poor and oppressed, and my failure to do what I could to feed the hungry.
All: I ask pardon, O Lord.

Leader: For the times I have failed to respond to the call of the Gospel by not doing what I could for those without clothing or shelter.
All: I ask pardon, O Lord.

Leader: For the times I have not respected members of my family, my neighbors, and those who work with me.
All: I ask pardon, O Lord.

Leader: For the times I have not been sensitive to another's needs and weaknesses.
All: I ask pardon, O Lord.

Leader: For those I have hurt by words of unkindness or untruth.
All: I ask pardon, O Lord.

Leader: For those I have discriminated against because of race, religion, nationality, age, profession, or gender.
All: I ask pardon, O Lord.

Leader: For the times I have caused pain and suffering in the lives of loved ones and friends through my abuse of alcohol, food, or drugs.
All: I ask pardon, O Lord.

Leader: For those who have suffered because of my misuse of money.
All: I ask pardon, O Lord.

Leader: For the times I have been selfish with the gifts God has given me.
All: I ask pardon, O Lord.

Leader: For the times I have been unforgiving.
All: I ask pardon, O Lord.

Leader: For the times I have been angry with others and have caused pain and suffering in their lives.
All: I ask pardon, O Lord.

Leader: Let us pause in silence and ask the Lord for forgiveness for what troubles us most. (*Allow a slightly longer period of silence.*)

Rite of Reconciliation
(Please stand.)

Priest: Let us pray in the words that Jesus taught us.
All: Our Father...

Priest: Let us pray. Lord, we come before you asking for mercy and forgiveness of our sins. We confess that we are sinners. Through the ministry of the Church, grant us pardon from all our sins. We give your thankful praise in the name of Jesus, our Lord and Savior.
All: Amen.

Suggested Hymn

Lord, Have Mercy or some other hymn asking for mercy and forgiveness.

Individual Confession and Absolution
(Please kneel or be seated.)

Concluding Rite

PROCLAMATION OF PRAISE

Psalms 1–2

I will give thanks to the Lord with my whole heart;
I will tell of all your wonderful deeds.
I will be glad and exult in you;
I will sing praise to your name,
O most High.

CONCLUDING PRAYER OF THANKSGIVING
(Please stand.)

Priest: Let us pray. All holy Father, you have shown us the way to forgiveness in the example of your son, Jesus Christ. Through the merits of his Passion and death on the cross, grant us pardon of our sinfulness. Make us living signs of your love for the whole world to see. We ask this through Christ our Lord.

All: Amen.

BLESSING

Priest: May the Lord guide your hearts in the way of his love and fill you with Christlike patience.

All: Amen.

Priest: May the Lord give you strength to walk in newness of life and to please God in all things.

All: Amen.

Priest: May almighty God bless you, the Father, and the Son, and the Holy Spirit.

All: Amen.

Dismissal

(A psalm of hymn may be sung or the sign of peace given in closing.)
Priest: The Lord has freed you from your sins. Go in peace.
All: Thanks be to God.

5. Traditional Examination of Conscience

A thorough examination of a person's conscience has been a traditional recommendation for those who are preparing for the confession of their sins. Within the spiritual tradition of the Church, there are occasions when the examination should be very detailed in preparation for the celebration of the sacrament. One such occasion when a detailed examination should take place is within the season of Lent.

The detailed examination of conscience begins with a prayer and a series of preparatory questions and then examines the behavior of a person in relation to the Ten Commandments and the Precepts of the Church. The detailed examination ends with particular questions for people in different "states in life," such as married, single, or religious, and, finally, particular questions for people who are doctors, lawyers, druggists, and so on. The examination that follows is from *The Mission Book of the Redemptorist Fathers*, a devotional manual routinely used by many Catholics until the Second Vatican Council. The examination will include edited questions pertaining to the Ten Commandments and the Precepts of the Church but will not include the questions for people in different states in life.

Preparatory Prayer

O God, Father of light, who enlightens everyone who comes into this world, give me light, love, and sorrow, that I may discover, detest and confess all the sins that I have committed.

O Most holy Virgin Mary, Mother of the Redeemer, so compassionate toward those who desire to repent, help me to make a good confession.

My dear guardian angel, help me to call to mind all my offenses. All the saints and angels, pray for me that I may now bring forth worthy fruits of penance.

Preparatory Questions

How long ago did you make your last confession? Did you receive absolution? Have you performed your penance? Did you willfully conceal a mortal sin or confess without true sorrow, without the purpose of amendment, or without intending to perform your penance?

First Commandment:
I am the Lord your God, you shall have no gods before me.

Have you disbelieved or willfully indulged in doubts against any article of faith or suggested or encouraged such doubts in others? Have you attended or joined in false worship? Have you exposed your faith to danger by evil associations? Have you remained a long time, a whole month or longer, without reciting any prayer, or performing any act of devotion toward God? Have you consulted fortunetellers or made use of superstitious practices, love potions, or charms?

Second Commandment:
You shall not take the name of the Lord your God in vain.

Have you been guilty of blasphemy by angry, injurious, or insulting words against God? Have you pronounced in a blasphemous or irreverent manner, or in anger, the holy name of God, the name of Jesus Christ, or that of any of the saints? Have you sworn a false oath? Have you cursed yourself or cursed a neighbor?

Third Commandment:
Remember to keep holy the sabbath day.

How often have you on Sundays and holy days of obligation willfully choose not to attend Mass, or come too late, or left before Mass was over? How often have you performed unnecessary servile work on Sundays and on holy days or caused others to do the same? How often did you desecrate these days by frequenting ungodly company, by sinful amusements, gambling, immodest dancing, or drinking to excess?

Fourth Commandment:
Honor your father and your mother.

Have you insulted, mocked, ridiculed, or cursed your parents? Have you threatened them, or even lifted your hand to strike them? Have you sorely grieved your parents by your ingratitude or misconduct? Have you neglected or refused to aid them in their wants? Have you neglected to pray for them? Have you neglected to pray for the repose of their souls?

Fifth Commandment:
You shall not kill.

Have you by act, participation, instigation, counsel, or consent been guilty of anyone's death or bodily injury? Have you intended or attempted to take another's life? Have you injured your health by excess in eating or drinking? Have you been drunk or been the cause of drunkenness in another? Have you by act, advice, or consent done anything to hinder or destroy life? Have you harmed the soul of another person by giving scandal? Have you by wicked words, deeds, or bad example ruined innocent persons, taught them bad habits or things they should not know?

Sixth and Ninth Commandments:
You shall not commit adultery.
You shall not covet your neighbors wife.

These commandments forbid everything that is contrary to purity. How often have you made use of impure language, allusions, or words of double meaning? How often have you voluntarily exposed yourself to the occasion of sin by sinful curiosity, by frequenting dangerous company, places, or sinful amusements? How often have you been guilty of improper liberties with others? Have far have you carried your sinful conduct? You must mention those circumstances that change the nature of your sin—the sex, the relationship, and the condition—whether married, single or bound by vow. Were you married or single at the time?

Seventh and Tenth Commandments:
You shall not steal.
You shall not covet your neighbors' goods.

Have you stolen money or anything of value? Is it still in your possession? What was its value? How much did you take each time and how often? Have you stolen anything belonging to God or to a sacred place? Have you charged exorbitant prices; made out false bills; or cheated in the weight, measure, quantity, or quality of your goods? Have you cheated in games? Have you been guilty of forgery? Have you kept things you found without inquiring for the owner? Have you bought, received, or concealed things you knew to be stolen?

Eighth Commandment:
You shall not bear false witness against your neighbor.

Have you taken a false oath or advised others to do so? Have you signed false papers or forged writings? Have you been guilty of malicious lying? Have you caused ill-feelings between others by tale-bearing? Have you attempted to repair the harm you have done by contradicting your false reports? Have you been guilty of unjust suspicions and rash judgments?

6. Prayer Before Confession

O most loving Jesus, dying on the Cross for my sake, remember that I am a soul redeemed by your most precious blood. Pardon me, I am sorry for my sins. I beseech you by your sacred wounds, by your loving heart, to receive the traitor who now casts himself in sorrow at your feet. My sins fill me with terror, I know that I deserve the flames of hell. But since you have died for me, I hope that you will have mercy on me now that I implore your forgiveness and am firmly resolved to sin no more. I promise to serve you faithfully all the days of my life, and to love you as much as I have offended you. O my most loving Jesus, you have died to save me, let not your blood be shed for me in vain. Grant me the grace to confess my sins humbly and sincerely. Give me the strength to avoid all of the occasions of sin and never more to offend you again.

Holy Virgin Mary, Mother of mercy, my holy guardian angel and all my patron saints, help me to lead from this day forward a truly Christian life. Amen.

7. A Visit to the Most Blessed Sacrament by Saint Alphonsus Liguori

At one time in the not-so-distant past, the practice of a daily visit to the Blessed Sacrament was not uncommon. The faithful on their way home from the fields would stop in the village church or coming home from work they would stop in the neighborhood church. Priests, monks, and religious women living in monasteries and convents with chapels would often stop into the chapel in the midst of their daily routine and make a quick visit to the Blessed Sacrament. Unfortunately, this practice, because of a variety of reasons, fell into disfavor. Today, however, the practice is being revived with a renewed interest, because of the establishment of the practice of Perpetual Adoration in many parish churches and because of a renewed emphasis on the doctrine of the True Presence of Christ in the Blessed Sacrament.

The *Visits to the Blessed Sacrament* by Saint Alphonsus is a perennial favorite. Each visit (the saint provides the faithful with an appropriate visit for each day of the month) consists of an opening prayer, a meditation on the Eucharist, a spiritual communion prayer, a visit to the Blessed Mother, and, finally, a closing prayer.

Opening Prayer

My Lord Jesus Christ, I believe that you are really here in this sacrament. Night and day you remain here compassionate and loving. You call, you wait for, you welcome, everyone who comes to you.

Unimportant though I am, I adore you. I thank you for all the wonderful graces you have given me. But I thank you especially for having given me yourself in this sacrament, for having asked your own Mother to mother me, for having called me here to talk to you.

I am here before you today to do three things: to thank you for these precious gifts, to make up for all the disrespect that you receive in this sacrament from those who offend you, to adore you everywhere in the world where you are present in this living bread but are left abandoned and unloved.

My Jesus, I love you with all my heart. I know I have displeased you often in the past—I am sorry. With your help I promise never to do it again. I am only a miserable sinner, but I consecrate myself to you completely. I give you my will, my love, my desires, everything I own. From now on, do what you please with me. All I ask is that you love me, that you keep me faithful to you to the end of my life. I ask for the grace to do your will exactly as you want it done.

I pray for the souls in purgatory—especially for those who were close to you in this sacrament and close to your Mother Mary. I pray for every soul hardened in sin. My Savior, I unite my love to the love of your divine heart, and I offer them both together to your Father. I beg him to accept this offering in your name. Amen.

Visit Appropriate for Lent

You are kneeling before a fountain. From its calm depths a voice whispers: *If you are thirsty, come to me.* It is Christ in the Blessed Sacrament. From this fountain of love, he pours out upon the world all the merits of his sufferings. From it, the saints drink deeply. The prophet predicted it: *You shall drink with joy from the Savior's fountain.*

A Spanish Poor Clare loved to make long visits to the Blessed Sacrament. The other nuns asked what she did during those long silent hours. "I could kneel there forever," she answered. "And why not? God is there. You wonder what I do in the presence of my God? I marvel, I love, I thank, I beg. What does a beggar do when he meets a millionaire? a sick person when he sees a doctor? a starving person when he sees food? What does a dry-throated hiker do at a drinking fountain?"

My Jesus: You are my Life, my Hope, my Treasure, my soul's only Love. A cruel death was the price you paid to be in this sacrament today. And even now you suffer insults from those who ignore you. Yet you remain because you want our love.

Come, my Lord, implant yourself in my heart. Lock its door forever. I want nothing cheap to enter it and take away the love that belongs to you. You alone must run my life. If I swerve from you, steer me straight once more. Make me search for one pleasure: the pleasure of pleasing you. Make me yearn for one joy: the joy of visiting you. Make me crave for one delight: the delight of receiving your body and blood. So many people chase after such hollow things! But all I care about is your love, and I am here to beg it from you today. Let me forget myself and keep you ever before my mind. Amen.

Spiritual Communion

My Jesus, I believe you are really here in the Blessed Sacrament. I love you more than anything in the world, and I hunger to feed on your flesh. But since I cannot receive communion at this moment, feed my soul at least spiritually. I unite myself to you now as I do when I actually receive you. Never let me be parted from you.

Visit With Mary

We have another fountain to drink from as well, our Mother Mary. Saint Bernard said that Mary is so rich in graces that everyone shares in them: "Of her fullness, we have all received." Mary was literally filled with grace, as the angel said when he greeted her. God filled her with such tremendous riches so that she could share them with her children. Cause of our joy, pray for us!

Closing Prayer

Most Holy Immaculate Virgin and my Mother Mary, to you who are the Mother of my Lord, the Queen of the World, the Advocate, the

Hope, the Refuge of Sinners, I have recourse today—I who am the most miserable of all. I render you my most humble homage, O great Queen, and I thank you for all the graces you have conferred on me until now, particularly for having delivered me from hell, which I have so often deserved. I love you, O most amiable Lady; and for the love which I bear you, I promise to serve you always and to do all in my power to make others also love you. I place in you all my hopes; I confide my salvation to your care. Accept me for your servant and receive me under your mantle, O Mother of Mercy. And since you are so powerful with God, deliver me from all temptations, or rather obtain for me the strength to triumph over them until death. Of you I ask a perfect love for Jesus Christ. From you I hope to die a good death. O my Mother, by the love which you bear to God, I beseech you to help me at all times, but especially at the last moment of my life. Leave me not, I beseech you, until you see me safe in heaven, blessing you and singing your mercies for all eternity. Amen. So I hope. So may it be.

8. Devotions in Honor of the Passion of the Lord

Among the many ascetical works of Saint Alphonsus Liguori, there is a little gem entitled *The Passion and Death of Jesus Christ*. This work is reflective of the fruits of the many meditations of Saint Alphonsus on the Passion of the Lord. Saint Alphonsus believed that "all of the saints learned the art of loving God" from the study of the Passion and death of Jesus. Or, to put it in yet another way, "who could love any other object besides Jesus when they see him dying in the midst of so many sufferings and insults in order to captivate our love?"

For our purposes, two small sections representative of the meditations found in *The Passion and Death of Jesus Christ* are included in this book. The first is a small litany prayer entitled *Steps of the Passion*. The second is a somewhat longer text entitled *Little Chaplet of the Five Wounds of Jesus Crucified*.

Steps of the Passion

My most loving Jesus, while praying in the garden you shed a sweat of blood, were in agony, and experienced sorrow until death. Have mercy on us. *Have mercy on us, O Lord, have mercy on us.*

My most loving Jesus, you were betrayed by Judas with a kiss, handed over to your enemies, taken prisoner by them and bound and abandoned by your disciples. Have mercy on us. *Have mercy on us, O Lord, have mercy on us.*

My most loving Jesus, declared guilty of death by the Council of Chief Priests, blindfolded in the house of Caiphas, struck, spat at, and ridiculed. Have mercy on us. *Have mercy on us, O Lord, have mercy on us.*

My most loving Jesus, led as an evildoer to Pilate, ridiculed by Herod and treated as a madman. Have mercy on us. *Have mercy on us, O Lord, have mercy on us.*

My most loving Jesus, stripped of your clothes, bound to a pillar and so cruelly scourged. Have mercy on us. *Have mercy on us, O Lord, have mercy on us.*

My most loving Jesus, crowned with thorns, clothed in a red robe, struck at and in mockery saluted as the King of the Jews. Have mercy on us. *Have mercy on us, O Lord, have mercy on us.*

My most loving Jesus, rejected by your friends, made lower than Barabbas and then unjustly condemned by Pilate to die upon a Cross. Have mercy on us. *Have mercy on us, O Lord, have mercy on us.*

My most loving Jesus, loaded with the wood of the Cross and as an innocent lamb led away to death. Have mercy on us. *Have mercy on us, O Lord, have mercy on us.*

My most loving Jesus, nailed to the Cross, placed between two thieves, ridiculed and blasphemed, and for three hours was in agony. Have mercy on us. *Have mercy on us, O Lord, have mercy on us.*

My most loving Jesus, dead upon the Cross and in the sight of your Holy Mother pierced on the side with a spear from which flowed blood and water. Have mercy on us. *Have mercy on us, O Lord, have mercy on us.*

My most loving Jesus, taken down from the Cross and placed on the lap of your sorrowing Mother. Have mercy on us. *Have mercy on us, O Lord, have mercy on us.*

My most loving Jesus, torn with a whip, bearing five wounds was laid in a tomb. Have mercy on us. *Have mercy on us, O Lord, have mercy on us.*

Lord, as we venerate your sacred Passion, by the power of your Cross and death, deliver us from being eternally lost and lead us where you led the thief crucified with you. We ask this of you who live and reign forever and ever. Amen.

Little Chaplet of the Five Wounds of Jesus Crucified

MEDITATION I

O my Lord Jesus Christ, I adore the wound in your left foot. I thank you for having suffered this wound for me with so much sorrow and with so much love. I feel compassion for your pain and for the pain of your afflicted Mother. By the merit of this sacred wound, I pray that you would grant me the pardon of my sins of which I repent with my whole heart, because they have offended your infinite goodness. O sorrowing Mother, pray to Jesus for me.

MEDITATION II

O my Lord Jesus Christ, I adore the wound in your right foot. I thank you for having suffered this wound for me with so much sorrow and with so much love. I feel compassion for your pain and for the pain of your afflicted Mother. By the merit of this sacred wound, I pray that you would give me the strength not to fall into mortal sin and to persevere in your grace until my death. O sorrowing Mother, pray to Jesus for me.

MEDITATION III

O my Lord Jesus Christ, I adore the wound in your left hand. I thank you for having suffered this wound for me with so much sorrow and with so much love. I feel compassion for your pain and for the pain of your afflicted Mother. By the merit of this sacred wound, I pray that you would deliver me from hell which I have so often deserved, a place where I could never love you again. O sorrowing Mother, pray to Jesus for me.

MEDITATION IV

O my Lord Jesus Christ, I adore the wound in your right hand. I thank you for having suffered this wound for me with so much sorrow and with so much love. I feel compassion for your pain and for the pain of your afflicted Mother. By the merit of this sacred wound, I pray that you would give me the glory of paradise where I shall love you perfectly and with all my strength. O sorrowing Mother, pray to Jesus for me.

MEDITATION V

O my Lord Jesus Christ, I adore the wound in your side. I thank you for having suffered this wound for me with so much sorrow and with so much love. I feel compassion for your pain and for the pain of your afflicted Mother, who alone felt all its pain. By the merits of this sacred wound, I pray that you would grant me the gift of holy love for you, so that I may love you in this life and in the other life, face to face, for all eternity in paradise. O sorrowing Mother, pray to Jesus for me.

A Rule of Life
Appropriate for Lent

W hat can a person do in order to live a holy life? What are the necessary choices a person must make to gain salvation and strive to live a life of perfection? Many of the saints have attempted to answer this question, and each of their answers contributes to the richness and the diversity of spiritual expression that is found in the Church. Saint Ignatius of Loyola has left us with the *Spiritual Exercises*, Saint Thérèse of the Child Jesus with her "Little Way," Saint Teresa of Ávila with the *Interior Castle*, and Saint Alphonsus Liguori with his *Way of Salvation and Perfection*. Each of these great saints has demonstrated, by their lives and their example, a particular path that we may follow that may also lead us to holiness.

1. Saint Alphonsus Liguori's Rule of Life

Buried in the *Way of Salvation and Perfection* is a short Rule of Life proposed by Saint Alphonsus. This short rule can serve as a helpful reference for a person's spiritual journey. Because it is so short, it can be easily followed and referenced. While by no means should it be understood as the complete reflection of the saint, or as a substitute for the *Way of Salvation and Perfection*, it is nevertheless a helpful guide.

Alphonsus Liguori's Rule of Life may be most appropriate for the season of Lent. For those who are looking for the time-tested spiritual guidance, the rule provides the necessary discipline. For those who may be looking for some insight into a particular spiritual practice or habit, the rule provides a context for understanding the spiritual tradition and practice.

Rule I

The first thing in the morning, immediately upon waking up, the following prayer should be prayed:

O my God, I adore you. I love you with all my heart and I thank you for all your gifts, in particular for preserving me through the night. I offer you all that I shall do or suffer throughout this day, in union with the actions and the sufferings of Jesus and Mary. I intend to avoid every offense against you, but I ask that you extend your protection to me so that I may continue to love you. Most Holy Mary, take me under your protection. My guardian angel and patron saints, come to my aid. Amen.

Rule II

As soon as possible in the day, make a half-hour meditation. Although meditation is not absolutely necessary, it is morally necessary in order to gain the grace of perseverance. Those who neglect meditation will find it very difficult to persevere in the grace of God. There are two reasons for this: the first is because the eyes of flesh cannot see the eternal truths, but rather through the eyes of understanding, which is reflection. The person who does not meditate will be unable to appreciate the importance of salvation and of the necessary steps which secure it and the obstacles which hinder it. The second reason is because the person who does not practice meditation will also not practice prayer. Prayer is necessary, not merely as a precept, but as a way to observe the commandments, since, as a general rule, God gives his grace only to those who ask for it.

Without meditation a person has a very small understanding of his or her spiritual wants, is often unaware of the necessity of prayer in order to overcome temptation, and because of the absence of the practice of prayer is eventually lost. The eminent Bishop Palafox said, "How will the Lord give us perseverance unless we ask for it? How shall we ask for it if we do not pray?" Saint Teresa of Ávila declares that it is not possible for a person who prays to remain in sin; such a person will either give up prayer or give up sin because they are incompatible. (You may wish to refer to Section Two, page 27, for a description of the Alphonsian method of meditation.)

Rule III

Attend Mass daily. We participate at Mass to honor Almighty God, to thank God for his gifts, to make atonement for the punishment due to our sins, and to obtain divine grace. As we prepare to participate in the Mass, we should pray, "Eternal Father, in this Mass, I offer Jesus Christ, with all the merits of his Passion. I honor your majesty. I thank you for all the gifts that you have given me. I attend this Mass because of my sins and the sins of all the living and of those who have died in your grace. I pray for the graces necessary for salvation." At the elevation of the sacred host pray, "By the blood of Jesus Christ, grant me the grace to love you in this life and in the next." When the priest takes holy Communion, pray, "My Jesus, I love you, and I long for you in my soul. I embrace you and pray that I will never be separated from you."

Rule IV

Read a spiritual book for a half hour, or at least a quarter of an hour, each day. It is best to read the lives of the saints.

Rule V

Every day, make a visit to the Blessed Sacrament. In the presence of the Lord pray, "O Lord, I thank you for your love in leaving yourself to me in this sacrament. With my whole heart, I love you, O God, above all else. Because I love you, I am sorry for all my offenses against you, whether great or small. I beg you to give me the grace of perseverance in your grace and in your holy love." At the same time, make a visit to our Blessed Mother, before one of her images, and beg of her the same graces of perseverance and the love of God.

Rule VI

In the evening, make an examination of conscience and then pray a prayer of faith, hope, and charity. Suggested prayers that you may use or adapt follow:

Act of Faith: My God, I believe in you and I hope in you. I love you above all things, with all my soul, with all my heart and with all my strength. I love you because you are infinitely good and worthy of being loved. Because I love you, I repent with all my heart of having offended you. Have mercy on me, a sinner. Amen.

Act of Hope: My God, I believe in you and I hope in you. Because of your infinite goodness and kindness, I hope for everlasting life, patience in my sufferings, and, above all, your gentle and guiding hand, leading me to everlasting peace and joy. Amen.

Act of Charity: O my Jesus, you who are love, enkindle in my heart that divine fire which consumes the saints and transforms them. Fill up that which is lacking in me and form me each day more and more into your divine image. Help me to love and serve my brothers and sisters and to recognize in them your loving presence. Amen.

Rule VII

Frequent reception of the sacraments of reconciliation and the holy Eucharist is recommended. Before confession, pray as follows:

I thank you, O my God, for having waited for me until now. I hope, through the merits of Jesus Christ, for the pardon of all of my sins. I am sorry for them, and repent of them with my whole heart. By my sins I have lost heaven and have deserved hell. Above all I am grieved, to the depths of my being, and hate and detest my sins more than all evils, because they have offended your infinite goodness. I would rather die than offend you any more.

Rule VIII

It is wise to choose a good confessor and to follow his direction in all spiritual matters and even in temporal matters of importance. The relationship should not be ended without a good reason. Saint Philip Neri teaches: "Let those who desire to advance in the way of God put themselves under the direction of an enlightened confessor, and let them obey their director as they would the voice of God. Whoever does this may feel assured that they will never have to render an account to God of what they choose." This teaching conforms to the words of Jesus Christ, "Whoever listens to you, listens to me" (Lk 10:16).

Rule IX

When you are tempted, do not trust yourself, and do not trust all the good resolutions and promises that you have made, but rely completely on divine assistance; have immediate recourse to God and the Blessed Virgin. In temptations against purity, the greatest care must be taken. The best plan to adopt on these occasions is to renew the firm purpose "to die than to offend God" (Rule VII) and to make the Sign of the Cross, calling on God and the Blessed Mother. It is also helpful to make frequent invocations to the most holy names of Jesus and Mary, which have a wonderful efficacy against filthy temptations and which should be invoked continually until the temptations pass. It should be remembered that we do not have the personal strength to overcome the attacks of the flesh, our most cruel enemy. God readily supplies the strength that we need to all that ask; the person who fails to ask will fall prey to the enemy. The same process is to be followed in combating temptations against the virtue of faith. On the occasion of such temptations, it is advised to make acts of love, contrition, and hope.

Rule X

If you commit a venial sin, make an act of love and of contrition, renew your firm purpose of amendment, and continue on in peace. To remain troubled after a fault compounds the fault, for a troubled soul is incapable of doing even the smallest good. If you commit a more serious sin, immediately make an act of contrition, resolve never to be guilty of the same sin.

Rule XI

In all the sufferings of life, such as illnesses, losses, and persecutions, always be aware of the necessity of resigning yourself to the will of God and reflect on these words: "God wills it, and so I will it also," or, in other words, "God wills that it be this way, so it shall be done." The person who behaves in this manner stores up immense treasure in heaven and always lives in peace. On the contrary, people who resist the will of God double their afflictions. A person has to endure suffering, whether they accept it or not, and if they resist it, by their impatience, they suffer even more.

Rule XII

Be very careful to observe a tender and obvious devotion to most holy Mary, by performing each day some exercise of piety in her honor. Never omit—the first thing in the morning and the last at night—to pray three Hail Marys in honor of her purity, imploring her to keep you from all sin. Read something every day, even if it is only a few lines, about the Blessed Virgin. Pray her litanies, pray her rosary, and meditate on the mysteries. When you leave or enter your house, ask her blessing with a Hail Mary and on passing by any of her images, pray in the same way. When the clock strikes the hour, pray a Hail Mary and then, "Jesus and Mary, I love you! Do not permit me to offend you!" With the advice of your confessor, fast on Saturday, on the vigils of the feasts of Mary, and make the novenas for these feasts (also remember to pray in a special way at Christmas, Pentecost, and on the feast of your patron saint).

Rule XIII

Say a daily prayer to Jesus Christ to obtain his holy love:

> My crucified love, my dear Jesus, I believe in you, and confess you to be the true Son of God and the Redeemer. I adore you from the abyss of my nothingness, and I thank you for the death you suffered for me so that I might obtain the life of divine grace. My beloved Redeemer, to you I owe all of my salvation. Through you I have escaped hell and received pardon for my sins. But I am so ungrateful that, instead of loving you, I have repeated my offenses against you. I deserve to be condemned, so as not to be able to love you any more; but, no, my Jesus, punish me in any other way, but not in this. If I have not loved you in times past, I love you now, and I desire nothing but to love you with all my heart. Without your help, I can do nothing. Since you have commanded me to love you, give me also that strength to fulfill this sweet and loving commandment.

> My Lord Jesus, you have promised to grant all that we ask of you. I ask, first of all, pardon for all of my sins and I repent, above all things, because I have offended you, O infinite goodness. I ask for holy perseverance in your grace until my death. But, above all, I ask for the gift of your holy love. Ah, my Jesus, my hope, my love, my all, inflame me with that love with

which you came upon this earth to light! For this end, make me always live in conformity with your holy will. Enlighten me, so that I may understand more and more how worthy you are of love, and that I may know the immense love you have for me, especially in giving your life for me. Grant, then, that I may love you with all my heart, and may love you always, and never cease to beg of you the grace to love you in this life so that I may one day come to love you in all eternity.

O Mother of beautiful love, my advocate and my refuge, Mary who are of all creatures the most beautiful, the most loving, and the most beloved of God, and whose only desire it is to see God loved, by the love that you have for Jesus Christ, pray for me, and obtain for me the grace to love him always, and with all my heart. This I ask for and hope for from you. Amen.

Traditional Prayers Appropriate for Lent

There are many different ways to choose prayers that are traditional and appropriate for the Lenten season. One way is to choose those prayers that appear in the many manuals of devotion that routinely appear during Lent. Another way is simply to ask a representative group of people to offer suggestions as to what their particular favorite Lenten prayer might be. Yet another way is to choose those prayers that accurately reflect the great themes of Lent, such as the Passion and death of the Lord, the confession of sins, and other themes that suggest repentance and conversion. No matter what manner of choosing might be selected, invariably any collection will miss a favorite prayer or devotion that a particular person might determine is essential. The collection that follow succeeds in including many traditional favorites, but undoubtedly omits many others.

1. "Cantata on the Passion" by Saint Alphonsus Liguori

The original text of this cantata (a dramatic scene set to music but not intended to be acted) was discovered in London in 1859. The words and the music were composed by Saint Alphonsus around 1760. The cantata presents a dialogue between the soul and the Redeemer. It is reproduced here with no attempt to update the language or the presentation in order to preserve as much as the original feeling as might be possible.

The Soul

Tell me, thou judge iniquitous, ah! tell me why
Thou didst so oft my Savior's innocence proclaim,
And yet, at length, condemn him to a death of shame,
Like vilest criminal upon a cross to die?
Of what avail the barb'rous scourges, cruel blows,
If, in thy heart, thou didst his future death decree?
Why not at once have doom'd him to the bitter tree

When the first cry of hate from surging crowds arose?
Since well thou knewest thou wouldst sentence him to die,
Why not at once make known his cruel destiny?
But what do I behold? An angry crowd draws near,
Confused cries are heard, and threat'ning groans resound;
Nearer still and nearer there comes a thrilling sound.
What is this clam'rous music breaking on mine ear?
Ah! it is the trumpet, whose shrill discordant breath
Proclaims aloud the sentence of my Savior's death.
Now, alas! I see him, along the rugged road
Painfully he's toiling with tott'ring step and slow,
Wounded, sore, and bleeding, he bears the heavy load
Laid upon his shoulder by his relentless foe.
At ev'ry painful step he makes
Fresh blood-drops mark the way he takes.
A cross of wood
Upon his wounded shoulder rests;
His bruised flesh is staining it with blood;
His venerable head a mocking crown adorns;
His aching brows are pierc'd with long and cruel thorns.
"Tis thy unfathom'd love, my dearest Lord,
That makes thee wear this crown of mockery.
Where goest thou, my God ador'd?"

The Redeemer

I go to die for thee.

The Soul

Dear Lord, it is for me
Thou goest forth to die?
How gladly, then, would I
Lay down my life for thee!

The Redeemer
Peace! Till thy dying breath
Think on my love for thee;
After my bitter death
Forever love thou me.
Remain, my turtle dove!
For my heart give me thine;
My faithful one! Be Mine.
And pledge me all thy love.

The Soul

My Lord! I thee adore,
To thee my heart I bring.
I'm thine, my treasur'd king,
I'm thine for evermore.

2. Prayers to Commemorate the Seven Last Words of Jesus

The seven last words of Jesus, as the tradition is known today, are not words in the strict sense, but rather utterances from the mouth of Jesus as he hung upon the Cross. These words are recorded for us in the gospels however no gospel contains all seven words and only one gospel, the Gospel of John, makes reference to Jesus giving his mother to the care of the apostle John and John to the care of his mother. Tradition places the root of this devotion in the tenth century, but it is not until the latter half of the nineteenth century, when many Churches adopted the devotion for Good Friday, that this devotion achieved widespread popularity.

V. O God, come to my assistance.
R. O Lord, make haste to help me.

V. Glory to the Father and to the Son and to the Holy Spirit.
R. As it was in the beginning, is now, and ever shall be. Amen.

First Word
Father, forgive them, for they do not know what they do.

Dear Jesus, who for my love, suffered upon the Cross in order to pay with your sufferings the debt of my sins and opened your divine lips to obtain for me their remission from the eternal justice of God, have pity on me and on all the faithful who are in their last agony. When I come to that last hour, by the merits of your most Precious Blood, which was shed for my salvation, give me such a lively sorrow for my sins that my soul will then expire in the bosom of your divine mercy. My God, I believe in you, I hope in you, and I love you. I repent of having offended you by my sins.

Second Word
This day you shall be with me in paradise.

Dear Jesus, who for my love hung in agony upon the Cross, and with such readiness and bounty responds to the Good Thief when he acknowledges you to be the Son of God, and assures him of paradise, have pity on me and all the faithful who are in their last agony. When I shall come to the end of my life, by the merits of your most Precious Blood, inspire in my soul a faith so firm and constant that it shall not waver at any suggestions of the evil one, so I may obtain the reward of holy paradise. My God, I believe in you, I hope in you, and I love you. I repent of having offended you by my sins.

Third Word
Behold your mother; behold your son.

Dear Jesus, who for my love hung in agony upon the Cross and who, forgetting your own sufferings, gifted me with your Holy Mother as a pledge of your love through her, I pray that I will be enabled to call upon you with confidence in my greatest need. Have pity on me and all the faithful who are in their last agony. Through the interior martyrdom of your dear Mother, inspire in my heart a firm trust in the infinite merits of your most Precious Blood, so that I may be able to escape the eternal damnation, which I have merited by my sins. My God, I believe in you, I hope in you, and I love you. I repent of having offended you by my sins.

Fourth Word
My God, my god, why have you forsaken me?

Dear Jesus, who for my love hung in agony upon the Cross and who, adding suffering to suffering, in addition to your bodily pains, endured with infinite patience the most painful affliction of spirit at being abandoned by your Eternal Father, have pity on me and all the faithful who are in their last agony. When I come to the hour of my own death, by the merits of your Precious Blood, grant me the grace of suffering with true patience all the pains and agony of my death struggle, so that by uniting my sufferings to yours, I may be able at last to share your glory in paradise. My God, I believe in you, I hope in you, and I love you. I repent of having offended you by my sins.

Fifth Word
I thirst

Dear Jesus, who for my love hung in agony upon the Cross, and who, not yet satisfied with so many reproaches and sufferings, suffered even more so that all people might be saved. The whole torrent of your Passion is not enough to slake the thirst of your loving heart. Have pity on me and all the faithful who are in their last agony, and upon me, so when I arrive at my final hour I will have lighted within me a fire of love so great that my heart will be filled with the desire of being united with you for all of eternity. My God, I believe in you, I hope in you, and I love you. I repent of having offended you by my sins.

Sixth Word
All is finished.

Dear Jesus, who for my love hung in agony upon the Cross, and from that pulpit of truth proclaimed that you had finished the work of our redemption, whereby humankind, from being children of wrath and perdition, have been made children of God and heirs of heaven, have pity on all the faithful who are in their last agony. When I arrive at my final hour, by the merits of your most Precious Blood, detach me completely from the world and from myself, granting me the grace to offer you from my heart the sacrifice of my life in expiation of my sins. My God, I believe in you, I hope in you, and I love you. I repent of having offended you by my sins.

Seventh Word
Father, into your hands I commend my spirit.

Dear Jesus, who for my love hung in agony upon the Cross, and in order to complete the great sacrifice embraced the will of your Eternal Father, resigning your spirit into his hands and then bowing your head and dying. Have pity on all the faithful who are in their last agony and upon me. When I have come to my final moment, by the merits of your Precious Blood, grant me a perfect conformity to your Divine Will, so that I may be ready to live or to die as it pleases you. I desire nothing else except the perfect fulfillment in me of your Divine Will.

Final Prayer to the Sorrowful Mother

Most holy Mother of Sorrows, by that soul-piercing martyrdom that you experienced at the foot of the Cross during the three hours of agony of your Son, Jesus, assist me in my time of need. I am a child of sorrows and when I am faced with my agony, intercede on my behalf so that I may be found worthy to pass from my deathbed to the blessed paradise of the Kingdom.

V. From a sudden and unprovided death,

R. Deliver me, O Lord.

V. From the snares of the devil,

R. Deliver me, O Lord.

V. From everlasting death,

R. Deliver me, O Lord.

3. Short Prayers and Invocations

May the Sacred Heart of Jesus be loved in every place.

Sweet Heart of my Jesus, grant that I may love you forever.

Heart of Jesus, burning with love for us, set our hearts on fire
with your love.

Heart of Jesus, I put my trust in you.

Jesus, meek and humble of heart, make our heart like unto yours.

Divine Heart of Jesus, convert sinners, save the dying,
and deliver the holy souls in purgatory.

Sweet Heart of Jesus, be my love.

We adore you, O Christ, and we praise thee,
because by your holy Cross you have redeemed the world.

Hail, O Cross, our only hope!

By the sign of the holy Cross, deliver us from our enemies, O God!

The Cross is my sure salvation. The Cross—it is that which I worship
forever. The Cross of our Lord is with me. The Cross is my refuge.

My Lord, and my God!

Behold the Lamb of God, behold him who takes away
the sins of the world!

All for you, O my Jesus, all for you!

My Jesus, mercy.

My sweetest Jesus, be not my Judge, but my Savior.

Jesus, my God, I love you above all things.

4. Litany of the Sacred Heart of Jesus

V. Lord, have mercy on us.
R. Christ, have mercy on us.
V. Christ, hear us.
R. Christ, graciously hear us.

God, the Father of Heaven, have mercy on us.
God the Son, Redeemer of the World, have mercy on us.
God the Holy Spirit, have mercy on us.
Holy Trinity, one God, have mercy on us.

Heart of Jesus, Son of the Eternal Father, *have mercy on us.*
Heart of Jesus, formed by the Holy Spirit in the Virgin Mother's womb,
    have mercy on us.
Heart of Jesus, united to the Word of God, *have mercy on us.*
Heart of Jesus, of infinite majesty, *have mercy on us.*
Heart of Jesus, holy temple of God, *have mercy on us.*
Heart of Jesus, tabernacle of the Most High, *have mercy on us.*
Heart of Jesus, house of God and gate of heaven, *have mercy on us.*
Heart of Jesus, glowing furnace of charity, *have mercy on us.*
Heart of Jesus, vessel of justice and love, *have mercy on us.*
Heart of Jesus, full of goodness and love, *have mercy on us.*
Heart of Jesus, abyss of all virtues, *have mercy on us.*
Heart of Jesus, most worthy of all praise, *have mercy on us.*
Heart of Jesus, King and center of all hearts, *have mercy on us.*
Heart of Jesus, keeper of the treasures of wisdom and knowledge,
    have mercy on us.
Heart of Jesus, where dwells the fullness of God,
    have mercy on us.
Heart of Jesus, in whom the Father is well pleased,
    have mercy on us.

Heart of Jesus, in whose fullness we have all received,
have mercy on us.
Heart of Jesus, desire of the everlasting hills,
have mercy on us.
Heart of Jesus, patient and rich in mercy, *have mercy on us.*
Heart of Jesus, fount of live and holiness, *have mercy on us.*
Heart of Jesus, bruised for our sins, *have mercy on us.*
Heart of Jesus, obedient unto death, *have mercy on us.*
Heart of Jesus, pierced with a lance, *have mercy on us.*
Heart of Jesus, source of all consolation, *have mercy on us.*
Heart of Jesus, our life and resurrection, *have mercy on us.*
Heart of Jesus, our peace and reconciliation, *have mercy on us.*
Heart of Jesus, victim for our sins, *have mercy on us.*
Heart of Jesus, salvation of those who hope in you,
have mercy on us.
Heart of Jesus, hope of those who die in you, *have mercy on us.*
Heart of Jesus, delight of all the saints, *have mercy on us.*

Lamb of God, you take away the sins of the world,
spare us, O Lord.
Lamb of God, you take away the sins of the world,
graciously hear us, O Lord.
Lamb of God, you take away the sins of the world,
have mercy on us.

V. Jesus, meek and humble of Heart,
R. Make our hearts like unto yours.
Let us pray. Almighty and everlasting God, look upon the heart of your beloved Son and upon the praise and satisfaction which he offers you in the name of sinners. In your goodness, grant all people pardon when they seek your mercy, in the name of your Son, Jesus Christ, who lives and reigns with you forever and ever. Amen.

5. A Lenten Prayer

This prayer, of unknown origin, has been adapted many times by many people, is a popular modern prayer that is used in a variety of Lenten settings. Known by many names such as "A Lenten Prayer," or, simply, "How To Fast," it provides a wonderful summary of the great themes of Lent. The prayer clearly illustrates that the season of Lent is more than a time of fasting, but is also a joyous season of feasting. Lent is a time to fast from some and to feast for others. It is a season that offers us the opportunity to practice what we say we believe.

Fast from judging others; feast on the Christ indwelling in them.
Fast from emphasis on differences; feast on the unity of all life.
Fast from apparent darkness; feast on the reality of light.
Fast from words that pollute; feast on phrases that purify.
Fast from discontent; feast on gratitude.
Fast from anger; feast on patience.
Fast from pessimism; feast on optimism.
Fast from worry; feast on trust.
Fast from complaining; feast on appreciation.
Fast from negatives; feast on affirmatives.
Fast from unrelenting pressures; feast on unceasing prayer.
Fast from hostility; feast on nonviolence.
Fast from bitterness; feast on forgiveness.
Fast from self-concern; feast on compassion for others.
Fast from personal anxiety; feast on eternal truth.
Fast from discouragement; feast on hope.
Fast from facts that depress; feast on truths that uplift.
Fast from lethargy; feast on enthusiasm.
Fast from suspicion; feast on truth.
Fast from thoughts that weaken; feast on promises that inspire.
Fast from idle gossip; feast on purposeful silence.

Gentle God, during this season of fasting and feasting, gift us with your presence, so we can be gift to others in carrying out your work. Amen.

6. Prayer to the Blessed Mother

Remember, O Virgin Mother of God, when you stand in the sight of the Lord, to speak good things for us and to turn away his indignation from us.

Holy Mother, pierce me through,
In my heart each wound renew,
Of my Savior crucified.
Let me to my latest breath,
In my body bear the death,
Of that dying Son of thine.
Be to me, O Virgin, nigh
Lest in flames I burn and die.
In that awful judgment day.
Christ, when thou shall call me hence,
Be thy Mother my defense.
Be thy Cross my victory.
While my body here decays,
May my soul thy goodness praise,
Safe in paradise with thee. Amen.

V. Pray for us, O most sorrowful Virgin,
R. That we may be made worthy of the promises of Christ.
Let us pray. Let intercession be made for us, we beseech you, O Lord Jesus Christ, now and at the hour of our death, before the throne of your mercy, by the Blessed Virgin Mary, your Mother, whose most holy soul was pierced by a sword of sorrow, in the hour of your bitter Passion. Through you, Jesus Christ, Savior of the world, who lives

and reigns with the Father and the Holy Spirit, world without end. Amen.

V. Our Lady of a happy death,
R. Pray for us.
V. Saint Joseph,
R. Pray for us.

7. Traditional Prayers for Each Day of the Week

The pious tradition and devotion of praying for the poor souls in purgatory is a practice that has been promoted by many of the saints. This practice, appropriate for all times during the year, is especially suitable for the season of Lent.

For those who wish to incorporate this devotion in their Lenten practice, two options are presented here. The first option is to pray a prayer assigned for each day of the week, along with the praying of the Our Father, the Glory to the Father, and Eternal Rest Grant Unto Them. For those who prefer a longer prayer, we have also provided an optional prayer for the deceased that may be prayed in place of the prayer of eternal rest. This optional prayer can be found following the prayers provided for Sunday; it is not repeated for the rest of the week, but can easily be referred to for those who prefer this option.

Sunday

O Lord God omnipotent, I beseech you by the Precious Blood, which your divine Son, Jesus, shed in the Garden, deliver the souls in purgatory, and especially that one which is the most forsaken of all, and bring it into your glory where it may praise and bless you for ever. Amen.

Our Father, who art in heaven, hallowed be your name. Your kingdom come, your will be done, on earth as it is in heaven. Give us this day our daily bread and forgive us our trespasses, as we forgive those who trespass against us, and lead us not into temptation, but deliver us from evil. Amen.

Hail Mary, full of grace, the Lord is with you. Blessed are you among women, and blessed is the fruit of your womb, Jesus. Holy Mary, Mother of God, pray for us sinners, now, and at the hour of our death. Amen.

V. Eternal rest grant unto them O Lord,
R. And let perpetual light shine upon them.
V. From the gates of Hell,
R. Deliver their souls, O Lord
V. May they rest in peace.
R. Amen.

V. O Lord, hear my prayer,
R. And let my cry come unto Thee.
Let us pray. O God, the Creator and Redeemer of all the faithful, grant to the souls of your servants and handmaids, the remission of all their sins, that through our devout supplications and prayers they may obtain the pardon they have always desired. We pray in the unity of the Father, the Son, and the Holy Spirit, world without end. Amen.

Monday

O Lord God omnipotent, I beseech you by the Precious Blood which your divine Son, Jesus, shed in his cruel scourging, deliver the souls in purgatory, and among them all, especially that soul which is near-est to its entrance into your glory, that it may soon begin to praise you and bless you for ever. Amen.

Our Father, who art in heaven, hallowed be your name. Your kingdom come, your will be done, on earth as it is in heaven. Give us this day our daily bread and forgive us our trespasses, as we forgive those who trespass against us, and lead us not into temptation, but deliver us from evil. Amen.

Hail Mary, full of grace, the Lord is with you. Blessed are you among women, and blessed is the fruit of your womb, Jesus. Holy Mary, Mother of God, pray for us sinners, now, and at the hour of our death. Amen.

Eternal rest grant unto them, O Lord, and let perpetual light shine upon them. May their souls, and all the souls of the faithful departed, rest in peace. Amen.

Tuesday

O Lord God omnipotent, I beseech you by the Precious Blood which your divine Son, Jesus, shed in his bitter crowning with thorns, deliver the souls in purgatory and among them all, particularly that soul which is in greatest need of our prayers, in order that it may not be delayed long in praising your glory and blessing you for ever. Amen.

Our Father, who art in heaven, hallowed be your name. Your kingdom come, your will be done, on earth as it is in heaven. Give us this day our daily bread and forgive us our trespasses, as we forgive those who trespass against us, and lead us not into temptation, but deliver us from evil. Amen.

Hail Mary, full of grace, the Lord is with you. Blessed are you among women, and blessed is the fruit of your womb, Jesus. Holy Mary, Mother of God, pray for us sinners, now, and at the hour of our death. Amen.

Eternal rest grant unto them, O Lord, and let perpetual light shine upon them. May their souls, and all the souls of the faithful departed, rest in peace. Amen.

Wednesday

O Lord God omnipotent, I beseech you by the Precious Blood which your divine Son, Jesus, shed in the streets of Jerusalem while he carried on his sacred shoulders the heavy burden of the Cross, deliver the souls in purgatory and especially the one soul which is richest in merits in your sight, so that, having soon attained the high place in glory to which it is destined, it may praise you triumphantly and bless you for ever. Amen.

Our Father, who art in heaven, hallowed be your name. Your kingdom come, your will be done, on earth as it is in heaven. Give us this day our daily bread and forgive us our trespasses, as we forgive those who trespass against us, and lead us not into temptation, but deliver us from evil. Amen.

Hail Mary, full of grace, the Lord is with you. Blessed are you among women, and blessed is the fruit of your womb, Jesus. Holy Mary, Mother of God, pray for us sinners, now, and at the hour of our death. Amen.

Eternal rest grant unto them, O Lord, and let perpetual light shine upon them. May their souls, and all the souls of the faithful departed, rest in peace. Amen.

Thursday

O Lord God omnipotent, I beseech you by the Precious Body and Blood of your divine Son, Jesus, which he himself on the night before his Passion and death gave us as food and bequeathed to his holy Church for the life-giving nourishment of the faithful, deliver the souls in purgatory, but most of all, that soul which was most devoted to this mystery of infinite love, in order that it may praise you, together with your divine Son and the Holy Spirit, in your glory forever. Amen.

Our Father, who art in heaven, hallowed be your name. Your kingdom come, your will be done, on earth as it is in heaven. Give us this day our daily bread and forgive us our trespasses, as we forgive those who trespass against us, and lead us not into temptation, but deliver us from evil, Amen.

Hail Mary, full of grace, the Lord is with you. Blessed are you among women, and blessed is the fruit of your womb, Jesus. Holy Mary, Mother of God, pray for us sinners, now, and at the hour of our death. Amen.

Eternal rest grant unto them, O Lord, and let perpetual light shine upon them. May their souls, and all the souls of the faithful departed, rest in peace. Amen.

Friday

O Lord God omnipotent, I beseech you by the Precious Blood of your divine Son, Jesus, shed this day upon the tree of the Cross, especially from his sacred hands and feet, deliver the souls in purgatory, and particularly that soul for whom I am most obligated to pray for, in order that I may not be the cause which hinders you from admitting it quickly to the possession of your glory where it may praise you and bless you for ever. Amen.

Our Father, who art in heaven, hallowed be your name. Your kingdom come, your will be done, on earth as it is in heaven. Give us this day our daily bread and forgive us our trespasses, as we forgive those who trespass against us, and lead us not into temptation, but deliver us from evil. Amen.

Hail Mary, full of grace, the Lord is with you. Blessed are you among women, and blessed is the fruit of your womb, Jesus. Holy Mary, Mother of God, pray for us sinners, now, and at the hour of our death. Amen.

Eternal rest grant unto them, O Lord, and let perpetual light shine upon them. May their souls, and all the souls of the faithful departed, rest in peace. Amen.

Saturday

O Lord God omnipotent, I beseech you by the Precious Blood which gushed forth from the sacred side of your divine Son, Jesus, in the presence and to the great sorrow of his most holy Mother, deliver the souls in purgatory and among them all especially that soul which has been most devout to this noble Mother, that it may come quickly into your glory, there to praise you in her, and her in you, through all the ages. Amen.

Our Father, who art in heaven, hallowed be your name. Your kingdom come, your will be done, on earth as it is in heaven. Give us this day our daily bread and forgive us our trespasses, as we forgive those who trespass against us, and lead us not into temptation, but deliver us from evil. Amen.

Hail Mary, full of grace, the Lord is with you. Blessed are you among women, and blessed is the fruit of your womb, Jesus. Holy Mary, Mother of God, pray for us sinners, now, and at the hour of our death. Amen.

Eternal rest grant unto them, O Lord. And let perpetual light shine upon them. May their souls, and all the souls of the faithful departed, rest in peace. Amen.

8. *Stabat Mater*

The opening Latin words of this ancient hymn, *Stabat Mater*, give this liturgical sequence its name. It celebrates the emotions of the Blessed Mother at Calvary and, because of the intensity and depth of the feelings expressed, it has proven to be very popular since at least the beginning of the fourteenth century. The authorship of this hymn has been ascribed to Saint Gregory the Great (d. 604), Saint Bernard of Clairvaux (d. 1153), Pope Innocent III (d. 1216), and Pope John XII (d. 1334). Modern scholarship seems to be in agreement that it was probably authored by Innocent III, but there are those who argue that he had "too great and too cold of an intellect" to author something that is so emotional. Regardless, this hymn has a revered place in the traditions and customs of Lent.

At the Cross her station keeping,
Stood the mournful Mother weeping,
Close to Jesus to the last.

Through her heart, his sorrow sharing,
All his bitter anguish bearing,
Lo! The piercing sword had passed.

O how sad and sore distressed
Was that Mother, highly blessed,
Of the sole-begotten One.

Woe-begone with heart's prostration,
Mother meek, the bitter Passion
Saw she of her glorious Son.

Who on Christ's dear Mother gazing,
In her trouble so amazing,
Born of woman, would not weep?

Who on Christ's dear Mother thinking,
Such a cup of sorrow drinking,
Would not share her sorrow deep?

For his people's sins rejected,
Saw her Jesus unprotected,
Saw with thorns, with scourges rent.

Saw her Son from judgment taken,
Her Beloved in death forsaken,
Till his spirit forth he sent.

Font of love and holy sorrow,
Mother, may my spirit borrow
Somewhat of thy woe profound.

Unto Christ, with pure emotion,
Raise my contrite heart's devotion,
Love to read in every wound.

Those five wounds on Jesus smitten,
Mother, in my heart be written,
Deep as in thine own they be.

Thou, thy Savior's Cross who bearest,
Thou, thy Son's rebuke who sharest,
Let me share them both with thee.

In the passion of my Maker,
Be my sinful soul partaker,
Weep till death and weep with thee.

Mine with thee be that sad station,
There to watch the great salvation,
Wrought upon the atoning tree.

Virgin, thou of virgins fairest,
May the bitter woe thou bearest,
Make on me impression deep.

Thus Christ's dying may I carry,
With him in his Passion tarry,
And his wounds in memory keep.

May his wound both wound and heal me.
He enkindle, cleanse, and heal me.
Be his Cross my hope and stay.

May he, when the mountains quiver,
From that flame which burns forever,
Shield me on the judgment day.

Jesus, may the Cross defend me,
And thy Mother's prayer befriend me,
Let me die in thy embrace.

When to dust my dust returneth,
Grant a soul that to thee yearneth,
In thy paradise a place. Amen.

9. Act of Faith

O my God, I firmly believe that you are one God in three divine Persons, Father, Son, and Holy Spirit; I believe that your divine Son became man and died for our sins, and that he will come to judge the living and the dead. I believe these and all the truths which the holy Catholic Church teaches, because you revealed them, who can neither deceive nor be deceived. Amen.

10. Act of Hope

O my God, relying on your infinite goodness and promises, I hope to obtain pardon of my sins, the help of your grace, and life everlasting, through the merits of Jesus Christ, my Lord and Redeemer. Amen.

11. Act of Love

O my God, I love you above all things, with my whole heart and soul, because you are all good and worthy of all my love. I love my neighbor as myself for the love of you. I forgive all who have injured me and I ask pardon of all whom I have injured. Amen.

12. Act of Contrition

My God, I am sorry for my sins with all my heart. In choosing to do wrong and failing to do good, I have sinned against you whom I should love above all things. I firmly intend, with your help, to do penance, to sin no more, and to avoid whatever leads me to sin. Our Savior Jesus Christ suffered and died for us. In his name, my God, have mercy. Amen.

13. Confiteor

I confess to Almighty God, to blessed Mary ever Virgin, to blessed Michael the Archangel, to blessed John the Baptist, to the holy apostles Peter and Paul, to all the saints, and to you, Father, that I have sinned exceedingly in thought, word, and deed, through my fault, through my fault, through my most grievous fault (*here strike your breast three times*); therefore I beseech the blessed Mary ever Virgin, blessed Michael the Archangel, blessed John the Baptist, the holy apostles Peter and Paul, all the saints, and you, Father, to pray to the Lord our God for me. May God have mercy on me, forgive me my sins, and lead me to eternal life. Amen.

14. Prayer to Jesus Crucified

Behold, my beloved and good Jesus. I cast myself upon my knees in your sight, and with the most fervent desire of my soul I pray and beseech you to impress upon my heart lively sentiments of faith, hope, and love, with true repentance from my sins and a most firm desire of amendment; while with deep affection and grief of soul I consider within myself and mentally contemplate your five most precious wounds, having before my eyes that which David the prophet long ago spoke about you, my Jesus: "They have pierced my hands and my feet; I can count all of my bones" (Ps 22:17–18).

15. Prayer to Our Redeemer

Soul of Christ, sanctify me; body of Christ, save me. Blood of Christ, inebriate me; water from the side of Christ, wash me. Passion of Christ, strengthen me. O good Jesus, hear me. Within your wounds hide me. Never permit me to be separated from you. From the evil one, protect me. At the hour of death call me, and bid me come to you that with your saints I may praise you forever. Amen.

Modern Practices and Prayers for Lent

Prayers and devotions are rooted in the lived experience of faith and spiritual practice. It should come as no surprise then that there are modern adaptations of old favorites and, in some cases, completely new and original expressions of the experience of Lent.

The modern prayers and practices that are collected here follow the established pattern. A new expression of the Stations of the Cross, intended to be prayed by the family, not as gathered in a church, but rather around the dinner table; a prayer to the Heart of Jesus from one of the foremost moral theologians of this century; and a original canticle that celebrates the joyful paradox of the Cross provide the core expressions of this collection. Only the passage of time will tell if they will one day make the transition from "modern" to "traditional."

1. A Family-Centered Way of the Cross

This cycle of short prayers is intended to present the Way of the Cross over the entire Lenten season. The first and second stations are presented for reflection during the week of Ash Wednesday, the third and fourth stations during the first week of Lent, and so on. The power of this Family-Centered Way of the Cross may be discovered in its simplicity and in its brevity.

Instructions: Every evening of Lent before the family retires, gather around the dining room table. Light a candle. One person announces the station and leads the response. Everyone then repeats the response. After a moment of quiet, the reader says the prayer and all repeat the common response.

Station One: Ash Wednesday
Jesus Is Condemned to Death

Reader: Lord, fill us with your love!
All: Lord, fill us with your love!

Reader: Lord, everyone condemned you to die. Sometimes in our family, Lord, we yell and condemn one another. Help us, Lord, to love one another more.

All: Lord, fill us with your love!

Station One: Thursday
Jesus Is Condemned to Death

Reader: Lord, fill us with your love!

All: Lord, fill us with your love!

Reader: Lord, the people were angry as they condemned you. Sometimes anger gets loose in our family, and we hurt one another. Help us, Lord, to love one another more.

All: Lord, fill us with your love!

Station Two: Friday
Jesus Takes Up His Cross

Reader: Lord, fill us with your love!

All: Lord, fill us with your love!

Reader: Lord, you lifted that very heavy Cross. Sometimes our family has heavy crosses to bear. Help us carry our family crosses with as much love as you carried yours.

All: Lord, fill us with your love!

Station Two: Saturday
Jesus Takes Up His Cross

Reader: Lord, fill us with your love!

All: Lord, fill us with your love!

Reader: Lord, you had to be very strong to lift that Cross and carry it. Give our family strength to lift up and carry one another, especially when we are sad or hurt.

All: Lord, fill us with your love!

Station Three: Sunday of Week One
Jesus Falls the First Time

Reader: Lord, lift us up!

All: Lord, lift us up!

Reader: Lord, it must have hurt when you stumbled. You must have felt bruised. Sometimes we bruise one another in our family. Help us heal those hurts, Lord!

All: Lord, lift us up!

Station Three: Monday of Week One
Jesus Falls the First Time

Reader: Lord, lift us up!

All: Lord, lift us up!

Reader: Lord, when you fell, it was very hard for you to get up and keep going. Help us pick one another up when we are tired and can't keep going.

All: Lord, lift us up!

Station Three: Tuesday of Week One
Jesus Falls the First Time

Reader: Lord, lift us up!

All: Lord, lift us up!

Reader: Lord, did the people who were watching help you pick up your Cross? In our family, we will pick up one another and keep loving.

All: Lord, lift us up!

Station Three: Wednesday of Week One
Jesus Falls the First Time

Reader: Lord, lift us up!

All: Lord, lift us up!

Reader: Lord, when we fall or fail, we need to rely on our mother, father, brothers, and sisters to lift us up, to hold us, to help us keep going.

All: Lord, lift us up!

Station Four: Thursday of Week One
Jesus Meets His Mother

Reader: Lord, lift us up!

All: Lord, lift us up!

Reader: Lord, as you loved your mother, help us today to love our mother. Make our love for our mother grow more and more.

All: Lord, lift us up!

Station Four: Friday of Week One
Jesus Meets His Mother

Reader: Lord, lift us up!

All: Lord, lift us up!

Reader: Lord, you gave us Mary as our Mother. She will help our family when we are suffering as you did. Mary, help us today.

All: Lord, lift us up!

Station Four: Saturday of Week One
Jesus Meets His Mother

Reader: Lord, lift us up!

All: Lord, lift us up!

Reader: Lord, help us to love as Mary, your mother, loved. She held you, she taught you, she prayed for you, she comforted you. Help us to love in this way!

All: Lord, lift us up!

Station Five: Sunday of Week Two
Simon Helps Carry the Cross

Reader: Lord, help us to care!

All: Lord, help us to care!

Reader: Lord, sometimes we feel drained and just can't go on. Be there for us, Lord, as Simon was for you. With you and our family helping, we can go on!

All: Lord, help us to care!

Station Five: Monday of Week Two
Simon Helps Carry the Cross

Reader: Lord, help us to care!

All: Lord, help us to care!

Reader: Lord, our family has to carry our crosses together. Lord, we share our family crosses and help one another carry them!

All: Lord, help us to care!

Station Five: Tuesday of Week Two
Simon Helps Carry the Cross

Reader: Lord, help us to care!

All: Lord, help us to care!

Reader: Lord, you felt relief when Simon took that heavy load from you. Lord, help us to relieve our mother and father when they carry a heavy load.

All: Lord, help us to care!

Station Five: Wednesday of Week Two
Simon Helps Carry the Cross

Reader: Lord, help us to care!

All: Lord, help us to care!

Reader: Lord, I have a very personal cross I need you to help me carry. Here is the name of the cross I bear (*time of quiet*). Help me, Lord!

All: Lord, help us to care!

Station Six: Thursday of Week Two
Veronica Wipes the Face of Jesus

Reader: Lord, help us to care!

All: Lord, help us to care!

Reader: Lord, we need someone to touch us with a loving, gentle hand. Lord, we need you to touch us today, as Veronica touched you!

All: Lord, help us to care!

Station Six: Friday of Week Two
Veronica Wipes the Face of Jesus

Reader: Lord, help us to care!

All: Lord, help us to care!

Reader: Lord, we need to give to each member of our family. We need to give without thinking about what we will get in return. Help us to be giving, Lord!

All: Lord, help us to care!

Station Six: Saturday of Week Two
Veronica Wipes the Face of Jesus

Reader: Lord, help us to care!

All: Lord, help us to care!

Reader: Lord, you gave Veronica a picture of yourself to carry. Lord, help us carry a picture of our family and their love for us in our hearts.

All: Lord, help us to care!

Station Seven: Sunday of Week Three
Jesus Falls a Second Time

Reader: Lord, hold us today!

All: Lord, hold us today!

Reader: Lord, in our family, we fall so many times. We need your help to get up, forgive one another, and begin again. Give us that love, Lord.

All: Lord, hold us today!

Station Seven: Monday of Week Three
Jesus Falls a Second Time

Reader: Lord, hold us today!

All: Lord, hold us today!

Reader: Lord, we sometimes say: "I told you so!" when we fall a second time! Help us, Lord, to just pick up one another and give one another a kiss.

All: Lord, hold us today!

Station Seven: Tuesday of Week Three
Jesus Falls a Second Time

Reader: Lord, hold us today!

All: Lord, hold us today!

Reader: Lord, crosses are heavy. It is hard to go even a few feet without falling. Lord, help us hold and carry our crosses.

All: Lord, hold us today!

Station Seven: Wednesday of Week Three
Jesus Falls a Second Time

Reader: Lord, hold us today!

All: Lord, hold us today!

Reader: Lord, it's hard to walk when we are carrying a heavy load. We stumble, we fall. We need our family and you, Lord, to walk very close to us!

All: Lord, hold us today!

Station Eight: Thursday of Week Three
The Women Weep Over Jesus

Reader: Lord, hold us today!

All: Lord, hold us today!

Reader: Lord, we also cry at times. We are sad or hurt or burdened, and we cry. Lord, wipe away our tears as the women wiped away yours!

All: Lord, hold us today!

Station Eight: Friday of Week Three
The Women Weep Over Jesus

Reader: Lord, hold us today!

All: Lord, hold us today!

Reader: Lord, the women were there to console you. Help our family console one another. We will hug and hold one another.

All: Lord, hold us today!!

Station Eight: Saturday of Week Three
The Women Weep Over Jesus

Reader: Lord, hold us today!

All: Lord, hold us today!

Reader: Lord, we use our tears to wash away the hurt and sadness. We hope, Lord, that you will cry for us, that you will wash away our hurt and sadness.

All: Lord, hold us today!

Station Nine: Sunday of Week Four
Jesus Falls the Third Time

Reader: Lord, be at our side!

All: Lord, be at our side!

Reader: When you fell so many times, it was so hard to get up and keep going. When we feel that way, Lord, pick us up and be at our side.

All: Lord, be at our side!

Station Nine: Monday of Week Four
Jesus Falls the Third Time

Reader: Lord, be at our side!

All: Lord, be at our side!

Reader: Lord, sometimes we see our mother or father filled with worry. Help us, Lord, to pick them up with a kiss and a smile!

All: Lord, be at our side!

Station Nine: Tuesday of Week Four
Jesus Falls the Third Time

Reader: Lord, be at our side!

All: Lord, be at our side!

Reader: Lord, when the cross is really heavy, we just can't walk straight. We stagger and limp. Your love for us can lessen the load. Love us, Lord!

All: Lord, be at our side!

Station Nine: Wednesday of Week Four
Jesus Falls the Third Time

Reader: Lord, be at our side!

All: Lord, be at our side!

Reader: Lord, when we wake up in the morning, help us be aware of which members of our family are carrying a cross that is too heavy for them. We will help!

All: Lord, be at our side!

Station Ten: Thursday of Week Four
Jesus Is Stripped of His Garments

Reader: Lord, be at our side!

All: Lord, be at our side!

Reader: Lord, you can see right through us. You know everything we do and everything we think. You love us over and over again.

All: Lord, be at our side!

Station Ten: Friday of Week Four
Jesus Is Stripped of His Garments

Reader: Lord, be at our side!

All: Lord, be at our side!

Reader: Lord, in our family, we are stripped of things that we might want. Help us give these things up willingly, as you did!

All: Lord, be at our side!

Station Ten: Saturday of Week Four
Jesus Is Stripped of His Garments

Reader: Lord, be at our side!

All: Lord, be at our side!

Reader: Lord, when we love one another, we cover one another with a special light. This love will heal the hurt and naked areas of our family.

All: Lord, be at our side!

Station Eleven: Sunday of Week Five
Jesus Is Crucified

Reader: Lord, take us in your arms!

All: Lord, take us in your arms!

Reader: Lord, you stretched out your arms, and you opened your hands to hold the whole world. Hold us now in your hands and arms!

All: Lord, take us in your arms!

Station Eleven: Monday of Week Five
Jesus Is Crucified

Reader: Lord, take us in your arms!

All: Lord, take us in your arms!

Reader: Lord, they lifted the Cross up, and you waited for God to come and take you. Help our family, Lord, always look to God.

All: Lord, take us in your arms!

Station Eleven: Tuesday of Week Five
Jesus Is Crucified

Reader: Lord, take us in your arms!

All: Lord, take us in your arms!

Reader: Lord, your mother Mary and other people gathered, watched, but could not help you. When we can't help, teach us to watch and love.

All: Lord, take us in your arms!

Station Eleven: Wednesday of Week Five
Jesus Is Crucified

Reader: Lord, take us in your arms!

All: Lord, take us in your arms!

Reader: Lord, you must have felt very alone on that Cross. When we feel alone, we will think of you and love even more, as you did.

All: Lord, take us in your arms!

Station Twelve: Thursday of Week Five
Jesus Dies on the Cross

Reader: Lord, take us in your arms!

All: Lord, take us in your arms!

Reader: Lord, you gave up your spirit to God who loves you. In our family, we want to love one another as much as you loved God.

All: Lord, take us in your arms!

Station Twelve: Friday of Week Five
Jesus Dies on the Cross

Reader: Lord, take us in your arms!

All: Lord, take us in your arms!

Reader: Lord, sometimes in our family, people die (*Here mention the names of those you wish to remember*). Lord, take them to paradise to live with you in peace and love.

All: Lord, take us in your arms!

Station Twelve: Saturday of Week Five
Jesus Dies on the Cross

Reader: Lord, take us in your arms!

All: Lord, take us in your arms!

Reader: Lord, when you died on the Cross, you filled the world with your love. Help us fill our family with love and caring!

All: Lord, take us in your arms!

Station Thirteen: Sunday of Passion Week
Jesus Is Taken Down From the Cross

Reader: Lord, hug us with your love!

All: Lord, hug us with your love!

Reader: Lord, other people had to untie you and carry you down from the Cross. In our family, help us rely on others to carry us and hold us.

All: Lord, hug us with your love!

Station Thirteen: Monday of Passion Week
Jesus Is Taken Down From the Cross

Reader: Lord, hug us with your love!

All: Lord, hug us with your love!

Reader: Lord, you went to heaven to prepare a place for your disciples and for us. Help us prepare a place for you in our hearts.

All: Lord, hug us with your love!

Station Thirteen: Tuesday of Passion Week
Jesus Is Taken Down From the Cross

Reader: Lord, hug us with your love!

All: Lord, hug us with your love!

Reader: Lord, we believe that you are with us—all day, every day. Help us want to be with our mother, father, brothers, and sisters as much as we can.

All: Lord, hug us with your love!

Station Thirteen: Wednesday of Passion Week
Jesus Is Taken Down From the Cross

Reader: Lord, hug us with your love!

All: Lord, hug us with your love!

Reader: Lord, it is your love for us that gave you the strength to face hurt and death. Help us remember that love when we feel hurt.

All: Lord, hug us with your love!

Station Fourteen: Holy Thursday
Jesus Is Placed in a Tomb

Reader: Lord, hug us with your love!

All: Lord, hug us with your love!

Reader: Lord, you were placed in a tomb to wait for Resurrection. Sometimes it is hard to wait for things. Lord, give us love to wait.

All: Lord, hug us with your love!

Station Fourteen: Good Friday
Jesus Is Placed in a Tomb

Reader: Lord, hug us with your love!

All: Lord, hug us with your love!

Reader: Lord, in the tomb, all is quiet and peace-filled. Help us be quiet and peace-filled in our family. Lord, teach us to quiet one another.

All: Lord, hug us with your love!

Station Fourteen: Holy Saturday
Jesus Is Placed in a Tomb

Reader: Lord, hug us with your love!

All: Lord, hug us with your love!

Reader: Lord, you knew that God would come, roll back the stone, and raise you up. We know that God will pick up our family, too! We will wait and love!

All: Lord, hug us with your love!

2. Lenten Family Graces

When a family makes the commitment to pray together, especially during this sacred season of Lent, they can expect special moments of grace and blessing because of their effort. The difficulty that many families experience preparing and gathering for a meal often exhausts the available energy. To expect a family to take the time to pray anything other than a quick traditional grace, without providing the resources to do so, is expecting too much. Families have the desire to pray, but they do not always have the necessary time to prepare and recollect.

Lenten Family Graces provides an easy way for families to make a special effort to pray together during Lent. It includes reflections and prayers for Ash Wednesday, all of the Fridays of Lent, the Triduum, and Easter Sunday. In addition it provides special prayers for the solemn feasts of the Chair of Saint Peter, the Annunciation, Saint Joseph, Husband of Mary, and one popular saint: Patrick. Each of these feast days usually occurs during the Lenten season.

Each day begins with a brief reflection followed by a prayer for the day. The designated reader can read the prayer, and the assembled family needs only to respond "Amen." The family does not need to have any extra booklets or to memorize any refrains or antiphons.

For those who want to expand this shared prayer time, two options are included. The designated reader can use the Scripture reference to look up the reading of the day, prepare it, and then read it to the family before the prayer. Also, the reflections include either activity suggestions or ideas about the Scripture and the season that the family may wish to discuss.

It is often difficult for families to do anything together because of all the pressures and demands that seem to be part of living in our society. It is hoped that the family that prays these prayers will enjoy the traditional blessing: "The family that prays together stays together."

Ash Wednesday
Matthew 6:1–6,16–18

The season of Lent begins with the traditional distribution of ashes and the admonition, "Remember that you are dust and to dust you shall return." Ashes remind us of the fragility of human life and the penance we are called to perform.

Encourage a family mealtime discussion about what Lenten penance each member of the family has chosen to help them prepare for Easter. The discussion does not have to be limited to what people choose to do without but can include what they have decided to *add* to their lives.

God of our beginnings, we enter this season of Lent in which we prepare for the rising of your Son at Easter. In the tradition of our ancestors, we have fasted and abstained this day. We hope that the hunger we feel in our stomachs will remind us of the hunger we feel in our hearts for your risen Son. Bless the food we now share, food that will not satisfy our hunger, but food that will strengthen us as we prepare and remember. Be with us during these forty days of Lent. Amen.

Friday After Ash Wednesday
Isaiah 58:1–9

Isaiah teaches us that fasting is something that is pleasing to God, but only if it helps those who are blessed with an abundance to understand the plight of the poor. To freely choose to experience the plight of the poor and then to commit ourselves to working to relieve the conditions that cause poverty is most pleasing to the Lord. To fast and then to ignore the poor is unacceptable to God.

God of our abundance, you have blessed us with more than we need. We often take what you have given us for granted. We are aware that we sometimes waste more than many of our brothers and sisters have for life. Help us through the gift of your grace to recognize all people as our family, to take nothing for granted, to rejoice in what is before us, and to be always grateful for what we have. Bless this meal that we share. Amen.

Friday, First Week of Lent
Ezekiel 18:21–28

The prophet reminds the people of Israel that repentance is necessary for salvation. It is only by conversion, by choosing to live a life patterned on God's law, that we can ever hope to enjoy eternal life.

God of the prodigal son, of the woman at the well, of Peter who denied you, and of all who are in need of repentance. We are the people who gather in your name. We are aware of our faults and weaknesses, conscious of our sins, but hopeful of your love and forgiveness. We ask that you change our hearts, liberate us from prejudice and judgment, and set us free from whatever keeps us from you. Enable us to reach out to one another with love. Permit us to recognize in this gift of nourishment the pledge of your love and faithfulness. Amen.

Friday, Second Week of Lent
Matthew 21:33–46

In the parable of the vineyard, Matthew reminds us that we should use God's gifts and not take them for granted. We are God's Chosen

People, called into the fullness of life through our baptism. But we must do more than simply claim an affiliation with God. If we take our relationship with the Lord for granted, we may soon hear the same warning that Jesus gave the people of his time: "The kingdom of God will be taken away from you" (Mt 21:43).

God of commitment, you are our rock, our fortress, and our strength. You have remained faithful to your people, even though we have sometimes wandered far from you. At times we feel unconnected and out of touch. We rejoice that in such moments, you are there, that you have never wavered, that you have remained steadfast. Help us to remember your loving presence and to recognize your guiding and patient Spirit. Bring us home to you, our loving God. Bless this time that we have together, this meal that we share, and our faith that it symbolizes. Let it be a moment that recalls for us the Eucharist that binds us to you forever. Amen.

Friday, Third Week of Lent
Hosea 14:2–10

The prophet Hosea lived around 750 B.C. By the time he became a prophet, Israel had already established a pattern that would play itself out again and again. The people would stray from the Lord, break the covenant, and experience great suffering because of their sins. Finally, a prophet would call them back into relationship with God. Today we hear Hosea remind the people that they have continually strayed from God, but God has remained faithful to them. If they wish to restore their relationship with the Lord, they need to seek forgiveness.

God of our longings, you know the deepest secrets of our hearts. We praise and thank you for sending us prophets, men and women who bravely witness to your truth, even when we may not want to hear or obey. We thank you for Jeremiah, Hosea, Ezekiel, and Isaiah, but also for Thea, Teresa, Joseph, and Martin, men and women who proclaim your love and call each of us to repent and to change. Prophets are not always perfect, are seldom welcomed, and are frequently ignored, but the truth they preach is a truth that we need to hear. Help us to open our hearts and our ears to those who may be proclaiming your truth in our world this day. Bless us, fill us, strengthen us, and nourish us with the food that we have before us and with the Word who walks among us. Amen.

Friday, Fourth Week of Lent
Wisdom 2:12–22

The Book of Wisdom reminds us that wickedness blinds us to the ways of the Lord. To be steeped in sin is to be drained of innocence and holiness. In such a state it is very difficult to hear God's word or walk in God's ways.

Throughout the first four weeks of Lent, we have heard reminders of the need to repent of our sins and to become people of conversion. The time is fast approaching when we will celebrate the great feast of Easter. If we have not yet recognized our own need for repentance, today seems to be a good opportunity to begin the process.

God of our innocence and holiness, you are the Father who calls us back, you are the Spirit who gives us life, you are the Son who shows us the way. Hear the prayers of your grateful people. We have not always remained faithful to you. Oftentimes we have preferred self-centeredness to listening, self-righteousness to mercy, stubbornness to understanding, and hardness of heart to conversion of spirit. You have gifted us with this season of Lent, a time in which your spirit can probe us and gently form us into your people. Be with us now. Use the days and the hours of this sacred time remaining to accomplish your will and to renew your kingdom. Bless the food that we share. Let it be for us a sign of your loving presence. Amen.

Friday, Fifth Week of Lent
Jeremiah 20:10–13

In today's reading we receive insight into the mind of a prophet. Jeremiah believes that God will remain with him, despite all the hardship and despite all the people around him who persist in their unbelief. The prophet clearly teaches us that conversion, walking in the ways of the Lord, is not always popular and is seldom easy. Others do not always appreciate the prophet's words and work.

I remember hearing a rule for living that made sense to me: "We should believe that our salvation depends only on God and work as if it depends only on us." We, too, are called to walk in the ways of the Lord, to accomplish God's will by sharing in the prophet's singlehearted belief and singleminded effort.

God of our comings and goings, you patiently wait for your people to return to you, to experience a conversion of mind and heart, to awaken to your gentle presence, and to become alive again in your love. We are sometimes numbed to the core, distracted by the demands and obligations that surround us. We often lose sight of the purpose and meaning of life, distracted far too often by anything that just happens to catch our attention. Help us as we stumble toward you, be patient with our grumbling, heal our blindness, and call us back to your loving hands. Bless this food that we now share. Let it be for us sustaining nourishment, giving us strength for the journey that lies ahead. Amen.

Holy Thursday
1 Corinthians 11:23–26

The evening Mass of the Lord's Supper commemorates the institution of the sacraments of the Eucharist and holy orders. It also celebrates the Lord's washing the feet of his disciples. In the reading for this Mass, Saint Paul proclaims to the Corinthians and to us the command of Jesus: "Do this in remembrance of me" (1 Cor 11:24). In addition to attending the liturgy, we can follow the Lord's command to remember him by making a single cup of wine and a special loaf of bread the centerpiece for this evening's meal.

> God who remembers, you call each of us to remember, and in the remembering, to recall your Word who walked among us. He was a light to the poor, he set captives free, he gave sight to the blind, and he forgave all our sins. He left us his body and his blood as a sign of the kingdom and a pledge of faithfulness. This night we remember all that he has done for us. We ask that you bless our family (that you bless this cup of wine and this loaf of bread) and that you bless the food that we now share. In our eating, let each of us remember through him, with him, and in him. Amen.

Good Friday
John 19:25–30 (or John, chapters 18 and 19)

Today is the celebration of the Lord's Passion and death. On this day of fast and abstinence, the evening meal should be as simple as possible. During Good Friday services, we pray traditional prayers of petition. Our blessing prayer for the evening meal reflects these ancient prayers of the Church.

God our Father, today your Son Jesus suffered and died. He became obedient for us. You raised him on high, and you have given him the name above all others.

In his name we pray for the Church throughout the world; for our Holy Father, the pope; for the clergy and laity of the Church; for those who are preparing for baptism; for the unity of all Christians; for our ancestors in the faith, the Jewish people, and for all non-Christians; for those who do not believe in God; for all in public office; and for those in special need. Hear our prayers for all these needs, for our family gathered here, and for the meal that we now share. We pray in the name of Jesus, the Lord. Amen.

Holy Saturday

On Holy Saturday, the Church patiently waits for the Resurrection that we know is to come. Mass is not celebrated today until the solemn vigil of Easter late this evening, well after the evening meal is concluded. There is no Scripture that is given for our reflection. Instead, the Church waits in silence for the Passover of the Lord, the period of time in which Jesus passed from death to life. We live in anticipation of one day sharing his victory over death.

God of our waiting, this is the night of vigil with the Lord. Tonight we patiently wait for the kingdom to be restored. We wait for the promises to be fulfilled, for the new life that is to come. We are not the people who jeered at your Son. We are not the people who wagged our heads in disbelief. We are the people of faith. We are the people who believe in the power of your Word and the promises of the Spirit who is to come.

Be with us now as we await the morning of Resurrection. Be with us as we take care of the details of our preparations for

Easter morning. Bless the meal that we share, and strengthen the faith that nourishes us. Amen.

Easter
John 20:1–9

The great feast of the Resurrection! Jesus, the paschal lamb, is risen. Let the Church sing alleluia!

Glorious God! Creator of the Universe, Spirit who enlivens our hope, Lord and Savior who leads us from death to life. Today we join with the hosts of angels to sing our songs of alleluia. Jesus is risen! He is no longer in the tomb. The chains of death cannot bind him. The Word lives and moves among us as he has promised. We gather in celebration, praying that your Easter blessing be on us. We ask that you bless this food that we now share. May it be for us a sign of your abiding presence. Amen.

Feast of the Chair of Peter, Apostle (February 22)
Matthew 16:13–19

The feast of the Chair of Saint Peter celebrates the teaching authority of the pope. From the earliest times, the chair in which a bishop presides has signified his authority, much as a throne signifies the authority of a king or queen. When the pope teaches a doctrine infallibly (a very rare occurrence), he speaks *ex cathedra*, literally "from the chair."

Although this feast is unknown to most people—except for those who attend daily Mass—it nevertheless celebrates something that is central to our traditional understanding of what it means to be a Roman Catholic.

Loving God, today we pray a special prayer of blessing in honor of your servant, our Holy Father. We ask that you bless Pope *N.*, and that you give him wisdom and guidance, the necessary grace to lead your Church, a listening heart to understand our cares and concerns, and a discerning spirit to know your will. Be with your people who are in union with the Church, but bless also your people who may be alienated, unwanted, or unable to hear your voice and recognize your love. Bless us today and the food that we share, so that we may continue to build your kingdom, faithfully living our vocations and walking in your ways. Amen.

Commemoration of Saint Patrick
(March 17)

Saint Patrick is known as the Apostle of Ireland. He was born in Scotland in 387 and in his youth was captured and sold as a slave in Ireland. He escaped and later returned, commissioned by Pope Saint Celestine to evangelize all of Ireland, something that he successfully accomplished over thirty-three years. The prayer that follows is suggested by the *Confession of Saint Patrick*.

Most intimate God, we cannot be silent about your grace. We must proclaim your love and turn our hearts to you, Lord and Savior. You have been faithful to us from birth. You formed us, and you know all that there is to know about us. And yet you continue to love us, calling us every day to yourself. We pray that we may never take you for granted. We pray that we may always enjoy your blessings, call upon you in prayer, walk with you in hope, and count on you for life and sustenance. Amen.

Solemnity of Joseph, Husband of Mary (March 19)
Luke 2:41–51

The feast of Saint Joseph, husband of Mary, has been celebrated in many countries since the tenth century. It was approved as a feast day for the universal Church in 1621.

Creator God, you are the God who rejoices in life, from the smallest unborn child to the oldest among us. You celebrate every breath, every thought, every action, seeing in each one of us songs of love and praise. To guide and protect, you have raised up mothers and fathers, parents who join with you in the symphony of creation. As once you blessed Saint Joseph and his family, bless each of us and our families, too. Let all that we do be a sign of your unwavering commitment to life lived in peace and joy, a sign of your kingdom that is to come. Amen.

Solemnity of the Annunciation of the Lord (March 25)
Luke 1:26-38

The feast of the Annunciation has been celebrated since the seventh century. It is the feast that celebrates the angel Gabriel's announcement to the Blessed Mother that she would conceive and bear a child.

God of our good news, as once you announced to Mary through the angel Gabriel that she was blessed to be the mother of your Son, so you announce to each of us today that you remain faithful, forgiving, and loving. Let your steadfastness be good news for us. Let it bring hope where there is doubt, clarity where there is confusion, and peace where there is anxiety and guilt. Be for us today the gospel that we need to hear. Bless the food that we share and the lives that we live. Amen.

3. Litany of Forgiveness

For the times I lacked compassion and concern for others,
forgive me Lord.

For not sharing my resources of time, talent, and treasure,
forgive me Lord.

For holding grudges and refusing to have a forgiving heart,
forgive me Lord.

For the times I have criticized and gossiped,
forgive me Lord.

For not reaching out to comfort and console others,
forgive me Lord.

For not caring for myself physically, emotionally, and spiritually,
forgive me Lord.

For the ways I misuse nature and damage the environment,
forgive me Lord.

For those times when I talked more than I listened,
forgive me Lord.

For my prejudices, biases, and deliberate acts of discrimination,
forgive me Lord.

For being greedy, forgive me Lord.

For the misuse and abuse of the wonderful gift of spirituality,
forgive me Lord.

For failing to see your face in the homeless and helpless,
forgive me Lord.

For believing that I could save myself, forgive me Lord.

For not living fully for you, forgive me Lord.

For doubting that you can and will forgive me unconditionally,
forgive me Lord.

For doubting that you love me with an everlasting love,
forgive me Lord.

Amen.

4. Prayer for Taking Risks

To laugh is to risk appearing the fool.

To weep is to risk appearing sentimental.

To reach out for another is to risk involvement.

To express your feelings is to risk exposing your true self.

To place your ideas, your dreams, before the crowd

Is to risk their loss.

To love is to risk not being loved in return.

To live is to risk dying.

To hope is to risk despair.

To try is to risk failure.

But risks must be taken because the greatest hazard

Is to risk nothing.

Those who risk nothing,

Do nothing,

Have nothing,

And are nothing.

They may avoid suffering and sorrow,

But they simply cannot learn, feel, change, grow, love, live.

Chained by their own fears, they are slaves:

They have forfeited freedom.

Only a person who risks is free.

5. Prayer Before Confession

Lord Jesus, open my mind and my heart to your Holy Spirit. Show me where I am failing to love your heavenly Father. Show me where I am failing to love you, failing to accept you as my Savior, failing to seek you and yield to you as my Lord. Show me where I am failing to love the Holy Spirit, failing to be open and to be led by Wisdom and Love.

Lord, Jesus, show me where I am failing to love any one of your brothers or sisters as you love me. Show me where I am failing to love myself as you love me. Show me where I am putting myself before God. Show me where I am seeking my own desires at the expense of a brother or a sister.

Your power finds its strength in my weakness; without you I can do nothing. Amen.

6. Prayer for Openness to Healing and Transformation

My love is like a wave breaking on the shore of eternity, forever washing over your weakness and wounds.

My mercy endures forever.

Every time you fail, I will forgive and heal you. Alone you can do nothing. With me you can do everything.

Let my grace transform you and heal your heart.

Know that I make everything work together for the good of those who love me. I can transform even your weaknesses and failures into blessings if you allow me.

Believe that you are filled with the healing presence of my Spirit.

Enter into my heart of divine compassion and let my love light a healing fire within your soul.

I release my power in your life now, and you will continue to grow in the depths and heights of my love.

Be at peace, my beloved, I am the God who dwells within you and embraces you with tenderness forever. Amen.

7. Canticle III: Joyful Paradox

To know you is paradox—
To apprehend the Cross
and to know that who is there is you,
To apprehend the Cross
and to know that who is there is me
And everyone else
And all of creation.

To apprehend the Cross and to know it
as unspeakable pain and suffering,
A nightmare from hell,
And to know that as you, as me,
as everyone, as all,
Far from your protecting us from harm.

Quite the contrary,
In order to fill its divine purpose
Everything must go to crucifixion—
You, me, all of us, the world, the earth.
There is such joy in this knowing,
Joy beyond pleasure and beyond delight
In this knowing.

To know you as the horror of the Cross
Is heartbreaking,
And yet to know the knowing
of that horrible
heartbreak of you
Is joy,
Is from the bottom of my feet joy!
Paradox.

Perhaps it is the utter truth of it all
that is so joyful.
Perhaps it is the sublimeness
of your willingness
to suffer yourself
that is so joyful.
Perhaps it is your need and desire
to invite us to suffer
and into the suffering of being your becoming
that is so joyful.
Perhaps it is because your tormented becoming
is so beautiful and so radically alive
that ferments the joy.

I don't know for sure, but I do know
that to gaze upon the Cross
And drink it in
Finishes itself in me as joy.
Thou shall love the Lord thy God
with all thy mind and with all thy soul.

Amen, amen, amen.

8. Heart of Jesus Prayer

In spite of our sinfulness and weakness, we have enough reasons to
be consoled, even to rejoice, for we can still praise you, dearest Lord.
It is right that we weep because of our sins, but it is more fitting to
rejoice because even our past sins tell us to praise your merciful love
with all our hearts because you have forgiven us. Our very pain—
that we came so late to love you—is one more sign that you do not
take away from us your loving kindness.

All of creation and the whole history of salvation tell us of your great love for us. The joyful and serene countenances of people who love you tell us with no need for words. Jesus, thank you for allowing us so often to meet people who, in the midst of most painful suffering, radiate joy and peace, people who so convincingly invite others to praise you. You offer your love as source of joy and peace to all who sincerely seek you. O divine Physician, heal us of all self-induced sadness. May we drink joyfully, from your springs of salvation!

Lord, let your countenance shine upon us! Send us your light and your truth. Make us wise enough to seek you at the purest fountain, your heart.

We are thirsty for your love, and we come to you. Let us drink as you promised, so that streams of living water will flow from within us. Send us your Holy Spirit and make us joyful messengers of your blissful love!

SECTION SIX

Daily Meditations
for Lent

A common Lenten spiritual practice that has proven to be quite popular is the commitment to a daily period of prayer and reflection. Although daily prayer and reflection is appropriate throughout the year, it seems to be especially appropriate during this spiritual season.

In the pages that follow a collection of daily meditations for Lent, along with the assigned Scripture references for each day of the season, are arranged for personal use.

There are many different ways to use the meditations that are provided. A suggested format would include the following steps, often considered essential for fruitful prayer and meditation.

The first step is to choose a particular time each day for your prayer. It is also helpful to choose a particular place that is conducive to reflection and to assume a position that is comfortable. Many people find fifteen or twenty minutes first thing in the morning, before the household awakens, to be very beneficial.

The second step is to quietly read the assigned Scripture for the day. It is not necessary to read the entire Scripture reference, the point is not to "get through everything," but rather to be open to the gentle prodding's of the Spirit of God. Some people choose to read just the suggested gospel, others choose just a few lines of text and find it very satisfactory.

The third step is to take some quiet reflection time, just a few moments, and let the Word of God be present to you. After a few moments of quiet you may then choose to read the meditation that is provided for the day. Again, after reading the meditation, take a few more moments of quiet.

The fourth step is to present to God, through prayers of petition, or thanks and praise, the "fruits" of your reflection. For example, the Scripture and the daily meditation might have helped you become aware of your gratefulness for the gift of life or the gift of family. A few simple words of praise and thanksgiving would then be appropriate. Perhaps you became aware of a relationship that needs mending; a prayer for the other person in the relationship might be appropriate. Whatever comes to you in prayer is considered the "voice of God" or the "gentle prodding of the Holy Spirit."

The fifth step is to conclude your period of prayer and meditation with the slow recitation of a familiar prayer. Some people routinely choose to pray the Our Father. Still others might choose a prayer from the collections provided in Section Four or Section Five of this book.

1. Choosing Meditations for the Appropriate Cycle of the Liturgical Year

The Church's liturgical year is regulated for three individual cycles for Sundays and two individual cycles for the weekdays. The Sunday cycle is identified as A, B, and C, while the weekday cycle is simply designated as Year I or Year II. This designation enables the Word of God as found in the Scriptures to be proclaimed on a rotating basis so that the faithful may have an opportunity to hear as much as the Word as possible within the liturgical context.

The Lenten meditations follow the Sunday cycle of A, B, and C. The lectionary cycle is presented below in order to help you determine which series of meditations to select for your reflection. By following the correct cycle, you will be reflecting on the readings that are used for that particular day throughout the universal Church. Of course, you may decide not to use the lectionary cycle and choose your own method for selecting the meditations that you prefer.

In order to be as complete and as useful as possible, the lectionary cycle will be noted for both Sundays and for weekdays.

LECTIONARY CYCLE

2000	2001	2002	2003	2004	2005	2006	2007	2008	2009	2010
B II	C I	A II	B I	C II	A I	B II	C I	A II	B I	C II

ASH WEDNESDAY

2000	2001	2002	2003	2004	2005	2006	2007	2008	2009	2010
3/8	2/28	2/13	3/5	2/25	2/9	3/1	2/21	2/6	2/25	2/17

EASTER SUNDAY

2000	2001	2002	2003	2004	2005	2006	2007	2008	2009	2010
4/23	4/15	3/31	4/20	4/11	3/27	4/16	4/8	3/23	4/12	4/4

Daily Meditations for Lent: Cycle A

My nephew is very good at putting together model kits. Last Christmas, I bought him a complicated space station with hundreds of pieces. I thought, *He will never be able to get this together.* On Christmas afternoon, after all the presents had been opened and the food eaten, I watched my nephew slowly spread out the pieces of the space station on the floor before him. He stared at the pieces, examined the instructions, and began deliberately building the space station. An hour later, to my astonishment, the space station was finished, and he was off to investigate another gift.

Many times, our lives end up in a hundred pieces, just like that unassembled toy. Our energies are scattered among our work, our homes, our kids, our spouses, our friends, our bills, and a host of other responsibilities. We need time to stop, take out the master plan, and put it all together into something that makes sense and gives us life. As we journey through the forty days of Lent, we can look at our lives and ask ourselves: *What is the spiritual sense of it all? What has the Lord been doing with me this last year?*

These meditations can help you as you walk this spiritual path. Each meditation begins with a story—to help you plug into your own story—and then continues with a connection to the liturgical readings for the day. A short prayer ends the meditation.

The purpose of these meditations is to help lead you to a place where God can speak to you about your life, so that your many pieces will find a permanent home. On Easter, may you rise with the Lord into a life that is spirit-filled, connected, and purposeful.

Ash Wednesday
Joel 2:12–18; 2 Corinthians 5:20—6:2;
Matthew 6:1–6, 16–18

In an acceptable time I heard you,
and on the day of salvation I helped you.
(2 Cor 6:2)

The professional football season is sprinkled with horrific tackles and some very serious injuries. Recently, after one such tackle, a player lay motionless on the ground. He had been upended and had landed head first, his neck bent at a very odd angle. Everyone feared that his neck had been broken. Both teams on the field knelt in small silent circles, their helmets off, their heads bent in prayer. Even on the sidelines the coaches and players were in prayer postures. Later in the game, the announcer gave the news—the player had suffered a bruised spinal column and would recover fully.

These big brutish players momentarily surrendered their power to prayer. Our readings for this Ash Wednesday are filled with directives to let go and surrender. Joel asks us to tear open our hearts and return to the Lord. In the gospel, Jesus directs his disciples to surrender their money in alms, their bodies in fasting, and their spirits in prayer. We even sign our heads with ashes today to remind ourselves that we ultimately will surrender to death. Jesus tells us that in this surrendering we will find God: "Your father who sees in secret will repay you" (Mt 6:6). As this Lent begins, let us surrender to the Lord, letting go of what we hold most tightly—prestige, power, possessions, resentments, or old bitter memories.

We pray with the rite of blessing: "Direct our hearts to better things, O Lord; heal our sin and ignorance."

Thursday After Ash Wednesday
Deuteronomy 30:15–20; Luke 9:22–25

If anyone wishes to come after me,
he must deny himself and take up his cross daily and follow me.
(Lk 9:23)

In some movies, the hero is shot, knifed, and beaten up many times. Yet the hero goes on as if the wounds weren't even there. Any of us who has bruised a rib, broken a finger, cut ourselves, or stubbed a toe knows that this movie magic is not true. The wound hurts! We limp, breathe delicately, cradle our hurt finger for protection. Unlike Hollywood, the real world does not allow us to live easily with physical or emotional wounds.

When Jesus asks us to take up our cross in today's gospel, we are challenged to take hold of our life and all it contains, including the many old wounds that still hurt us. It is for our redemption and our liberation that we live actively with hurt and pain. With the Israelite people in the first reading, we, too, "choose life." In reclaiming our life, wounds and all, we believe that we will live.

We pray: Lord, I place my hope in you. Help me this Lent to embrace my life and carry my cross. Amen.

Friday After Ash Wednesday
Isaiah 58:1–9; Matthew 9:14–15

Then your light shall break forth like the dawn,
and your wound shall quickly be healed.
(Isa 58:8)

Last winter, I was driving to visit my family. At the corner, four cars ahead of me, a woman was begging for money. She held a sign that read: "I am a single mother. I need food, money, or work." The light turned green, but the driver in the first car was lowering his window and giving this woman money. I was immediately annoyed that he was holding up traffic. But when the woman received the money, she fell on her knees, raised her hands to heaven, and began to pray loudly in thanksgiving to God. My annoyance turned to embarrassment. I had hoarded my love. This woman challenged me to give of the love I have.

In our gospel today, Jesus proclaims himself the bridegroom. A new love is born, one that will not be contained by rules or expectations. This love will spread like fire and beget new life. Isaiah echoes this same sentiment; we are called to love so powerfully that our love breaks forth like the light of dawn.

We pray: Today, Lord, open a path between my heart and my eyes. Let my love flow outward and bring light and birth to another. Amen.

Saturday After Ash Wednesday
Isaiah 58:9–14; Luke 5:27–32

Then you shall delight in the LORD,
and I will make you ride on the heights of the earth.
(Isa 58:14)

In the 1998 Olympic Women's Figure Skating competition, two contestants were favored to win the gold medal. The first skater performed beautifully and should have taken home the gold, but her rival skated beyond beautiful. When they asked the winner about her performance, she said that when she positioned herself for the beginning of the program, she entered an altered state. She, the ice, and the music became one. Skating was pure joy!

In today's readings, Jesus and Isaiah give us images of what the kingdom of God is. We must liberate ourselves from prejudice and enter the glory of the great banquet hall. Here the rich and the poor can dine together without distinction. Here there is pure joy in being part of the family of God. Isaiah uses words like *delight, honor-*

able, light, and *strength* to describe this altered state that is the kingdom of God. In the gospel, Jesus uses the image of a banquet. Jesus is the healer, and all who need mending come to the great banquet.

We pray: Lord, help me be honorable, filled with light and delight. Make me a pillar of your strength. Draw me into the joy of the kingdom. Amen.

First Sunday of Lent
Genesis 2:7–9; 3:1–7; Romans 5:12–19; Matthew 4:1–11

> *Have mercy on me, God, in your goodness;*
> *in your abundant compassion blot out my offense.*
> *(Ps 51:3)*

Saint Teresa of Ávila was once asked, "What is a Christian?" She replied, "A Christian is one who falls, to get up, to fall, to get up again." Saint Teresa had come to the personal opinion that the end to temptation and sin would certainly not occur within her lifetime. The best effort of the Christian is to stay in the race, always getting up after a fall with eyes fixed on the goal.

Our readings for this First Sunday of Lent show us a mini-history of temptation and sin. In Genesis, Adam and Eve failed miserably when faced with temptation and sin and so were exiled from the garden as punishment. In our gospel, Jesus is faced with temptation, and he succeeds admirably. In the second reading, Saint Paul assures us that Jesus, because of his success, will end our exile and bring us acquittal and life.

We pray: Lord, help me to understand where I fit into this history of temptation and sin. I repent of my wrongdoing and join forces with you this Lent against my sin. I choose to walk with you through death to new life. Amen.

Monday, First Week of Lent
Leviticus 19:1–2, 11–18; Matthew 25:31–46

I assure you, as often as you did it for
one of my least brothers, you did it for me.
(Mt 25:40)

I found myself traveling on an expressway in Los Angeles at the exact moment when the president of the United States was in his motorcade on the way to a political fund-raiser. It was an eerie sight. There were no cars on the expressway in either direction for as far as you could see. Police had barricaded every entrance. If the president had chosen to leave the freeway and enter the side streets, he would have seen the poor, the abandoned, the struggling, the crowded. Instead, he followed the isolated path we tend to create for our leaders, keeping them far from the needing crowds.

The kingdom of Christianity is built not on isolation but on justice and caring. If Jesus had been in the motorcade, he would most likely have gotten out to walk among the less popular and most marginalized, seeking not to receive political funds but to give prolific love. Our readings today carry the message of renewal. If you have become indifferent to the misfortune of others and perhaps even isolated yourself from it, then your heart is frozen, and you have no place in the kingdom.

We pray: Being perfectly just and absolutely loving is very difficult, but we can begin in small ways. Today, if you find a grudge in your heart, let it disappear. If you find yourself at odds with anyone, move to a position where there is no judgment. Encourage yourself to let go of your ties with the powerful and renew your preference for the weak.

Tuesday, First Week of Lent
Isaiah 55:10–11; Matthew 6:7–15

So shall my word be that goes forth from my mouth;
It shall not return to me void, but shall do my will.
(Isa 55:11)

Every February, northern places are blessed with a few days of warm weather. Crocuses respond to this temperate breath of God by boldly jutting their bright green stems out of the earth. They always keep their delicate yellow flowers sheathed and protected during this stage, waiting for the next touch of God's mild hand. Seeing this first sign of the cyclic seasons gives us hope as we look ahead to the end of winter and the beginning of spring.

Today's readings are like crocuses, signs of hope at the beginning of Lent. The first reading from Isaiah reminds us that the cycle of God's life is much like the cycle of nature. God's Word (the power of God) is constantly in motion between earth and heaven. In our gospel, Jesus reveals to us that we are called to be a part of that movement. The Our Father is the "word" that will sweep us into this spiritual cycle. This prayer gives us hope that as surely as spring follows winter, so God's love will lead us from darkness to light, sadness to joy, death to life.

We pray: Lord God, let your word come down from the heavens and rest in me. Empower your word to fill me with light, joy, and new life. Let your will be done in me this day. Amen.

Wednesday, First Week of Lent
Jonah 3:1–10; Luke 11:29–32

A clean heart create for me,
God; renew in me a steadfast spirit.
(Ps 51:12)

Every priest can tell you about the mystery of the preaching experience. God will do what God wants with your words. Once, when I was preaching at a cathedral parish, I had prepared my homily with extra diligence. I delivered the homily with great excitement and fervor. I thought the homily was great—insightful and prayerful with touches of humor. Afterward, one of the parishioners told me: "If I had wanted to see Bob Hope I would have turned on my TV set!" On another occasion I had prepared my homily poorly. It was not insightful, prayerful, or humorous. My delivery was lackluster. Afterward a woman told me that my words had changed her life.

All miracles and all redemption happen in God's time, not ours. In the readings today, Jonah has no energy for preaching, but God sends him to a town of pagans where his halfhearted words convert the whole town. And although Jesus, the long-awaited Messiah, preaches to his own Chosen People who claim to love Yahweh, they won't listen to Him.

Many areas of our lives are like preaching. We have little or no control over sickness, death, aging parents, abrupt losses, and unexpected changes. On the Lenten journey, we give over our control to God. We ask God to use our words, thoughts, and actions to bring forth the mystery of love and redemption.

We pray: Lord, use my words this day as vehicles of love that will carry the light of you and your goodness to others. Into your hands, Lord, I commend my life. Amen.

Thursday, First Week of Lent
Esther C:12, 14–16, 23–25; Matthew 7:7–12

*Be mindful of us, O LORD. Manifest yourself in the time
of our distress and give me courage.*
(Esth C:23)

The Unsinkable Molly Brown earned her reputation because she forced her lifeboat to go back toward the sinking *Titanic* to look for survivors in the frigid waters. She did this in spite of the fears, cries, and opposition of the people in her boat.

In our first reading, Esther shows us the face of courage, in spite of her own feelings of helplessness and aloneness. In her isolation, she calls on the faithful Yahweh who has always been there for her people. Esther finds the courage she needs; she faces her enemies and saves her people. In our gospel, Jesus asks us to seek the courage we need to live, to face the task of heroically taking on the events of daily life. We may be just as filled with feelings of aloneness and helplessness as Esther was. Many times we are overwhelmed, emotionally exhausted, or afraid to act. In that difficult moment, the Lord asks us to knock on the door, to cry out like Esther, to seek, and to ask. We believe that the faithful Lord who bolstered Esther in her moment of need will also fortify us.

We pray: Lord, you are the faithful God. For thousands of years you have always been there, giving help to your people. Be with me on this day, O Lord. Strengthen my spirit to seek and to ask. Help me find the courage to act. Amen.

Friday, First Week of Lent
Ezekiel 18:21–18; Matthew 5:20–26

Unless your righteousness surpasses that of the scribes and Pharisees,
you will not enter into the kingdom of heaven.
(Mt 5:20)

At a recent wake, the children of the deceased woman told me that a baby girl had been born into their family just that week, a granddaughter to the deceased grandmother. They named the baby after the grandmother and even remarked that some of the facial features of the granddaughter resembled those of the grandmother. While this scene of family connectedness was going on inside, a scuffle broke out in the parking lot. The grandfather, who had been divorced from the deceased for many years, was trying to make his way in to pay his respects, and some angry family members were trying to stop him.

Hate and love can exist side by side. Our two readings today direct us down the road to ever-increasing love. The prophet Ezekiel says that following the laws is enough to preserve our lives and keep us in Yahweh's heart. But Jesus says we must go beyond the law and form an inner determination to do everything we can to win back our brother and sister. We forgive them, we talk to them, and we offer them a continual bond of affection and mutual help. In this way, we commit ourselves to dispelling hate and encouraging love.

We pray: Lord, we are all brothers and sisters in your life. Give us the heart to extend ourselves in love to those who are estranged from us. Give us the gentleness that brings forgiveness. Amen.

Saturday, First Week of Lent
Deuteronomy 26:16–19; Matthew 5:43–48

You will be a people sacred to the Lord,
your God, as he promised.
(Deut 26:19)

The wedding ceremony is alive with symbols that proclaim to the couple and to the community that this is a heart-and-soul experience. We see the couple and their friends dressed in beautifully complementary colors and patterns. This connects to the deeper wonder of the two people who now choose to flow forward in one pattern of love. The wedding rings point to the richness of the love between the couple and their commitment that it will last forever. In lighting the unity candle together, the two signify that they share one life.

The heart-and-soul experience of God's kingdom is symbolized in today's readings. In Deuteronomy, the symbols take the shape of statutes, commandments, and decrees. If we embrace these symbols, God will truly give us ears to hear God's voice. Jesus expands this and proclaims that the new symbol must be more than just obedience. The new symbol is the love that goes beyond the law and beyond the ordinary. Our actions of love are the heart and soul of God's kingdom.

We pray: Lord, draw me into your presence. Create in me the symbols that make me a heart-and-soul Christian. Help me to hear your voice and to act with great love. Amen.

Second Sunday of Lent
Genesis 12:1–4; 2 Timothy 1:8–10; Matthew 17:1–9

This is my beloved Son; listen to him.
(Mt 17:5)

As soon as the first warm days of late March arrived, my mother would declare a spring cleaning day. She owned our time for that day! We threw open windows and doors to blow out all the stale air that had accumulated through boarded-up winter. Dust rags, floor and furniture polish, soap, water, and window cleaner made quick appearances. At the end of the day, as the last rug was rolled back in place, we rested amid sweet smells of cleanliness. We were now ready for the spring and summer ahead.

In today's readings, we hear how God breathes new life and freshness into us, almost like God declaring a day of spring cleaning. Abram, even though very old, leaves his home so he can begin a great nation. Jesus brings Peter, James, and John up to the mountain of God. There God breathes a new life and spirit into them. God also gives Jesus a new direction, and when Jesus comes down from the mountain, he is ready for Jerusalem where he will suffer and die.

We pray: Open my heart to your fresh new word, O Lord. May this Lent be a sacred spring to me, as I throw open the windows and doors of my life to you. May your fresh voice bring me a new sense of purpose and direction. Amen.

Monday, Second Week of Lent
Daniel 9:4–10; Luke 6:36–38

But yours, O Lord, our God,
are compassion and forgiveness!
(Dan 9:9)

Have you seen the advertisements for "The Best of ____" videotape from a popular daytime talk show? The advertisements show people whose hatred of each other erupts into violence. They leap out of their chairs screaming, punching, and tackling each other. So many talk shows portray this uglier side of life—people openly speaking about their lying, cheating, abandonment, and hatreds. Have we become a culture of condemnation and violence?

The prophet Daniel condemns himself and his nation for departing from God. But Daniel knows that God is a God of constant forgiveness and mercy. Daniel hopes that God will lift his nation out of self-condemnation. Jesus reminds his people that it is a sin to condemn and judge. We are invited to be like God, to journey away from condemnation and toward compassion. Unlike the talk shows, we move away from violence and toward pardon.

We pray: Lord, I stand before you now with my hands and heart open. Take the condemnation and judgment from my heart. Fill me, Lord, with your compassion and pardon. Challenge me to act lovingly toward all, especially those I most condemn. Amen.

Tuesday, Second Week of Lent
Isaiah 1:10,16–20; Matthew 23:1–12

Wash yourselves clean!
Put away your misdeeds from before my eyes;
cease doing evil; learn to do good.
(Isa 1:16–17)

One of the most startling pictures of 1997 was that of Mother Teresa embracing Princess Diana. If you did not know them, you would guess that it was a picture of opposites. Mother Teresa, small and frail looking, stood with her head bowed. She was dressed in the simple clothes of an Indian peasant, her hair covered and her face wrinkled beyond the help of cream. Princess Diana stood elegant and tall, dressed in the most expensive outfit, skin radiant and hair perfect. Both women were representing the plight of the poor— Mother Teresa by attending to the dying and Princess Diana by helping those injured by land mines. Their inner goodness shone far beyond their personal appearance.

The Word of God today proclaims that we must change our ways. Our conversion must be an inner one, not based on fine clothes and radiant skin but on a depth of love for the widow and orphan, for all the lost and helpless of the world. Because we serve the lowly, we will be gathered into the company of the great saints. Today we ask God to help us mine our inner wealth.

We pray: Lord, I look to my inner self, and I seek conversion. I ask you, Lord, to help me find the strength to reach out to the helpless and lost. I remember them now in my prayer. Amen.

Wednesday, Second Week of Lent
Jeremiah 18:18–20; Matthew 20:17–2

Free me from the net they have set for me, for you are my refuge.
(Ps 31:5)

Our century is distinguished by the fanatical murders of good people. Two of the most famous are Mahatma Gandhi and Archbishop Oscar Romero. Both worked for the poor and for peace. Both were murdered by nationalists who supported the existing government and opposed change. There are many other good people who gave their lives while serving the poor and working for peace—the sisters who were murdered in Liberia, the teachers who were executed in Central America, the Irish priests who disappeared in the Philippines. Many times good deeds are not merely left unrewarded but are met with criticism, punishment, or even death.

In both our readings today, we are faced with the cost of discipleship. Those who follow Jesus, work for peace, and strive to raise up the poor will be criticized, will suffer, and perhaps will be killed. Jeremiah asks God to explain to him why good must be repaid by evil. Jesus presumes that the way of the servant is a way of suffering. Disciples accept this "cup" as part and parcel of their call.

We pray: Lord, many times I struggle in accepting the suffering that comes with my good deeds. Help me to see this hurt as rooted in your call to me. Encourage me to drink the cup that you drink. Amen.

Thursday, Second Week of Lent
Jeremiah 17:5–10; Luke 16:19–31

Blessed is the man who trusts in the Lord,
whose hope is the Lord.
(Jer 17:7)

Lottery fever is sweeping through our land. Even the smallest gas station and convenience store have lottery tickets available. Recently, an international newspaper did a survey, asking their readers what they would do with the money if they won the lottery. The results showed that the focus of spending was very selfish. It centered on paying off bills, buying new cars and homes, and quitting jobs to travel. Only 2 percent of the people surveyed said that they would give any money to charity.

The gospel story of Lazarus is a stinging commentary on selfishness, especially characterized by the neglect of the poor by the rich. Jesus says that if we neglect or reject the less fortunate now, then we will be neglected and rejected in the afterlife. The message is not to give away all that we have but to share what we have and trust God as the source of our wealth. Jeremiah says it well: If we trust in humans we become a desert; if we trust in God we become a fountain (see Jer 17:5–8). This Lent let us become aware of how needy of God we are and thereby become rich in God's eyes.

We pray: Lord, take our selfish ways and turn them into visions of brotherhood and sisterhood. Let us become a fountain of your love, giving this treasure freely to others. Amen.

Friday, Second Week of Lent
Genesis 37:3–4, 12–13, 17–28;
Matthew 21:33–43, 45–46

By the Lord has this been done,
and it is wonderful in our eyes.
(Mt 21:42)

Earlier this year I went into the hospital for a surgical procedure. I was alone in the hospital chapel trying to pray away my presurgery nervousness when a teenager came in and sat down. At first he fidgeted, nervously chewing his gum. After a few minutes he calmed down and became still and quiet. Finally, he raised his head, looked around, saw me, and said: "It sure is peaceful in here!" In the midst of his bondage, he had discovered God's presence.

Our readings today present us with two stories of young people who have entered bondage—the Genesis story of Joseph sold into slavery with his coat of many colors and the gospel story of the vineyard owner's son killed by the tenant farmers. Both stories ask us to see beyond the bondage of the moment to the power of God. The Lord turns evil into good, confusion into sense, and despair into meaning. God's light-filled providence reaches into the darkest pockets of our existence.

We pray: Lord, take the dark moments of our present. Give us peace, and lead us to trust that you will rescue us and bring sense to the winding pathways of our lives. Amen.

Saturday, Second Week of Lent
Micah 7:14–15, 18–20; Luke 15:1–3, 11–32

You will show faithfulness to Jacob, and grace to Abraham,
As you have sworn to our fathers from days of old.
(Mic 7:20)

One of the most-watched programs on cable television is *Biography*. People are fascinated by family histories. When we can research our roots, many times we can find new life. But some people are not so lucky. One of our priests, who had converted from Judaism, was disowned by his family. They even went so far as to bury a symbolic coffin. As far as they were concerned, their son was dead. Even though he could never return to his own family, he spent his life as a Catholic priest working with other Jewish Christians.

Today's gospel reminds us that we can always return to our God, who never disowns us. God is like a grandpa sitting on the front porch in his rocking chair, his eyes glued to the road, waiting for our arrival. The prophet Micah tells his people of the wonderful history of the "days of old." God has always been and will always be faithful to us.

We pray: Lord, sometimes I find myself far away, cut off, and almost dead. I need you, Lord, to come to me and be my guide. Bring me back home, Lord. Amen.

Third Sunday of Lent
Exodus 17:3–7; Romans 5:1–2, 5–8; John 4:5–42

Sir, give me this water, so that I may not be thirsty.
(Jn 4:15)

One dramatic picture of the flooding in recent years was of an earthen dike breaking. The water found the weakest point in the dam and broke through, covering thousands of acres. The water could not be stopped! Farms, homes, and businesses were carried away as if they were cardboard.

In our readings today, water becomes a sign of the unstoppable power and presence of our God. In the water of Exodus, the people see that their God wants them to live, not die. God chooses life for them by giving them water in the dry desert. The divine presence in their lives will not be blocked! In the gospel, water is again a sign of God's presence but even more than that, of God's eternal life overflowing on us. Eternal life cannot be contained in a water jar but flows out of the well of Jesus to all believers. As we stop today to take a drink of water or offer a glass to spouse, child, or friend, we ask Jesus to make us a fountain of his life for others.

We pray: Jesus, I believe that you are the living water. This day I will drink fully from you! Amen.

Monday, Third Week of Lent
2 Kings 5:1–15; Luke 4:24–30

My being thirsts for God, the living God.
(Ps 42:3)

The Today Show interviewed a mother and father whose daughter, twenty years old, had died in a car accident. The hospital asked the parents if they would consider donating their daughter's heart and lungs for organ transplants. The parents knew that if their daughter were dying they would beg for organs to keep her alive. They said "Yes," believing that their daughter's death could now have meaning. Their daughter's heart went to another young woman of a similar age. Her lungs went to a young man who had already entered a coma and would die without a transplant. These two recipients survived their transplants, met, married, and were on *The Today Show* with the donor's parents. The recipients and the parents had become a new family.

Today's readings tell the story of life in the family of God. Naaman, in the first reading, needed to believe. Others helped him come to that place of belief. In our gospel, Jesus challenges and chastises his own community about their lack of belief in him. Jesus knows that miracles are abundant and are ours for the believing.

We pray: Lord, today I commit to believing in you. You bring healing, and you bring life out of death. You are my Lord! Amen.

Tuesday, Third Week of Lent
Daniel 3:25,34–43; Matthew 18:21–35

Remember your compassion and love, O LORD; for they are ages old.
(Ps 25:6)

Last spring, a homeowner on the shores of Lake Michigan woke up hearing the crashing of the waves against the sea wall. He grabbed his morning coffee and moved to the deck to watch the storm. In that moment, he heard the sea wall buckle. Quickly the deck on which he was standing began to collapse. He had barely enough time to grab his dog and run out the front door. As he cleared the door, the churning waters ate his house. He had lost everything but was glad to be alive!

Today's readings offer us two responses to the tragedies of life. Daniel, in the first reading, writes in a time when his nation has been destroyed. All that is left for Daniel and his people is hope. Those who would not convert to paganism were being burned in a furnace! In the midst of the fire, Azariah utters a prayer of hope. He believes that even in his greatest difficulty God will renew the covenant with him. In the gospel, Jesus proclaims that lack of forgiveness is as catastrophic in the spiritual realm as having our house destroyed or our land conquered. The true response to this inner spiritual darkness is forgiveness, forgiveness that is offered freely and often! Today let us choose hope and forgiveness as our responses to life.

We pray: Lord you are the key to my life. Open my heart that I may forgive. Cast the darkness of hatreds, grudges, and lack of forgiveness away from me, and give me a heart of love and caring. Amen.

Wednesday, Third Week of Lent
Deuteronomy 4:1, 5–9; Matthew 5:17–19

Now, Israel, hear the statutes and decrees
which I am teaching you to observe, that you may live.
(Deut 4:1)

One side of my family still preserves the ancient practice of arranging marriages. They send over to the "old country" for a suitable spouse for their son or daughter and then bring the future partner to the United States to see the intended for the first time. In this initial encounter, the future spouses may feel a combination of fear, shock, happiness, satisfaction, and acceptance, but whatever they feel, obedience to the family is a greater value than natural attraction or heart-pounding love. The family becomes the intermediary of love.

In both readings today, obedience to the law is placed as the highest value in Jewish culture. For Jewish people, who can neither see God face to face nor speak God's name, the law is an intermediary, a way of both seeing God and obeying God. In the Book of Deuteronomy, obedience to the law and successful living go hand in hand. Jesus goes one step further and proclaims that he himself is the fulfillment of all law. From now on, obedience to Jesus and successful living go hand in hand.

We pray: Lord, open my ears today that I might listen to your law written in my heart. I choose to obey you, Lord, in my life this day. Amen.

Thursday, Third Week of Lent
Jeremiah 7:23–28; Luke 11:14–23

If it is by the finger of God that [I] drive out demons,
then the kingdom of God has come upon you.
(Lk 11:20)

Some time ago, the scientific community predicted that in the year 2020 a mile-wide meteorite would pass dangerously close to the earth. For a few days after this prediction, the news reports all centered on the destruction the meteorite would cause when and if it hit the earth. To add to the confusion, two Hollywood movies about earth getting hit by a meteorite were released at about the same time the prediction was made. But further research showed that the meteorite will not be a danger to the earth after all. It will pass harmlessly by the earth at a distance of several hundred thousand miles.

In our gospel today, Jesus wants his people to know that there is no guessing, estimating, or ambiguity in who he is. Jesus is the living presence of the reign of God. His voice is the finger of God from which even demons run. The prophet Jeremiah also conveys to his people the determination of Yahweh to have a people absolutely committed to Yahweh. Even our psalm of today sings out: "Oh, that today you would hear his voice: / Do not harden your hearts" (Ps 95:7–8).

We pray: Lord, I do believe in you totally and without reservation! You are the Son of God. You are the conqueror of evil. Make my faith firm today! Amen.

Friday, Third Week of Lent
Hosea 14:2–10; Mark 12:28–34

Straight are the paths of the LORD, in them the just walk.
(Hos 14:10)

Many times we need others to show us the path that leads to life. For the first several years of my priesthood, I counseled a young married couple with a small baby. When they first came to see me, their marriage was in trouble. They were at odds with each other. They didn't know how to be a couple or a family. When I talked to their parents, I realized that their family systems were poor models for them and could offer them little help. The four of us were on our own. But the couple was gifted with love and a desire to make things work. Over the following year, together we found a path. They discovered a new way to be partners and family.

In today's readings, God offers us the path to true spiritual union with God and with each other. Hosea tells us that the path to the Lord our God is through conversion and return. This means turning our faces, eyes, and words to the Lord. It means saying "Lord, I see you, I hear you, I love you." The Lord will do the rest. Jesus proclaims that the path to God is a commitment of love. Love God totally, and love your neighbor with the same intensity as you do yourself.

We pray: Lord, you are the way, the truth, and the life. Open before me the path of life. Call me to return to you and to love totally. Renew your way within me. Amen.

Saturday, Third Week of Lent
Hosea 6:1–6; Luke 18:9–14

He will come to us like the rain,
like spring rain that waters the earth.
(Hos 6:3)

Fairy tales usually have a wizard or a magician in the story. These special people, like Merlin in *Camelot*, have magical formulas that only they know. Their incantations may bestow a curse or a blessing, or even rearrange history or change someone's shape. Merlin uses his magic to change the young King Arthur into various animals. This helps Arthur see the world with new eyes and a new understanding.

Jesus makes it clear in our gospel today that there is no magic formula for prayer that is possessed by only a few. Prayer is a gift that is open to all. Jesus gives us the model for prayer: we are sinners, totally dependent on God for our salvation. We must lower our heads and ask God to pour mercy on us and rub that mercy, like oil, into our muscles and bones. We must allow ourselves to feel God's hands on us. Hosea tells us that this is the love that God demands of us. God doesn't need our frantic activity. God does want us to know God as the one who directs our comings and goings.

We pray: Lord, I approach you with my head bowed and my hands open. Pour your mercy upon me this day. Let me feel myself loved and honored by you. I need your strong hand to be near me, directing me and leading me. Amen.

Fourth Sunday of Lent
1 Samuel 16:1,6–7, 10–13; Ephesians 5:8–14;
John 9:1–41

I am the light of the world. Whoever follows me will not walk in darkness, but will have the light of life.

(Jn 8:12)

A woman with teenage children had just gone through a very painful divorce. Feeling alone and buried in responsibility, she said, "I feel I am at the end of a dark tunnel. There is so little light, and I am so trapped!" Thus begins her journey, a journey from darkness to light. Each of us makes this journey hundreds of times in life, until we finally journey through the darkness of death to the brightness of eternity.

In today's gospel, John presents us with the journey of one man born blind. His is a journey into physical light and spiritual faith. As the First Book of Samuel 16:13 reminds us today, when we are ready, when we are called, the Spirit does not hesitate but rushes upon us. The choice before us is to accept the Lord's word and so become children of light or to continue to bang around in the darkness. The key that opens the door of light is the gospel phrase, "I do believe, Lord!"

We pray: Lord you are the giver of light. Send the light quickly to me, so I may see and believe! Amen.

Monday, Fourth Week of Lent
Isaiah 65:17–21; John 4:43–54

The man believed what Jesus said to him and left.

(Jn 4:50)

I was visiting some friends on the occasion of their daughter's eighth birthday. She received a small diary with a silver lock and key from her girlfriend. I could see from the love in her eight-year-old eyes that this was a treasure. Later that evening, I asked her if she would let me read her diary. She told me, "No! It's a secret diary, and only a secret friend can read it." I found out later that this secret friend was her girlfriend.

Life is a matter of trust. The more we trust, the more of life's treasures will be opened for us. In today's first reading, the prophet Isaiah proclaims that there will be a new heaven and a new earth. Life will be full of joy and happiness. Isaiah doesn't say exactly how this will happen; but in the gospel, Jesus gives us a demonstration. By healing the royal official's child, Jesus shows us that trust will be the bridge carrying us to a new heaven and a new earth. Trusting in him is the key to our happiness.

We pray: Lord, so many times I need your word to come to me and to create in me a new heaven and a new earth. Send your word to me this day that I might trust in you and feel your new life. Amen.

Tuesday, Fourth Week of Lent
Ezekiel 47:1–9, 12; John 5:1–3, 5–16

*Streams of the river gladden the city of God,
the holy dwelling of the Most High.*
(Ps 46:5)

In the 1998 Academy Award-winning movie *Titanic*, an old woman, the ship's last living survivor, tells the story of a love that changed her life. She keeps her memories alive throughout her life until finally, old and frail, she allows her memories to find a resting place with her lover at the bottom of the sea. This story is so powerful that one woman has seen the movie over one hundred times.

Today Ezekiel tells us another powerful love story, the story of the waters that flow from God's temple, changing everything they touch. They cleanse people's eyes, giving them new vision and renewing youth, enthusiasm, and energy. Jesus is the new temple. He possesses these waters that give life. When Jesus bathes the sick man in his word, the waters of Jesus flow over the waiting man and heal him.

We pray: Lord, over and over again I need you to purify and renew me. You are the living water. Pick me up this day, Lord, and let the waters of your love flow over me. Amen.

Wednesday, Fourth Week of Lent
Isaiah 49:8–15; John 5:17–30

The LORD supports all who are falling
and raises up all who are bowed down.
(Ps 145:14)

After Mass, a mother was holding her little daughter who was screaming out her protest in great sobs and bellows. When the mother saw me, she said, "I don't know, Father, sometimes she seems like such an angel and other times like such a devil!" I smiled and thought, *How can such opposites be in this small bundle of love?* Our lives seem to consist of opposites—birth and death, loss and triumph, joy and depression, anger and love, compassion and hatred.

Our readings today present us with opposites. Isaiah shows us a God who splits the mountains yet is as tender as a mother with her child. Jesus, in the midst of persecution, prays that those who attack him will have faith in him and will honor him. In the midst of a difficult time—when we may even be sobbing and bellowing like a small child—we raise our eyes and pray to God. Like Jesus, we say that all we have comes from God, and we trust that God will honor us and continue to give us a deep faith.

We pray: Lord, when I feel the scorching heat of life or when I am rubbed bare by the wild wind of living, lead me back to you. Give me the springs of water that will refresh me. Amen.

Thursday, Fourth Week of Lent
Exodus 32:7–14; John 5:31–47

Remember me, LORD, *as you favor your people.*
(Ps 106:4)

Last summer I decided to stroll through our local zoo. It was a blisteringly hot day, and even walking was almost too much of an effort. As I ventured along, I saw an exhausted mother sitting on a park bench with two boys, one on either side of her. They were reaching across her, grabbing and fighting for each other's ice-cream cones. The mother's eyes and mine met for an instant. She gave a sigh that said, "What can I do? They're mine!"

In both of today's readings, Moses and Jesus hang in there with the people. Both leaders see that their people are weak and have taken the wrong direction. The Chosen People have become like small boys fighting over ice-cream cones. Moses, like a good parent, pleads with God to give the people another chance. Jesus tries to help his people understand why they should believe in him. Both leaders show devotion and loyalty to those they are called to serve.

We pray: Lord, I know that you are always there with me. You hang in there with me and give me life. Help me to extend my loyalty, love, and devotion to others today. Amen.

Friday, Fourth Week of Lent
Wisdom 2:1, 12–22; John 7:1–2, 10, 25–30

And they knew not the hidden counsels of God
nor discern[ed] the innocent souls' reward.
(Wis 2:22)

In *The Color Purple,* the main character says, "I think that God would get angry if we walk through a field of flowers and not notice the color purple." Purple is the color that our eye tends to pick up least readily, so we really have to concentrate if we are to find this most delicate color in the vast blooming meadow.

Both readings today present us with evil people who do not look beyond the surface. These "wicked" condemn what they do not see and cannot understand (as the Book of Wisdom says, "Their wickedness blinded them" [2:21]). Most of the prophets were at the mercy of these surface-seers, and many prophets died because of them. Jesus knows the history of the prophets, so he challenges the ignorance of these narrow-minded condemners. The way of Jesus is to view each person as a great cathedral full of mystery and depth that would take a lifetime to understand. Or to treat each person as a field of flowers full of an eternity of shades and variances. It is certainly a challenge to us to recognize the great depth that we have because we are children of God and to respect that beauty in others by loving even their tiniest and most subtle qualities.

We pray with the psalmist, "The LORD redeems the lives of his servants; / no one incurs guilt who takes refuge in him" (Ps 34:23).

Saturday, Fourth Week of Lent
Jeremiah 11:18–20; John 7:40–53

A shield before me is God who saves the honest heart.
(Ps 7:11)

Who can forget the drama that surrounded the recent execution of a woman on death row in Texas? What made this event newsworthy was that this woman had become a born-again Christian. She had come to believe that Jesus was her personal Messiah. She had asked forgiveness from the families of her victims, and she did not fear her coming death. She not only had become a model prisoner but also had taught others about Jesus and his mercy. Many people thought that her life should be spared.

Each reading today shows us a condemned person: Jeremiah was condemned by the very people he preached to, and the same Chosen People condemned Jesus. Both Jesus and Jeremiah were fearless of the winds of hatred that swirled around them because they believed that God would be with them. As Jeremiah (11:20) says: "To you, I have entrusted my cause." In our lives we will meet disapproval, hatred, and even condemnation. We, like Jesus and Jeremiah, plant ourselves in the Lord and let go of our fear of whatever comes.

We pray: Lord, many times I journey in a forest with brutal branches and hurting thorns. Help me in these times of condemnation to place my trust completely in you. Amen.

Fifth Sunday of Lent of Lent
Ezekiel 37:12–14; Romans 8:8–11; John 11:1–45

I am the resurrection and the life.
(Jn 11:25)

When my mother died, my then six-year-old niece Sarah looked into my mother's casket and said: "That's not Grandma. Grandma lives in heaven now with God!" Her grandmother's death made my niece sad, but with her child-faith, she accepted the transition between this life and the next.

The Jews of the Hebrew Scriptures did not believe in this transition from death to life but only that on the last day the divine force would come, shake the universe, and open the graves. Then the dead would rise. Martha in today's gospel echoes that belief when she tells the Lord, "I know he [Lazarus] will rise, in the resurrection on the last day" (Jn 11:24). But the great truth in the raising of Lazarus is that we don't have to wait until the last day to rise again. Because Jesus has the power to raise people to life, anyone who believes in Jesus passes immediately from death to life. Physical death becomes only a changing of worlds.

We pray: Today I renew my belief in you, Lord, who make of me a

169

new creation. For me there is no waiting for some death event. My resurrection is now! Amen.

Monday, Fifth Week of Lent
Daniel 13:1–9,15–17,19–30,33–62; John 8:1–11

Even though I walk through a dark valley,
I fear no harm for you are at my side.
(Ps 23:4)

When I was a young priest, I had my first of many humbling confessional experiences. I was hearing a woman's confession, and after she was done, she became very still and quiet. When I asked if there was anything else she wished to say, she started to cry. Her soft cries slowly became louder until finally she burst into great heaving sobs. She felt guilty, accused, powerless, and sinful. I felt humbled to sit before someone who was so sorrowful.

We are guilty, and we are sinners. But we are also saved and forgiven. In today's first reading, Susanna is saved by her trust in God: "Through her tears she looked up to heaven, for she trusted in the Lord wholeheartedly" (Dan 13:35). And in the gospel, the adulterous woman is saved through the gentle, forgiving action of Jesus. When we feel accused, guilty, sinful, or powerless, we are called to come before the Lord Jesus, the eternal seat of mercy. No one returns from the Lord unforgiven.

We pray: Lord, I know that you wash me clean of guilt. I am weak, Lord, but I trust your strength. I am in darkness, Lord, but I trust your light. Amen.

He is rewarded with God's covenant forever. Jesus asks his followers also to trust in his Word. The early martyrs not only trusted but also found joy in Christ's Word. As their captors led them to slaughter, they sang glad songs of faith.

What does God's Word say to us today about our living and our dying? Can we take deeply to heart the invitation of Jesus to a life without end? Can we truly live today with a joy that speaks of our being true to the Word of Jesus that always gives life?

Friday, Fifth Week of Lent
Jeremiah 20:10–13; John 10:31–42

But the LORD is with me, like a mighty champion.
(Jer 20:11)

A few years ago, I flew to Phoenix for meetings. Next to me was a man with his Seeing Eye dog, which was curled quietly under the seat. This eight-year-old dog was ready to retire, so the man was returning it to its original owners. Then the man would go on to Los Angeles to receive a new two-year-old dog companion. When we arrived in Phoenix, the family was there with cameras, welcome signs, and tons of hugs for the retiring dog. The dog wagged his tail joyfully. He was home.

There is a sacred place deep within us where God lives, a place where we are most profoundly at home. In today's readings, Jeremiah is secure in the Lord despite the terror that surrounds him. Jesus is about to be stoned by the Jews but has confidence in knowing that God and he are one.

We pray: Lord, like Jeremiah and Jesus, I feel burdened and attacked by life. In this time of struggle I return to you, Lord, as the source of my well-being. Amen.

173

Saturday, Fifth Week of Lent
Ezekiel 37:21–28; John 11:45–57

He who scattered Israel, now gathers them together,
he guards them as a shepherd his flock.
(Jer 31:10)

Recently, I attended a woman's wake at which the family presented a video of photos of her, tracing her life from infancy through her last sickness. As I watched the pictures, I could sense the pattern and the meaning behind her life, a life full of hope, laughter, and purpose.

Both readings today speak to us about the purpose of our living and our dying. Ezekiel tells us that life is covenant—an agreement of peace and oneness between God and us. The gospel shows us a conspiracy against Jesus. Though the people will arrest and kill him, Jesus brings a deep peace to their hearts.

We pray: Lord, in you I place my restlessness. I place the burden of aging and dying into your hands. I know that in you everything has meaning and purpose. Amen.

Passion (Palm) Sunday
Matthew 21:1–11; Isaiah 50:4–7; Philippians 2:6–11;
Matthew 26:14—27:66 or 27:11–54

I will proclaim your name to the assembly;
in the community I will praise you.
(Ps 22:23)

In some ancient eastern Christian traditions, Palm Sunday is a day for children, the innocent ones, who go forth with palm branches to welcome Jesus, the innocent Lamb. All the children gather and lead the procession shouting "Hosanna!"

This tradition is a call to enter Holy Week through the gates of our childhood, to absorb all parts of Christ's Passion with innocent eyes and open hands, to drink with our emotions from the waters of this week. We keep the holy memory of this week alive with our sight as we witness the various celebrations, with our smell as we inhale the incense and the lighted Easter fire, with our hearing as we listen to the ancient Scripture proclaimed, with our touch as we lift the Good Friday cross to our lips, and with our taste as we receive the Holy Thursday Eucharist. "Do this in remembrance of me" (1 Cor 11:24). Keeping the memory of this week alive in our own hearts and in the hearts of our children is the sacred tradition of each Christian. This is how we participate in our own redemption and hand on that redemption to those we love.

We pray: Lord, today I raise my palm branches in praise of your kingship. I will follow you, both in exaltation and in suffering. I will be a living memory of the events of this week. Amen.

Monday of Holy Week
Isaiah 42:1–7; John 12:1–11

Here is my servant whom I uphold, upon whom I have put my spirit.
(Isa 42:1)

A very old couple comes to daily Mass at our monastery. She is ninety-two years old and he is eighty-nine. They always enter the church at the same time and sit in the same pew. In the last year she has developed Alzheimer's disease. When she comes to church now she always turns to her husband and asks, "Shall we sit here today?" He smiles at her, nods yes, takes her arm, and leads her into the pew. There is a gentle, loving devotion they share in their aging and in her sickness.

In the gospel, Mary anoints Jesus' feet and dries them with her hair, betraying her total love of and devotion to the Lord. In the first reading, Isaiah speaks of the quiet, gentle victory of "the servant."

175

Both readings encourage us to act toward Jesus with both the fierce devotion of Mary and the gentleness of the suffering servant.

We pray: Lord, you have formed me, you grasp me by the hand and lead me. Today, Lord, let me attend to you. Let my thoughts be on you during my work and my leisure. Amen.

Tuesday of Holy Week
Isaiah 49:1–6; John 13:21–33, 36–38

> *I will make you a light to the nations,*
> *that my salvation may reach to the ends of the earth.*
> *(Isa 49:6)*

Most parents experience disappointment, suffering, and betrayal at the hands of their teenage children. A couple told me the story of one night when they discovered that their daughter had sneaked out the house. They turned off the house lights and waited on the stairwell for their daughter to return. About one in the morning, she climbed back into the house, took off her shoes, and ran right into her parents sitting on the steps. You can imagine the hurt and the excuses that followed.

What do we do when we face frustration, disillusionment, disappointment, and hurt? Today's readings tell us that Jesus' path to light, resurrection, and glorification are to come through betrayal, disappointment, and suffering. We travel with the Lord. When we find ourselves journeying through the darker woods, we know that there will be a light beyond. We imitate the Lord in knowing only that the deepest night holds a promise of the brightest day.

We pray: Lord, we journey this week with you through betrayal and death. We believe, as you did, that there is a great life beyond this moment of darkness. Lord, walk with me this day as I walk with you. Amen.

Wednesday of Holy Week
Isaiah 50:4–9; Matthew 26:14–25

The Lord GOD is my help, therefore I am not disgraced.
(Isa 50:7)

As a Catholic grade-school child, I watched a movie about Saint Joan of Arc. Rather than crying out as she is burned at the stake, she is filled with peace and dignity. Nothing outside of us, even death, can rob us of that inner peace and dignity.

In today's gospel reading, Jesus maintains an inner peace and calm even though betrayal is near. How does Jesus keep his quiet in the midst of the whirlwind? It is through his lifeline to the God who is Jesus' Father. Jesus knows that God is with him. It is also our call to be deeply connected to God amid the storms that rage around us. Through "amazing grace" we will emerge from the worst struggles if we stay close to the Lord.

We pray: Lord, I enter this week of suffering and struggle aligned with you. You are the chain that holds me to life, the tree that roots me to God. Lord, this day I will stay deeply connected to you. Amen.

Holy Thursday, Easter Triduum
Exodus 12:1–8, 11–14; 1 Corinthians 11:23–26;
John 13:1–15

If I, therefore, the master and teacher, have washed your feet,
you ought to wash one another's feet.
(Jn 13:14)

A woman at our workplace is due to give birth any day. She tells us that she is impatiently waiting for her liberation. She also wants to love this child in a new way, to touch the child, bathe the child, nurse the child, and hug the child.

Our Holy Thursday readings take us on a journey from slavery to liberation and new life. In the Exodus account, we hear the story of our Hebrew ancestors breaking the chains of slavery and embracing freedom. Jesus challenges his disciples to break the bonds of selfishness and embrace a love that serves others. The Eucharist is the living reminder of our pilgrimage from slavery to new life. "As often as you eat this bread and drink the cup, you proclaim the death of the Lord until he comes" (1 Cor 11:26). We hold in our body and spirit the ongoing liberation of Jesus. This day we proclaim that Jesus' body and blood liberate us to love and serve one another.

We pray: Lord, today I will receive your body and blood. I believe that you take my feet in your hands and wash me gently. You command me to keep the memory of your body and blood sacred and living through my love and service. Amen.

Good Friday, Easter Triduum
Isaiah 52:13—53:12; Hebrews 4:14–16; 5:7–9; John 18:1—19, 42

Yet it was our infirmities that he bore, our sufferings that he endured.
(Isa 53:4)

One beautiful part of the baptismal rite is when the minister traces the sign of the cross on the child's forehead and invites the parents, godparents, and family to do the same. At a recent baptism, the child was not too fond of this signing: she screamed her displeasure at the top of her lungs. Although the mother wanted to take the child out of church to quiet her, I told the mother: "You can't leave with her— it's her baptism!" The cross is the symbol of our victorious faith. We trace the cross to remind ourselves of the legacy of faith that each child inherits.

Isaiah today tells us that "by his stripes we were healed" (53:5). The Book of Hebrews proclaims that Jesus is the high priest who intercedes for us forever. Scripture, liturgy, doctrine, and community all proclaim the Lord's protection of the baptized. His endurance of the pain and shame of the cross has set a seal on each of us. We don't have to be sinful, guilty, or filled with shame. We can be holy, loving, and filled with hope. It is the Lord who has done this for us.

We pray: Lord, on the cross you bore not just your own weight but mine as well. You have broken the bonds of death and sin for me. I will today seek to live as a free person, innocent and holy. Amen.

Holy Saturday, Easter Triduum
Genesis 1:1—2:2; Genesis 22:1–18; Exodus 14:15—15:1; Isaiah 54:5–14; Isaiah 55:1–11; Baruch 3:9–15, 32—4:4; Ezekiel 36:16–28; Romans 6:3–11; Luke 24:1–12

God looked at everything he had made, and he found it very good.
(Gen 1:31)

Every spring and fall my family goes to our cottage in Canada where we have buried the remains of my mother and sister. We tend to the flowers that surround the granite markers bearing their names. We wait in this world of darkness and light, looking to the time when we will all be one in the light of the Lord. Until that time we live in hope and tend the flowers.

Rabindrath Tagore says, "Faith is the bird that feels the light and sings when the dawn is still dark." Tonight we stoke the fire and light the Easter candles. Though we sense the coming light, we must still wait. We keep vigil in our circles of artificial light, waiting for the real light of the Word to break upon us.

We pray: Lord, this day and night we wait with you in the tomb. We are a people of hope, and we know the dawn is coming. Let us be still this day, Lord, as we await the light. Amen.

Easter
Acts of the Apostles 10:34, 37–43; Colossians 3:1–4;
John 20:1–9 (morning Mass);
Luke 24:13–35 (evening Mass)

Yes, Christ my hope has arisen! To Galilee he goes before you.
(Easter Sequence)

I received an announcement of the arrival of a new child. What made this announcement unusual was that this child was not born into the family but adopted. I went to the celebration with my small gift. The house was decorated, the new parents were beaming, the child was all smiles, and the friends were full of gifts and congratulations. It was an amazing and beautiful transformation from the quiet and sometimes sad home I used to visit to a vibrant place full of hope. New life always carries with it the seeds of new beginning and new dreaming.

Our Easter Lord is about transformation. His new life carries with it the gift of new beginnings and new dreaming for us. The readings today combine amazement and belief. If the Lord has risen, what will this mean for the dispirited band of disciples? It took the disciples some time to learn about their own transformation. Today we celebrate with joy our new life in the Lord and, like the disciples, we wonder what this will mean and how we will be transformed.

We pray: Lord, in you all life has become new. Your life spreads its light and warmth even to my darkest and coldest places. Lift me up today, Lord. Transform me. Amen! Alleluia!

Feast of the Chair of Saint Peter, Apostle (February 22)
1 Peter 5:1–4; Matthew 16:13–19

You are Peter, and upon this rock I will build my church.
(Mt 16:18)

One highlight of any visit to London is the Tower of London and its guarded museum that holds the crown jewels. An amazing amount of precious metals, priceless stones, and precise workmanship went into each crown. Of course, the crowns are more than just fancy-wear hats. They are the traditional sign of power and authority passed on from monarch to monarch through the centuries.

Today in our Catholic faith, we celebrate the power and authority that Jesus has passed down through the centuries to our present pontiff. This supremacy is based not on gold and jewels but on the word of Jesus, first given to Peter and then handed down to each of his successors. This word is not locked up in museums and guarded by guns. It is visible in the person and presence of our pope, the Vicar of Christ. Jesus wanted a visible church with a visible leader so his word would always be enfleshed. Today let us align ourselves with God's vicar on earth, believing in the word of Jesus that rests on him and, through him, on us.

We pray: Lord, you choose a person of flesh and blood to be the head of your Church. Help me believe in your ongoing word of life and in the men and women you choose to lead us. Amen.

Solemnity of Joseph, Husband of Mary (March 19)
2 Samuel 7:4–5, 12–14, 16; Romans 4:13, 16–18, 22;
Matthew 1:16, 18–21, 24

> *Joseph, son of David, do not be afraid*
> *to take Mary your wife into your home.*
> *(Mt 1:20)*

Every room in our Catholic grade school had the traditional picture of Saint Joseph. He was working with the young boy Jesus, planing a board in their carpenter shop. The painting gave me the impression that Jesus and Joseph spent a lot of quality time together. As a young boy, I liked this idea of father and son bonding.

This feast of Joseph is a time to look at our own bonding with Joseph. He is a carpenter, the spouse of Mary, the foster father of Jesus, a just man, and the patron of the Church. We bond with Joseph because we also, like Jesus, are members of the Holy Family. Because we are brothers and sisters to Jesus through baptism, Joseph is our foster father as well.

We pray: Loving Saint Joseph, you shared a deep bond with the Lord Jesus. I ask you to help me deepen my own personal bond with the Lord. Help me, like you, to be a builder, a just person, a patron of our church, and a loving companion of Jesus and Mary. Amen.

Solemnity of the Annunciation of the Lord (March 25)
Isaiah 7:10–14; Hebrews 10:4–10; Luke 1:26–38

Here I am; to do your will is my delight.
(Ps 40:8–9)

Long before I can remember, my mother and dad decided to become engaged and to marry. He proposed to her, and she said "yes." If my mother had said "no," then I might not be here today. I am very happy she said "yes." It was a decision that changed her life forever.

In each of our lives, there is a moment when we say "yes" and our lives are forever changed. Mary's "yes" changed her life from that of a single young girl to that of the Mother of God, with a spouse and a child. Mary's "yes" also changed the life of the whole earth. Dates would now be marked from the time of her child's birth, millions of people would follow her son, even giving their lives for him, and nations would dedicate themselves to the image of Mary as the Mother of God. On this day, we can also say "yes" to what brings the Incarnate Jesus to life within us. Our "yes" might not change the direction of the world, but it can change us.

We pray: Lord, on this feast of your conception when you vest yourself with flesh through the "yes" of Mary, lead me to bring you more alive within my heart and spirit. Amen.

Daily Meditations for Lent: Cycle B

The older couple always sat close to the aisle in the second-to-last pew. On this particular day the young parish priest greeted the people as they entered for the weekday Mass. When he saw the couple sitting in the back, he approached them and asked if they would like to move closer. He told them that they could see and hear better if they were closer to the front. The older man looked at his wife and then at the priest. When the man spoke, it was with gentle tones born out of years of experience: "You know, Father, I would like to move up closer, but my wife here wouldn't. So I choose to sit back here with her. Jesus can still hear me and my wife will still love me!"

Prayer to God in the heavens has to be rooted in the earth. Our prayer should flow out of the everyday motion of our lives. The stories that burst on the morning news, the feel of the heat or cold of the day, the ordinary banter of our spouses, children, and coworkers—this is the stuff of prayer and reflection.

As you approach the Scriptures of Lent, first think about the day at hand. What is happening around you and inside of you right now? Then take time to slowly read the Scripture. See if the Scripture has anything to say to your life today. Quietly allow Scripture and your life to build a bridge to each other. It is then that the Word of God and the word of life intermingle in a blessed fashion.

In these Lenten meditations, I have tried to take everyday stories and connect them in some way with the Scripture for the liturgy of the day. In some instances the bond is quite powerful, in others the connection is a lingering tiny thread. I hope that you will use these meditations as a foundation for your own bridge between the Scripture of the day and your life.

God is indeed most profound when God speaks to you about you.

Ash Wednesday
Joel 2:12–18; 2 Corinthians 5:20–6:2;
Matthew 6:1–6, 16–18

Rend your hearts, not your garments,
and return to the Lord, your God.
(Joel 2:13)

Sometime during March we notice the news media turning their attention to the annual Academy Awards. We watch fascinated as the stars arrive on the evening of the awards. They come in chauffeured limousines, wearing the latest hairdos, the most fashionable clothes, and the most extravagant jewelry. For days afterward, commentators discuss who was the best-dressed star and who was the worst, proof of America's absolute fascination with externals.

In the readings for Ash Wednesday, both the prophet Joel and the Lord Jesus condemn superficiality. It is not a pathway to the kingdom. The pathway back to God is through the valleys of deep inner renewal. This renewal requires a change of heart, not of clothes or hairstyle. If we fast, we do so to experience a deeper hunger, a hunger for what is just and holy. If we give alms, we do so to experience a sense of solidarity with those who are poor and abandoned by our hollow society. If we pray, we do so because we acknowledge our complete and utter dependence on God who gives us all we have.

In his Second Letter to the Corinthians, Paul tells us in earnest that we can't dillydally any longer: "Now is the day of salvation!" (6:2). We receive our ashes to help us grasp the urgency of personal renewal. Now is the moment to act justly, to take the hand of the poor, to rely on our God for everything.

Thursday After Ash Wednesday
Deuteronomy 30:15–20; Luke 9:22–25

"Whoever wishes to be my follower must deny his very self,
take up his cross each day, and follow in my steps."
(Lk 9:23)

Recently in New York, a Jewish woman died leaving millions of dollars to a religious college for women. The surprise was that she had any money at all. She lived a simple, very frugal life. She would even walk to the library every day after work where she would read the daily paper rather than buy one for herself. In the midst of self-sacrifice, she had stored up great wealth that she never used for personal gain.

Today in our readings, God asks us to choose the door of life. It is the doorway of resurrection, of life forever with God. Jesus gives us the key to that door in the way we act: whoever wishes to be his follower must deny themselves, take up their cross each day, and follow in his steps (Lk 9:23). The prayer of Saint Francis recasts the idea in this way: "Let me seek not so much to be consoled as to console, to be understood as to understand, to be loved as to love."

As Christians, we deny ourselves to give others what they need. We choose to take the key of life and open the door into the kingdom. In a world where so many waste their lives acquiring power, prestige, and money, let us be the ones who take the road less traveled. We bear the loss of a self-centered life so we can embrace the glory of acceptance and giving.

Friday After Ash Wednesday
Isaiah 58:1–9; Matthew 9:14–15

This, rather, is the fasting that I wish: releasing those bound unjustly,
untying the thongs of the yoke; setting free the oppressed.
(Isa 58:6)

When we were tiny, someone taught us proper Catholic etiquette—how to dress for church, how to genuflect, how to bow our heads and fold our hands in prayer. Most of us continue to use these same practices today as we enter and leave church. Traditions of religious dramatics sometimes make us feel holy, many times make us feel prayerful, and most often make us feel secure. If we act in the correct way, then we think we deserve the just reward!

In the first reading, Isaiah turns the world of religious acting upside down. He tells his tradition-bound people that God has no stake in their religious perfumery. Isaiah challenges them to establish a new religious tradition based on opposing oppression rather than multiplying movements. This new tradition is not complicated. It is simply helping another who has less than we have—less food, less shelter, less clothing, less love, less chains. In this way our light will shine!

Jesus tells us that not only will our light shine but also we will be chosen to enter paradise if we care for those who have less than we have (Mt 25:34–36). If we choose to ignore the less fortunate, we will be condemned by God. Jesus is the bridegroom, the feast of heaven is here! What we have is not ours to hoard. We must share it equally with all.

Saturday After Ash Wednesday
Isaiah 58:9–14; Luke 5:27–32

If you bestow your bread on the hungry and satisfy the afflicted;
Then light shall rise for you in the darkness.
(Isa 58:10)

In today's gospel, Jesus calls Levi, a tax collector, to be one of his followers. Levi holds a specially gifted spot in the history of the Catholic faith. Who is this famous Levi? Levi is Saint Matthew. Jesus changes Levi's name to *Mattai,* which means *gift of God.* Matthew wrote his gospel to lead the Jewish leaders—who rejected Matthew as a sinner—to Jesus.

Jesus' call to discipleship liberates us from the prejudices by which we classify people. The religion teachers of Jesus' time did not consider tax collectors, foreigners, or sinners as part of their religious family. They, the religious elite, classified these people as outcasts. Jesus, on the other hand, announces his intention to include these outcasts as partners with him in his kingdom.

We seem to have at least as much trouble with prejudice as the people of Jesus' time had. For many years in the American Catholic Church, barriers of prejudice have existed. Anglo-Americans often would not worship in the same parish as people of different ethnic or racial backgrounds. Many times Anglo-Americans would choose not to live in the same neighborhoods as people of color and not to work in the same jobs. Let us hope that these barriers are now breaking down. If we do not live as one, then we have no place in Jesus' kingdom. This Lent open your heart, your mind, and your spirit to those you consider not worthy to be members of your religious family.

First Sunday of Lent
Genesis 9:8–15; 1 Peter 3:18–22; Mark 1:12–15

I set my bow in the clouds to serve as a sign of the covenant
between me and the earth.
(Gen 9:13)

Sometimes you have to just trust the Lord tugging at your heart, let go, and take a risk. Twenty years ago, Suzy Yelh became a single parent. Her marriage had ended. She had watched the devastation that this breakup caused her children. Rather than give in to despair she established "The Rainbow Program," a support group for children who are experiencing divorce or death. Ms. Yelh says, "There has to be a rainbow for all God's children!" The Rainbow Program is now in many countries and has aided over fifty thousand children.

Our readings this first Sunday of Lent are full of hope, covenants, and rainbows for those who trust in the Lord. In the ark of hope, Noah established a new covenant with the Lord. Through it, people could trust in God, and God would continue to give them life. Peter tells us that Jesus continues this covenant with us. It is a covenant of the spirit that is not limited by fleshly existence. Jesus is the living rainbow of that covenant. In him, both animals and angels find an abode of comfort. Evil has no place.

It is time to make or renew our personal covenant with the Lord. Our covenant is a simple covenant that says, "I will trust always in you, Lord, in all things, through all temptations. No evil will have a place in me. I will be a living rainbow of your radiance!"

Monday, First Week of Lent
Leviticus 19:1–2, 11–18; Matthew 25:31–46

I assure you, as often as you did it for one of my least brothers,
you did it for me.
(Mt 25:40)

Recently the president of the United States traveled the expressways of Los Angeles in his motorcade on the way to a political rally. It was an eerie sight. There were no cars on the expressway in either direction for as far as you could see. Police had barricaded every entrance. If the president had chosen to leave the freeway and enter the side streets, he would have seen the poor, the abandoned, the struggling, the crowded. Instead, he followed the isolated path we tend to create for our leaders, keeping them far from the needing crowds.

The kingdom of Christianity is built not on isolation but on justice and caring. If Jesus had been in the motorcade he would most likely have gotten out to walk among the less popular and most marginalized, seeking not to receive political funds but to give prolific love. Our readings today carry the message of renewal. If you have become indifferent to the misfortune of others and perhaps even isolated yourself from it, then your heart is frozen, and you have no place in the kingdom.

Being perfectly just and absolutely loving is very difficult, but we can begin in small ways. Today, if you find a grudge in your heart, let it disappear. If you find yourself at odds with anyone, move to a position where there is no judgment. Encourage yourself to let go of your ties with the powerful and renew your preference for the weak.

Tuesday, First Week of Lent
Isaiah 55:10–11; Matthew 6:7–15

Your Father knows what you need before you ask him.
This is how you are to pray: "Our Father."
(Mt 6:8–9)

Christian parents have a strong tradition of teaching their children how to pray. Saying a short prayer before bed in thanksgiving for all God's gifts or a prayer of blessing before the evening meal is the beginning point of the prayer journey. Children easily recognize that the parents are over them and God is over the parents. The child flows easily between asking the parent for things and asking God for things.

In the gospels, one of the first demands of Jesus' disciples is for Jesus to teach them to pray. They want to know how to ask God for things. Jesus' response in today's gospel is that the value of prayer does not lie in the quantity of words or the mere repetition of formulas as if we were accomplishing a task. The value of prayer lies chiefly in our inner attitude. We believe in God. We surrender our lives into God's loving hands. Then God will shower us with goodness as surely as the heavens water the earth.

There is a Zen saying: "Show me the person who has forgotten words. That is the one I wish to speak with!" As you approach your prayer this Lent, put your mind and heart on God as creator and friend, a God who loves you and is always willing to share a quiet moment with you. From this stance, let your requests rise softly from your dry soil to God's verdant ears.

Wednesday, First Week of Lent
Jonah 3:1–10; Luke 11:29–32

For at the preaching of Jonah they reformed,
but you have a greater than Jonah here.
(Lk 11:32)

Many of the tent revival preachers earlier in this century had to be part orator, part singer, and part magician to bring the people to believe. The people came expecting some excitement, some miracle. The preacher had to make someone see without glasses, hear without an aid, or even walk without a wheelchair. Usually, the crowd could not be swayed to worship the Lord unless they saw proof positive of God's power.

In the gospel today, Jesus feels the same frustration all preachers feel. Words are not enough to bring the people's faith alive. The crowds demand more. They want a sign. Make someone walk, make the blind see, make the deaf hear. Jesus' frustration is even more compounded by the story of Nineveh. That whole pagan, sinner-filled town converted because of Jonah's message. But these faithful Jews will not budge at Jesus' message.

The next time you are in church resolve not to ask for any more than you hear. Listen to the words of the Scriptures and then resolve to act on them. Be a sign for your generation of the power of God's spoken word!

Thursday, First Week of Lent
Esther C:12, 14–16, 23–25; Matthew 7:7–12

Ask, and you will receive. Seek, and you will find.
Knock, and it will be opened to you.
(Mt 7:7)

When you were younger, you may have had the experience of your mother or father opening the door of the house and calling you home for dinner. You could tell from the tone of your parent's voice whether or not they wanted to have you home at that moment. As one small child remarked, "My mother never sounds serious until the third call!"

Today Jesus gives us a window into his own prayer. Jesus' self-chosen style of prayer was the prayer of petition—asking God to help him out. Jesus gives us a second insight into his own prayer with his insistence on persistence. Petition plus persistence will eventually bend God's ear. God gets serious after the third call. If our prayer to God is to be successful, then we must not lose heart easily. Fervent and frequent prayer is a way of letting God know how deep our soil is. When God ultimately gives us the seed of response, God will be able to plant it so deep that it will take good root and grow strong and tall. We will then receive the fruits of God's response and share them with others.

Take the prayer of Queen Esther in the first reading and make that prayer yours. It is a prayer of petition asking for God to breech the heavens with the divine power and come to her aid. Let it be your prayer this day and this Lent.

Friday, First Week of Lent
Ezekiel 18:21–28; Matthew 5:20–26

Unless your holiness surpasses that of the scribes and Pharisees you shall not enter the kingdom of God.
(Mt 5:20)

A husband cared for his wife all through her last year until she died of cancer. Before his wife was diagnosed with cancer the man had been an adamant worker, spending long hours on the job both weekdays and weekends. His wife's sickness and death was a purification process that moved him from a work ethic to a love ethic. His wife's passing brought him a new realization of the beauty and value of life. He is now a changed man. He lives more in the moment and spends much more time with his children and grandchildren. He stops and talks to everyone at work and on his way home. He goes out of his way to give a street person a kind word or some money.

The whole of chapter 5 of Matthew's Gospel is the Lord's plan of purification, which moves us from being strict followers of the law to being generous givers of love. Jesus hopes that his words will help us find a new way of living with our families, friends, and community. We come to know Jesus' golden rule—that we do unto others as we would have them do unto us.

Lent is a time of turning to the Lord, a process of purifying ourselves so that we become more like Jesus in the way we act. Today would be a good day to read chapter 5 of Matthew's Gospel. Pick one of Jesus' instructions in that chapter and decide to live it this week.

Saturday, First Week of Lent
Deuteronomy 26:16–19; Matthew 5:43–48

If you love those who love you, what merit is there in that?
(Mt 5:46)

One unusual gift that I received for my ordination was a loaf of freshly baked bread. The woman who gave me this gift was a constant presence in our parish community. Some weeks after my ordination I discovered that her bread-baking extended not only to gifts at celebrations but also to gifts for the poor, for the sick, and for the hungry. I learned that wherever this woman saw a need, she gave her freshly baked bread.

This bread-baking woman embodies the New Testament theme of love found in today's gospel. In the Hebrew tradition, the people loved and cared for those they saw as being their own kind. The Hebrews considered those of other nations to be aliens and enemies. They were suspect and certainly not cared for or loved. Jesus throws this notion overboard and tells his followers to decide who to love based on need. Your neighbor is not necessarily the person who lives next-door but the person who needs your help, your concern, and your bread. This person could just as easily be an enemy as a friend!

The law book of Deuteronomy declares that if we obey the rules, then God will give us honor, renown, and glory. Jesus reinterprets this obedience as the face of love. If we give love freely to all who need it, like the heavens give the rain to all—just or unjust—then God will honor us. So today let us extend our bread of love beyond our narrow neighborhoods to embrace all those who are in need.

Second Sunday of Lent
Genesis 22:1–2, 9, 10–13, 15–18; Romans 8:31–34;
Mark 9:2–10

He was transfigured before their eyes
and his clothes became dazzlingly white.
(Mk 9:2–3)

We all need a lift sometimes, something to renew us and transfigure our lives. In the Middle Ages during the Black Plague when one-third of Europe was dying, a small book was written entitled *The Imitation of Christ*. It helped people reach beyond the constant death that surrounded them and look to heaven as their goal. Even today this little book continues to be a consolation for those who suffer.

Today we celebrate the Transfiguration. In the midst of the disciples' fears, Jesus reveals to them a tiny sliver of what the resurrection will be like. In this vision can we see the unity of all life? There are Moses and Elijah representing the Hebrew tradition. There are James, Peter, and John, the future writers and preachers. There is God in the mystery of a voice coming from a cloud. There is Christ in glory. This vision gives the apostles hope to carry them through the journey to Jerusalem and the suffering that will occur. We still celebrate this vision of the Transfiguration today when at Easter we drape the cross with a dazzlingly white cloth.

Is it possible that we might be transfigured today? Is it possible for us to glimpse a sliver of God's glory and then be renewed to carry on with our Christian lives? Let our prayer today be, "Lord, transfigure me!"

Monday, Second Week of Lent
Deuteronomy 9:4–10; Luke 6:36–38

Be compassionate, as your Father is compassionate.
(Lk 6:36)

Mother Teresa tells the story of walking the streets of Calcutta and coming upon a woman dying. She felt an overwhelming need to alleviate the woman's suffering by offering her a bed, a peaceful and dignified place to die. Mother Teresa took the dying woman with her. This act of mercy led Mother Teresa to open a home for the dying. She called the home *Nirmal Hriday* ("Home of the Pure Heart").

Our readings for this day call us to reexamine our image of God. Is God really touched by our depressions, worries, sicknesses, and dyings, or is God a passive spectator who allows the laws of nature and humankind to go their own way? Both our readings reveal the face of God as one who constantly bends low to us and is touched by our needs and wants. God has an overwhelming need to alleviate our suffering. We share this perfect love of God when we feel the anguish of another and reach our hands out to help. The gospel images compassion as a waterwheel that constantly returns to the giver more than what is given (see Lk 6:38).

This Lent believe first in the compassion of our God, a God who has eyes that cry, ears that hear, and hands that reach out. Next challenge yourself to act in the image of the Compassionate One. Then you will hear Mother Teresa clearly as she says, "God has created us so we do small things with great love."

Tuesday, Second Week of Lent
Isaiah 1:10, 16–20; Matthew 23:1–12

Come now, let us set things right, says the Lord.
(Isa 1:18)

In the early part of our century, the town of Tombstone, Arizona, was synonymous with drinking, gambling, prostitution, and lawlessness. If you go there today, you will see a tourist town built to show off its vice-laden past. In Jesus' day, the towns of Sodom and Gomorrah had a reputation like that of Tombstone's. Their names were synonymous with impenitent sin and their fall with the just manifestation of God's wrath. In Genesis 19, God destroys both cities by brimstone and fire.

Both Isaiah and Jesus used the towns of Sodom and Gomorrah as examples of how angry God can become in the face of evil. But the God of anger can turn instantly to the God of forgiveness: "Though your sins be like scarlet, / they may become white as snow" (Isa 1:18). Jesus spends the whole of Matthew chapter 23 condemning religious leaders for their sins, almost going to the point of saying that God will destroy them for their false leadership and sinful, flaunting behavior. But in the midst of this condemnation, Jesus suggests the pathway back to God's forgiveness: the leader must become the servant (23:11).

We are each a small city. Many times the evil patterns of dominance and decadence can take over. We wonder if forgiveness can ever be ours again. At this crucial moment, we turn to the Lord. We ask humbly for forgiveness and recommit to serving our spouse, children, and community.

Wednesday, Second Week of Lent
Jeremiah 18:18–20; Matthew 20:17–28

Anyone among you who aspires to greatness must serve the rest.
(Mt 20:27)

During a presidential election year, the news media display hundreds of examples of what our candidates say, how they act, what their family and friends are like, and how presidential they look, dress, and sound. The news coverage is a mini-course on what makes a leader. We vote for the candidate we begin to trust, the one we believe will act on our behalf.

In today's readings, we have two styles of leadership that are both rejected by the public. Jeremiah's style of leadership was to stand apart from the crowd and confront them with the fact that they had turned from the Lord. For this, they threw Jeremiah into a cistern and later killed him. Jesus' style was to walk and talk with the people and remind them that the way of God is to serve one another. Like Jeremiah, Jesus also was killed by the people.

When we are baptized, we are baptized into the death of the Lord. In these waters, we embrace Jesus' style of being a leader—not lording, bossing, demanding, and commanding, but serving, asking, seeking, and helping. An old Chinese poem says, "What have the river and sea done to be kings of the hundred valleys? They put themselves below them and that is why they reign." The waters of baptism call us to flow humbly and lovingly through one another's lives.

Thursday, Second Week of Lent
Jeremiah 17:5–10; Luke 16:19–31

At his gate lay a beggar named Lazarus.
(Lk 16:20)

In our society we only have to open the paper to read about people of wealth and influence. They appear in the sports pages as owners and financiers of professional athletic teams or in the business pages as they wheel and deal to create more wealth for their companies. They are in the society pages as they move from political fund-raisers to AIDS-awareness cocktail parties. The names of the poor and the abandoned are never mentioned. Our society has made them nameless!

In today's gospel, Jesus reverses this name-dropping order of society and gives the poor beggar a name, Lazarus. The rich man remains nameless. It is the Lord's way of saying that the person who counts in this story is the beggar, not the rich man. The rich man has no friends in the afterlife, whereas Lazarus finds himself in the presence of angels and of Abraham, the father of millions. In the gospel, the rich man's sin was not that he denied a few crumbs to Lazarus, it was that he didn't even notice Lazarus.

If we are to be Christian, then we must not only care for the poor, but we must also name the poor. We must know the poor as we know our neighbor, by name. When we know someone's name, then that person stands out from the mass of humanity as an individual, as someone like us. Let us encourage ourselves to believe the Lord's message that the poor are more important than the rich. Then let us act on that message in knowing the poor in our midst!

Friday, Second Week of Lent
Genesis 37:3–4, 12-13, 17–28;
Matthew 21:33–43, 45–46

Israel loved Joseph best of all his sons, for he was the child of his old age.
(Gen 37:3)

Who among us doesn't have some part of us that feels rejected, attacked, displaced, or killed? A wife once mentioned that she and her husband were at a wedding banquet. She wanted so much to dance with her husband. She felt so close and loving to him at that moment. She stood up and took his hand and began to move toward the dance floor. The husband stood his ground. He wouldn't budge. He rejected her offer. Amid anger, pain, and shame the wife sat back down.

In both the Book of Genesis and the gospel parable of the property owner, we have a loving father who sends his beloved son out to do some work. In both stories the son is attacked and either sold into slavery or killed. But in the end all things are set straight. Joseph returns to free his family from hunger. The vineyard of Christ's parable is taken away from the tenants and given to others for harvesting. In the rejected son lies the true power of the spiritual life.

Lent is the time when we look to those parts of us that are rejected and in them find the seeds for a deeper spiritual renewal. Just as Joseph saves his family, so we recognize that our trials can bring us to a deeper spiritual realm. As we share our spiritual power with others, our family life and our life in society become more fruitful.

Saturday, Second Week of Lent
Micah 7:14–15, 18–20; Luke 15:1–3, 11–32

Let us eat and celebrate because this son of mine
was dead and has come back to life.
(Lk 15:23–24)

How many times have you heard the words "Grow up!" or "Act your age!" These words could have been directed to you when an adult thought you should have been acting more responsibly. Or maybe you have heard yourself echoing these words in frustration to your own children. One task of children is to grow up and become adults, to leave the parental nest and establish a life of their own.

In Jesus' parable of the Prodigal Son, we have the story of a child who demanded to grow up. So he took his inheritance, left home, and established himself as an adult. Yet the highlight of the story comes when the new adult returns home and reclaims his position as a child! The great spiritual journey that Christ presents to us in this parable is the rediscovery that we are God's children. We are never too old to have a happy childhood! The quality of childhood that God cherishes in this story is open honesty. The child in humility asks to be brought back into the family once again. Micah is correct in the first reading when he tells us that there is no one like our God who removes all our guilt and pardons all our sins.

Yes, it is time to return to God's family, to reclaim our position as God's child. Today open your heart and your hands to the Lord and ask humbly to be given life once again.

Third Sunday of Lent
Exodus 20:1–17; 1 Corinthians 1:22–25; John 2:13–25

Zeal for your house consumes me.

(Jn 2:17)

Where do we go to meet God? Every culture has built temples, shrines, or churches where people can go to meet God and obtain God's favor. Often we have a favorite spot where we feel God's presence in a special way. It could be sitting by a lake in the early morning, walking through a forest at sunset, or visiting the grave of a loved one with flowers in hand.

There was nothing more sacred to the Jewish people of Jesus' time than the Temple in Jerusalem where they kept the Scriptures and the Ark of the Covenant. God's presence dwelt in the Temple, making it the only legitimate place of worship in Israel. In our readings today, Jesus establishes himself as the new temple. God has made Jesus the temple of God's presence. Through Jesus, God hears our prayers and delivers favors to us. In his First Letter to the Corinthians, Saint Paul says it this way: "Christ [is] the power of God and the wisdom of God" (1:24).

This Lent, when you go to your church for worship, know that you unite with the person of Jesus in this sacred spot. The familiar walls that surround you are a passageway leading into the heart of the Lord Jesus. Unlike the church building that will only stand for a time, your union with the Lord is timeless.

Monday, Third Week of Lent
2 Kings 5:1–15; Luke 4:24–30

Go and wash and your flesh will heal.
(2 Kgs 5:10)

When Franklin Delano Roosevelt was president, he was afflicted with an incurable illness. He discovered that bathing in hot springs was a way to relieve some of his pain. With his own money, he built a huge health resort around the hot springs. He made it possible for children with incurable illnesses like his own to come and be soothed in the hot flowing waters.

Naaman the Syrian appears in both our readings on this Monday. Like FDR, Naaman is a man of good will afflicted with an incurable disease. He comes to the prophet seeking health. The prophet sends Naaman to the hidden source of life—the water—and Naaman is cured. In our gospel, Jesus himself is the hidden source of life. Jesus expects us to come to him with those incurable diseases that we carry within ourselves. The only medicine that Jesus asks us to bring with us is our belief that we can be cured. Action and belief are the cornerstones of our discipleship of Jesus who is the living water.

Baptism is the first time that we are bathed in the healing waters. But that immersion must happen over and over again. We ask the Lord to cleanse us of the injustice or disbelief that might linger deep in our seemingly incurable selves. Lord, cure us in your healing waters that we might walk with justice and belief!

Tuesday, Third Week of Lent
Daniel 3:25, 34–43; Matthew 18:21–35

Lord, when my brother wrongs me, how often must I forgive him?
(Mt 18:21)

The recent years of their marriage had been filled with accusations, anger, loneliness, and fear. Finally they had declared a separation from each other. They could now both get a feel for living separately before any more drastic decisions were made. Before he left, he tore all the phones from their plugs. Weeks later, he wanted to return to the house to collect some clothing. She put the clothing on the front drive and flattened it under the car wheels. It was a time of revenge!

The anger of the Jewish people in the Hebrew Scriptures was many times expressed in revenge (see Gen 4:24). Jesus breaks this cycle. He proclaims that forgiveness must replace the thirst for revenge. Those who yearn for a just society will not obtain it through accusations and hatred but through constant care and forgiveness of others from the heart. This should and can begin with those closest to us.

Today let us, like Azariah, stand up amid the fires that burn in the vengeful recesses of our spirit. Let us pray to the Lord to hand us kindness and great mercy. We can then step away from our vengefulness and treat all with the forgiveness born of God.

Wednesday, Third Week of Lent
Deuteronomy 4:1, 5–9; Matthew 5:17–19

Take care not to forget the things which your own eyes have seen.
(Deut 4:9)

An older gentleman once told me, "I always sleep like a baby when I return to the house where I grew up." As we grow from child into adult, we carry within us the sights, smells, tastes, and sensations that are rooted in the house of our infancy and youth. If we are able to return to that house, we may find that the smells are still there speaking to us of a time when we were protected and loved.

In our first reading, Moses tells the people "not to forget the things which your own eyes have seen but teach them to your children and to your children's children" (Deut 4:9). What is so important that we need to have it ingrained in our senses for centuries? The Lord's providence and the Lord's protection of us.

In the gospel, when Jesus says that he has come to fulfill the law and prophets, he is speaking about being the center point of that love and protection that has encompassed the Chosen People through their centuries of laws and prophets. Who will continue to give us manna in the desert and a light to guide us in the darkness? The Lord Jesus!

In this time of Lent, return to old familiar spiritual places and stir up within yourself those smells, tastes, sights, and sensations that speak of the Lord's caring and love of you!

Thursday, Third Week of Lent
Jeremiah 7:23–28; Luke 11:14–23

If it is by the finger of God that I cast out devils,
then the reign of God is upon you.
(Lk 11:20)

In the movie *The Exorcist*, a priest is called on to drive out the demon that has possessed a small child. Like Jesus, the priest sees himself as a lone pillar standing straight and tall against this evil. In the end, the devil is routed but at the expense of the priest's life. Does this story represent today's gospel in which Jesus sets his house against the house of the devil?

As Catholics, we believe that the Lord, who individually conquered evil, has now handed that power on to his Church. Our private prayer, the insistent and constant prayer of the community at Eucharist, and the courageous action of Christians are effective in repulsing the diabolical presences embedded in our culture. These evils lurk in the hoarding of money, the exploitation of others, the use of drugs, the acts of violence, and the frenzy of sex in our media. No person needs to be a lone pillar any longer. We stand with the Church and we stand against the evil one.

This Lent renew your own dedication to be one with the praying and witnessing Catholic community. Here the kingdom of justice and peace has taken root.

Friday, Third Week of Lent
Hosea 14:2–10; Mark 12:28–34

You shall love the Lord your God.
(Mk 12:30)

Cardinal Newman was once reported as saying, "Life is change, and those who have changed often are perfect!" Change is often very difficult and the older we become the more trapped we are in our patterns of seeing and acting. Confucius spoke of this when he commented on how supple and flexible were the limbs of infants and how as we age our limbs become stiff and brittle until at last we die and become rigid from head to toe. Life is flexibility, death is rigidity.

The great commandment to love God above all else is a commandment directed to helping us change. Our love of neighbor cannot be understood or fulfilled without love of God. In our love of God, we begin to look at our brothers and sisters the way God looks at them. We can give our brothers and sisters what God would give them. We can work with our brothers and sisters the way God would work with them. Solidarity with all God's children and creation is first solidarity with God.

This day, realign your own focus on God. Become flexible, grow young, and see all in the light of God's eyes.

Saturday, Third Week of Lent
Hosea 6:1–6; Luke 18:9–14

O God, be merciful to me a sinner!
(Lk 18:13)

Phony people have all the external appearances of happiness, success, or friendliness, but when you push beyond the veneer, you find no substance, no heart. People like this are only one-inch deep. Hollywood movies portray the classic used–car salesman as such an individual. In the time of Hosea and Jesus, the religious professionals had become phony people. They had lost their connection with God.

What God wants for us is so great that we can never buy it with religious practices or good works. We can never force God to reward us because we are doing everything in the correct and proper manner. In God's version of reality when there is a contest between the heart and the law, the heart always wins. In the gospel, the tax collector with the repentant heart wins, and the Pharisee with the outwardly correct practice loses. Over and over again in the gospels the people who throw themselves on Christ's mercy win—Peter after he had denied Christ, the thief on the cross, the blind beggar screaming out for sight, the sisters of Lazarus in tears at the tomb. Hosea in our first reading says it this way: "It is love that I desire, not sacrifice."

In Lent, we journey past our externals to see if we are planted in the heart of God. Take time today to throw yourself at the Lord and say: "Lord have mercy on me, a sinner!"

Fourth Sunday of Lent
2 Chronicles 36:14–17, 19–23; Ephesians 2:4–10; John 3:14–21

So must the Son of Man be lifted up,
that all who believe may have eternal life in him.
(Jn 3:14,15)

In the sanctuary of my home parish stands a huge crucifix. It is fifteen feet high and looms above as people walk into the church. As a small child I remember many times rushing past that image of Christ. At times I was too scared even to look up. Fear is not new to our Christian tradition. For many centuries, Christians used fear to prod themselves to a more faithful style of life. Religious scrupulosity flowed out of many such fears—a fear of damnation, a fear of not being worthy enough for God's kingdom, a fear that our sins killed Jesus, a fear that Jesus was actually looking for our every mistake.

Today's gospel offers a different version of the Cross. The Cross here is a pathway that can lead to belief, light, and eternal life. The Cross in the gospel is lifted up over us. But instead of being a dark, looming presence, it is a healing presence. The shadow that is cast over us is not of darkness or fear but of freedom and light. This Cross inspired one older woman to tell me, "Every time I look up at Jesus on the Cross I know he is healing another person."

In our first reading from the Book of Chronicles, King Cyrus is a symbol of Jesus. The king releases the people from their exile and invites them to return and rebuild the house of God! This Lent stand under the Cross of Jesus and be set free from your fears and chains. Allow his shadow of light to lift your spirit!

Monday, Fourth Week of Lent
Isaiah 65:17–21; John 4:43–54

I am about to create new heavens and a new earth.
(Isa 65:17)

In growing up as Christians, we have developed a personal vision of heaven that changes and matures as we age. As little children, we may have imagined heaven as the pearly gates, puffy clouds, beautifully winged angels, and a kindly old man sporting a long beard seated on an ornate throne. We may not have given much thought to what we did in heaven except we knew that it would be fun.

The Jewish people of Isaiah's time had a vision of heaven that was related to their present prosperity. Heaven was the place from which God ruled the entire universe, listening to the cry of the Chosen People and offering them a prosperous life. If some were not prosperous, then they or their relatives must have sinned somewhere along the way. People believed that God had simply stopped listening to them. In today's first reading, Isaiah is proclaiming that God is going to look toward the Chosen People again and pour down truth, faithfulness, and grace upon them. More than this, God will "rend the heavens and come down" (Isa 63:19).

Jesus is the living proof of Isaiah's vision. In the person of Jesus heaven has come down to earth, and earth has come up to heaven. The healings and other signs that Jesus gives us in the gospel are the proof that the kingdom of God is at hand!

Today is a day to open ourselves to the Jesus who has come down from heaven. We need the new life that he freely offers to all who believe in him. We need Jesus to say to us, "Return home. You will live!"

Tuesday, Fourth Week of Lent
Ezekiel 47:1–9, 12; John 5:1–3, 5–16

I saw water flowing out from beneath the threshold of the temple.
(Ezek 47:1)

Each winter there seems to be an arctic freeze that extends from Canada all the way down to Florida. During such deep freezes the evening news shows the farmers in Florida spraying water on their orange crops. The water hardens into a ball of ice around each orange and insulates the crop from dropping below freezing and thus being destroyed. Water saves the day!

In our first reading, Ezekiel describes the water that flows out of the Temple toward the Dead Sea. Everything the water touches bursts into life! This water symbolizes the life-giving power of God, the Spirit of God, which can transform the desert into a flowering orchard and the unfaithful people into a true Israel. Jesus is the rock of the Hebrew Scriptures who carries within himself the living water. When this rock is struck (Jn 19:34), water pours forth that quenches our thirst on the way to the Promised Land. In today's gospel, Jesus is the new pool of Bethsaida. Jesus' waters are always pouring forth. No longer must we wait, for the kingdom of heaven is at hand.

Today ask the Lord to again pour his living water over you as he did when you were baptized. Open your mouth and drink of that living water that always brings new birth and flowering life!

Wednesday, Fourth Week of Lent
Isaiah 49:8–15; John 5:17–30

Can a mother forget her infant, be without tenderness for the child of
her womb? Even should she forget, I will never forget you.
(Isa 49:15)

Our family had the tradition of spending most of the summer at a campground. My mother would stay with us at the camp, but my dad would drive up to the campground on Friday night after work and return to the city on Monday morning. Late Friday afternoon, my brothers and I would begin our vigil. We would wait by the side of the road and watch for dad's car to round the bend. When we spotted the car, we would jump, cheer, wave, and rush toward it. One weekend, my dad had car trouble and couldn't make the trip. We stayed out past dark that night with our eyes riveted on the bend. My dad never came. As we slowly made our way back to the tent, we cried. Where was he? Had he left us forever?

Isaiah presents us with an image of God as a devoted parent who will never, never leave us. The people of Israel had felt abandoned by God, thrown away by the very Creator who made them. But their perception was false. God was there holding them as close as ever. In the gospel, Jesus presents himself as one with God. Just as God loves, so does Jesus love. Just as God is an ever-vigilant parent, so is Jesus. Jesus' words are a cry from God and Jesus to us. We are to run to them as a child would, throw ourselves in their arms, and allow their quilt of love to wrap us up.

There is no being a Christian without this reciprocal relationship between us as the protected child and God as the loving parent. If we are ever to learn God's ways of justice, we first must be wrapped within the all-encompassing arms.

Thursday, Fourth Week of Lent
Exodus 32:7–14; John 5:31–47

If you believed Moses you would then believe me,
for it was about me that he wrote.
(Jn 5:46)

Sometimes when there has been a diplomatic hot spot that needed delicate care and nurturing, former president Jimmy Carter has volunteered his services as a negotiator. He does not carry the full weight of the United States diplomatic corps. He carries only the prestige of his person and the power of faith. The amazing fact is that with so little he has been so successful!

In our first reading from the Book of Exodus, Moses, armed only with words, negotiates a tricky pact between an angry God and an unfaithful people. It is amazing that with so little Moses is able to change God's mind. Moses is God's chosen intercessor who has the authority to ask in the name of the people. But Moses' term as mediator ends with his death. Moses is an anticipated figure of Jesus, the one true mediator and intercessor. Unlike Moses, Jesus' death only solidifies his role as our mediator, the one who will never leave us.

In today's gospel, Jesus displays to the people his credentials that mark him as the eternal mediator. These credentials are his miracles, John the Baptist's testimony, and the words of the Bible. Jesus shares with his Church his role as mediator. You and I now possess the proper credentials to mediate between God and others. When we believe deeply and act in justice toward others, we bring the presence of God to earth.

Friday, Fourth Week of Lent
Wisdom 2:1, 2–22; John 7:1–2, 10, 25–30

Let us beset the just one, because he is obnoxious to us.
(Wis 2:12)

So much hatred and suffering arises out of prejudice. All over the earth we see people trying to exterminate or enslave other people. Sometimes people who belong to the same race but to different tribes, clans, countries, or religions try to wipe one another out. Many times people of one race enslave or kill off people of another, as when American immigrants enslaved Africans and fought Native Americans and Mexicans. Sometimes people use more sophisticated means of dominating and impoverishing others—downsizing, corporate takeovers, and cutting back programs for the poor and disadvantaged.

Both readings today talk about the hatred that arises from labeling others as different. In the Book of Wisdom, we see the people setting out to kill the just one because he claims to be a child of God. People hate Jesus because he claims to be from God and only accidentally from Nazareth. One mission of Jesus was to erase prejudice and announce that the kingdom of God is all inclusive: we are all children of God. For this announcement Jesus was killed.

We have difficulty erasing prejudice from our own hearts, prejudice that we were raised with and that has been in our families and society for many generations. Yet the mark of the true disciple is this movement away from separateness and prejudice into solidarity and inclusion. Let us pray this day to wipe the blight of persecuting others from our spirits.

Saturday, Fourth Week of Lent
Jeremiah 11:18–20; John 7:40–53

O LORD, my God, in you I take refuge!
(Ps 7:2)

Many prospectors rushed to California and Alaska in the 1800s to find gold. Some found it, but many found only fool's gold—gold that looked and felt like the real thing but was not! Many times today we hear about people who were duped by fake jewelry, an imposter, or a get-rich-quick scheme.

In Jesus' time, many people paraded around claiming to be the messiah. As Jesus' popularity grew, so did the opposition to him. Jesus' opponents presented every reason they could think of to debunk his claim to be the messiah. The Pharisees wanted to destroy Jesus and his claims in the same fashion as the people of Jeremiah's day tried to destroy him. Throughout history, people who were closely connected with God were often persecuted, seen as false guides, condemned, and put to death.

Out of persecution arose the core of Jesus' spirituality. As a prophet Jesus expected to be "reviled and put to scorn." Yet through Jesus' suffering, he expressed the tremendous power of God's love. Our task as true disciples is to find within ridicule the pathway of God. This Lent we renew our commitment to living like the Lord Jesus in the midst of division and false claims.

Fifth Sunday of Lent
Jeremiah 31:31–34; Hebrews 5:7–9; John 12:20–33

Then a voice came from the sky: "I have glorified it,
and will glorify it again."
(Jn 12:28)

Sometimes God just can't contain God's own self. God gets very excited and needs to speak and act. We see this at the first moments of creation when God needed to speak over and over again. Every time God spoke there was another awesome dynamic created—light, air, earth, animals, plants, seas, and humans. During Jesus' prayer in today's gospel, God just can't hold back. God's jumps in and yells out how much God likes what Jesus is saying and doing. It is like the theater owner jumping up before the performance is over and yelling, "Bravo! Bravo!"

What was Jesus saying that caused so much excitement in God? Jesus was speaking about exploding forth like a seeding dandelion held up to the wind. In one moment—the moment of Jesus' death— all creation would be changed! Death would cease to be an ending and would become a new creation, like the first moment of creation! No wonder God cheered!

Let this new law be written on our hearts. The days of the new covenant have arrived. Even in our dying we will know the Lord. For it is here that, like Jesus, we also will make all things new.

Monday, Fifth Week of Lent
Daniel 13:1–9, 15–17, 19–30, 33–62; John 8:1–11

Nor do I condemn you. You may go.
(Jn 8:11)

The perfection that Jesus demands of his disciples (Mt 5:48) is being merciful as "your Father is merciful" (Lk 6:36). Mercy is the essential condition for entering the kingdom of God (Mt 5:7). A merciful attitude and stance make us like the Good Samaritan, like the tender father in the story of the Prodigal Son, like Jesus who raises the widow's son and who forgives the woman caught in adultery. Mercy is acting with tenderness toward the hurt in others! When Jesus spoke of mercy, he echoed the Hebrew tradition that when you extend mercy you become attached to the other, like being in a womb together—a tender, heartful attachment.

Right after the story of the woman caught in adultery comes Jesus' proclamation—"I am the light of the World" (Jn 8:12). Mercy is the handle that opens the door to the light. Saint Patrick is one person who understood this. He returned to the country where he was originally enslaved and extended to the people first mercy and then the gospel.

In Lent, we look within ourselves, at the parts of us that are hardened, revengeful, and law-minded. We seek to chisel away these callouses and bring mercy to bear on all our actions.

Tuesday, Fifth Week of Lent
Numbers 21:4–9; John 8:21–30

Because he spoke this way, many came to believe in him.
(Jn 8:30)

It is amazing to watch a mother and father hold a tiny baby and talk to the baby. As they speak the baby stares up at their eyes and lips, seemingly hanging on every word. The baby learns early on the nuances of love, anger, sorrow, questions, and statements. In growing, the baby will begin to trust the meaning of the parent's words, as well as the feeling they carry.

When we believe in another, we trust in their words. Jesus uses the words "I AM" to pound home to the people again that he is one with the God of the Israelite nation. This union expresses itself in activity, with an immediate and total spontaneity that is never tired or weary (see Isa 40:28). Jesus is like the Lord "who slumbers not nor sleeps" (Ps 121:4), who reacts the moment anyone touches his followers (see Num 21:1–3). Jesus demands that we trust not only the meaning of the words spoken but also the feeling behind them.

In the reading from Numbers, the Israelites stop trusting in God's word of salvation. Because of their disgusting condition they doubt God. To this doubt God brings anger and mercy to bear immediately.

Today let us look to our souls. Is there a space within us where we doubt that God is, where we are disgusted and complaining? Can we let the "I AM" of Jesus fill that cavity?

Wednesday, Fifth Week of Lent
Daniel 3:14–20, 91–92, 95; John 8:31–42

If you live according to my teaching, you are truly my disciples.
(Jn 8:31)

How many times in recent years have we heard the cry, "Free at last, free at last; thank God Almighty we're free at last!" It is the dream of all people who suffer slavery to be set free. Sometimes that slavery is physical bondage, sometimes it is the mental slavery of anguish, and sometimes it is the spiritual slavery of sin.

In our first reading from Daniel, we see that even though the Israelites were bound and then thrown into the furnace to suffer and die, just the opposite happened. Their faith set them free to walk amid the flames without pain. Their bodies were in bondage but their spirits were free.

In the gospel, Jesus tells the Jews that even though they do not suffer physical bondage, their spirits are still slaves to sin. The Jews were not, in Jesus' mind, living in accordance with their vocation as children of God. Because of that, they did not "know the truth," they were not truly free. They were still slaves! The Jews excelled in wealth, power, knowledge, and status. They believed that these things made them free. Jesus believed that these very things chained people to a life of sin. Jesus tells the Jews that freedom can only be found now in his Word.

Let us this day break the chains that bind us to wealth, power, knowledge, or status. Let us set our spirits free so we can listen to the Word of Jesus and let that Word find a deep root in our souls.

Thursday, Fifth Week of Lent
Genesis 17:3–9; John 8:51–59

I solemnly assure you, if a man is true to my word
he shall never see death.
(Jn 8:51)

Across from a golf course in a major American city is a facility where human bodies can be frozen, supposedly forever. People who do this believe that future generations will thaw them out when a cure for their fatal disease has been found. We do like to try to cheat death!

Our readings for this day speak of some people who have cheated death. They follow a man named Jesus who states, "I solemnly assure you, / if a man is true to my word / he shall never see death." To join this death-defying group takes no money, only belief. Abraham laid the groundwork for this belief by trusting in God's Word to him. He is rewarded with God's covenant forever. Jesus asks his followers also to trust in his Word. The early martyrs not only trusted but also found joy in Christ's Word. As their captors led them to slaughter, they sang glad songs of faith.

What does God's Word say to us today about our living and our dying? Can we take deeply to heart the invitation of Jesus to a life without end? Can we truly live today with a joy that speaks of our being true to the Word of Jesus that always gives life?

Friday, Fifth Week of Lent
Jeremiah 20:10–13; John 10:31–42

O LORD of hosts, you who test the just,
who probe mind and heart to you I have entrusted my cause.
(Jer 20:12)

What does it mean to be free? Some think that being free means they have no responsibilities. They can come and go as they choose, do what they want when they want. There is no one and no thing to chain them down.

Christians choose the demanding responsibility of preaching the gospel. In being faithful to this mission we become free. Just before the passage we have today, Jeremiah speaks about being seduced by Yahweh. The Lord takes him by force and obliges him to preach the Word of God. In doing this, Jeremiah becomes free. In being linked to Yahweh's Word, Jeremiah becomes indifferent to the jeers, threats, mocking, and violence of the people around him. Jeremiah can proclaim that the Lord has rescued the life of the poor from the power of the wicked!

Jesus also speaks about his commission to be God's Son. Jesus speaks the Word of God and does the work of God. In doing this, he is free from being trapped by the expectations and fears of the people.

So many times in our lives God calls us to be free to preach the gospel. God calls us to rise above the petty fears, threats, murmurings, and violence that appear around us, to truly speak God's word of justice to a civilization encrusted with greed. Spend a little time today praying with 1 Corinthians 9:16. Let this Lenten Scripture empower you to embrace the call to freedom.

Saturday, Fifth Week of Lent
Ezekiel 37:21–28; John 11:45–57

Jesus would die for the nation—and not for this nation only,
but to gather into one all the dispersed children of God.
(Jn 11:51–52)

As little children most of us had a place that we called "home," a place we could go to and feel part of a family. As adults, we commit ourselves to creating new homes, new places of unity, love, and caring.

Both readings today speak about making a home. In Ezekiel, God speaks about making a home among the Israelite people: "My dwelling shall be with them; I will be their God, and they shall be my people" (37:27). The message of Jesus is also evident: he will bring home all the dispersed children of God. Christ's Resurrection has a universal effect, uniting all of humanity in a renewed creation. As Jesus says: "When I am lifted up from the earth, I will draw everyone to myself" (Jn 12:32). We call our church "catholic," meaning "embracing the whole," because here believers of all races and cultures find a common home, a place of kinship and communion. This home is a small indication of what will take place at the end of time when the whole of humanity will be reunited in Christ (see Rev 7).

Since we share the same home, the same history, and a common destiny, we have a duty to fight against violence, injustice, inequality, and any ideology that opposes unity. This day rededicate yourself to stand with all who lack freedom or unity.

Passion (Palm) Sunday
Mark 11:1–10; Isaiah 50:4–7; Philippians 2:6–11;
Mark 14:1–15:47

They brought the colt to Jesus and threw their cloaks
across its back, and he sat on it.
(Mk 11:7)

For all of Jesus' public life he refused to be proclaimed or crowned by the people as the messiah. Most often Jesus directed them to silence concerning his messiahship. Other times when they tried to lift him up and carry him off in procession, he would slip through their midst. Jesus knew that the people had a very warlike image of the messiah, expecting the messiah to bring liberation from Roman oppressors. Jesus also knew that his messiahship was of a different kind. Jesus' messiahship would announce liberation into the kingdom of heaven. This liberation would occur through pardon, nonviolence, suffering, and death.

Today, on Palm Sunday, Jesus makes public the announcement that he is the true Messiah, the Anointed One. During Jesus' time people considered the palm tree a princely tree and its branches symbols of victory and well-being. So the people throw palm branches in front of Jesus to proclaim his anointed leadership. And yet Jesus rides on a donkey as peaceful people did, not on a war-horse like the generals of that time.

How many times have we hoped for a more powerful messiah, one who would change our lives for us? How many times have we moved from pardon and nonviolence into anger and revenge? Today, like Jesus, let us process in peace and forgiveness. Let us seek the kingdom of Jesus, the true Messiah.

Monday of Holy Week
Isaiah 42:1–7; John 12:1–11

Then she dried his feet with her hair,
and the house was filled with the ointment's fragrance.
(Jn 12:3)

We usually take great pains to prepare for big occasions. The greater the occasion, the more personal preparation time we need. Brides take all day to prepare for their weddings; a teenager spends the afternoon dressing for the prom; the coroner spends a day dressing and perfuming a body for viewing. During Holy Week, we watch Jesus face the greatest events in his ministry—his Passion, death, and Resurrection. In our gospel today, Jesus allows Mary to begin his preparation. The costly perfume she uses to anoint Jesus symbolizes her love and the love of his friends who will stay with Jesus through the tumultuous week ahead. For Judas, who has no love or intention to stay with Jesus, the perfume becomes a sign of conflict.

As this Holy Week begins, who will we be? Will we be Mary, who has a passionate love for Jesus and respects his mysterious personality? Can we, like Mary, take the expensive perfume of our lives and lay it at the feet of Jesus? Can we choose to love Jesus with all of our being (using even our very hair to dry his feet)? This is the love Jesus will display to us through this week!

Or will we be Judas? Will we be concerned about all the exterior things? Will we worry about how our money is used and what others will say? Will we avoid the journeys through suffering and death, eventually living more in the dark than in the day?

Renew this day your passionate love for the Lord. Choose to stay with the Lord and with yourself through the sufferings of the week.

Tuesday of Holy Week
Isaiah 49:1–6; John 13:21–33, 36–38

I tell you solemnly, one of you will betray me!
(Jn 13:21)

Throughout Jesus' ministry he always spoke of love without limits, forgiveness instead of revenge, and service over domination. In our gospel, Jesus struggles with his own commitment to live those words that he has spoken so often and so fervently. We see that Jesus is "deeply troubled," his depression arising from the betrayal of Judas and the lying of Peter. Now Jesus must forgive the betrayal and deceit that has torn and ripped apart the fabric of love between him and his friends. Jesus realizes that he must stand alone to face his sufferings and death. It will not be his disciples or his friends that see him through, but only his trust in God. Jesus believes God will not fail him.

The words of Isaiah give Jesus hope that there is an anchor in this sea of deceit: "The LORD called me from birth, / from my mother's womb he gave me my name./ God is now my strength!" (Isa 49:1,5).

We also are not free from the disciples' flaws. How often have we been like Judas, rejecting the call to love and entering the darkness, or like Peter, lying to protect our own skins? We ask forgiveness and renew our fidelity to the Lord who walks alone.

Wednesday of Holy Week
Isaiah 50:4–9; Matthew 26:14–25

I looked for sympathy, but there was none; for comforters,
and I found none.
(Ps 69:21)

Many great spiritual writers have written about "the dark night of the soul." This is a time when we experience a sense of complete abandonment and aloneness. We are slowly being surrounded by the darkness with no one there to help us or even walk with us. One religious sister told me of her experience with the dark night. She was in chapel praying and was overcome with a sense of God's complete absence. There was nothing there to pray to. She was so scared she had to run from the chapel!

Of all the days in Jesus' life, today is one of the darkest. The readings show us a Jesus who is abandoned and betrayed. He is facing his most difficult moment, his death, and the people he most relied on are deserting him. Isaiah prophesies that the messiah will face his pain and tortures alone. The responsorial psalm echoes his soft cry for help: "Lord in your great love, answer me!"

We have all faced dark nights of the soul when everything seems lost and we are forsaken. In this darkness, we stand with Jesus and with Isaiah. We rely on our belief that, as it did in the first moments of creation, the voice of God will create a dawn in the darkness.

Holy Thursday, Easter Triduum
Exodus 12:1–8, 11–14; 1 Corinthians 11:23–26; John 13:1–15

But if I washed your feet then you must wash each other's feet.
(Jn 13:14)

People often say "Seeing is believing." But on Holy Thursday Christ turns it all around. On Holy Thursday believing is seeing. Today the Lord establishes his greatest gift to his disciples, the Eucharist, the gift that has carried the Lord's presence to his followers throughout the centuries. Here in the Eucharist we humble human believers see and taste God.

If you go to the Holy Land and visit the room of the Last Supper, you will probably be surprised at how plain it is. No great church surrounds it, and nothing in the room would give a hint of the majestic event that occurred there. It is a simple upper room. This simplicity reflects our gospel reading that calls us to be servants of one another. Jesus' act of washing the disciples' feet was a sacred rite that prepared and purified them for the bread of life. If they did not serve one another as Jesus was serving them, then they could not receive the bread of life.

The poor of Jesus' day did not wear sandals, so their feet needed to be washed before entering a house. The poor of our day do not have sandals, food, a home, or political power. Once we have seen Christ in the Eucharist, we also see the poor who need us to wash their feet, call them into our home, lead them to the bread of life.

Good Friday, Easter Triduum
Isaiah 52:13–53:12; Hebrews 4:14–16; 5:7–9; John 18:1–19, 42

Yet it was our infirmities that he bore, our sufferings that he endured.
(Isa 53:4)

Jesus stretches out his hands between heaven and earth. The curtain in the Temple that separated the people from God is ripped in two. A new bridge has been established between God and us. The bridge is Jesus who, now crucified, will never die again. He lives forever as our passageway to the living God! From his Cross the Lord also gives us Mary to be the Mother of all believers. Through this last deed of Jesus we discover that the nature of the Church is to be a spiritual family. Mary helps to solidify in the spiritual family of the Church the values of humility, joy, interior peace, and simple piety.

The readings present us with the end of a stage of history. No longer must humanity be dragged by its fears, sit in unforgiven sins, and live at the mercy of the evil spirit. Now begins the era of the New Covenant of God with humanity marked by the Spirit of God. When Jesus gives up his Spirit, the Spirit doesn't die but instead fills the Church. As Isaiah prophesies: "See, my servant shall prosper, / he shall be raised high and greatly exalted" (Isa 52:13).

In this year of the new creation make forgiveness and peace hallmarks of your life.

Holy Saturday, Easter Triduum
Genesis 1:1–2:2; Genesis 22:1–18; Exodus 14:15–15:1; Isaiah 54:5–14; Isaiah 55:1–11; Baruch 3:9–15, 32–4:4; Ezekiel 36:16–28; Romans 6:3–11; Mark 16:1–8

He has been raised up; he is not here.
(Mk 16:6)

Most families gather together after a funeral. It is a time to console one another, share memories of the deceased one, and offer one another support during the healing days ahead. So today the Christian family gathers after the death of Jesus. The nine readings used in the Easter Vigil call us to remember the great deeds of God that prepared the way for Jesus. Over and over again we hear how God dramatically intervenes in human affairs to create, to save, to reprimand, and to form covenants. As we listen to stories of the pervasive presence of God in our lives, we know that we will never be abandoned. In this comfort we turn to one another and give our support to whatever healing we might need in the days ahead. We can only love one another because God has first and continuously loved us!

The Easter-Vigil memories carried through the readings end with Mark's quiet Resurrection gospel. It was early in the morning, the dawn was just breaking. In the faintness of that first light, we hear of the resurrected Jesus who already has moved ahead into Galilee. Yes, God again has dramatically intervened! The young man in the white robe asks the disciples to follow Jesus once more. Our vigil is over, the night has ended. It is time to put on the armor of day and join Christ in his mission to be the Light of the World.

Easter
Acts 10:34, 37–43; Colossians 3:1–4 or 1 Corinthians 5:6–8; John 20:1–9 or Mark 16:1–8

Christ indeed from death is risen, our new life obtaining.
(Sequence of Easter Sunday)

In the first words of Genesis, God ends the reign of darkness and chaos and replaces that reign with dawn and order. So the first day came to be! Jesus rises in the morning on the first day after the Sabbath. Again God conquers darkness and chaos. Light and order reign. In John's Gospel, the believers are called to silently contemplate the risen Lord. Mary Magdalene does not at first recognize Jesus and later Jesus has to show his wounds to the disciples before they acknowledge that it is the Lord. These stories convince us that every Christian has the spiritual task of contemplating the person of Jesus and coming to know him as the Resurrected One.

Through his death and Resurrection, Jesus is transformed. That is what we will become. Jesus' transformation took an instant as he shed his mortal body. Our transformation will take a lifetime, but in the end, like Jesus, we will rise transformed! Knowing the risen Jesus transformed the early Christians who then went out and witnessed to others. We, too, are transformed as we witness to the wonders that Jesus has done in our lives.

Let us then rise to the new dawn! As we contemplate the risen Lord and share him with others, we become an Alleluia people on the path to transformation!

Feast of the Chair of Peter, Apostle (February 22)
1 Peter 5:1–4; Matthew 16:13–19

I for my part declare to you, you are "Rock,"
and on this rock I will build my church.
(Mt 16:18)

Since 1065, every British monarch has been crowned in Westminster Abbey. During the coronation ceremony, the ruler sits in an ancient chair hewn from rough lumber with a large, very ordinary looking stone bolted to the bottom of the chair. This stone is believed to hold the power of the monarchy. Once long ago the stone was stolen by the people of Scotland, who at the time were considered northern enemies of the state, who then held the power to install the rightful monarchs of England. Amid great bloodshed, the stone was finally recaptured and returned to London.

Today we celebrate the Feast of Saint Peter's Chair. This feast commemorates Saint Peter's profession of faith: "You are the Messiah the Son of the living God!" (Mt 16:16). This feast also recalls the promise of Jesus to Peter that his faith would be a rock foundation upon which the Church would be built. Luckily for us the power to build the kingdom of Christ is not limited to a piece of stone but extends to all Christians who share in Peter's rocklike faith and spirit-filled charism.

Peter's commission to be a foundation stone is based on being a servant. Remember the Lord told the disciples that the one who leads must serve the rest (see Mt 20:25–28). This office, which continues today in the person of the pope, is dedicated to serving all of God's people. Today we act in unison with Peter and the pope when we profess our faith in Christ and renew our energy for building the kingdom of God on earth.

Solemnity of Joseph, Husband of Mary (March 19)
2 Samuel 7:4–5, 12–14, 16; Romans 4:13, 16–18, 22; Matthew 1:16, 18–21, 24

Jacob was the father of Joseph the husband of Mary.
(Mt 1:16)

In most marriages, the time of pregnancy presents special challenges. Physical, psychological, and emotional changes all affect the relationship between the husband and wife as they prepare the nest for their newest member. Chosen by God to be Mary's husband, Joseph became able to trust deeply in the mystery behind Mary's virgin-pregnancy. God, speaking to Joseph in dreams, became as real for him as Mary's growing body. Through Joseph's trust and faithful action, God was able to protect both Mary and her child.

In 1870 Pope Pius IX declared Saint Joseph to be Patron of the Universal Church. Joseph had found an authorized place in the spiritual life of the Roman Catholic Church. Matthew portrays Joseph as a just man, the model of trust in God and openness to God's plan.

Every so often on our journey we get glimpses of God's mysterious ways. Like Joseph, we and the Church are called to protect those entrusted to us, trusting that God is leading the way.

Solemnity of the Annunciation of the Lord (March 25)
Isaiah 7:10–14; Hebrews 10:4–10; Luke 1:26–38

Rejoice, O highly favored daughter! The Lord is with you.

(Lk 1:28)

There is a famous painting by Jean-Francois Millet called *The Angelus*. This painting, done in 1857, shows a husband and wife stopping for midday prayer in their newly planted field. The painter invites us to hear the bells of that distant church ringing out the Angelus just as his subjects did. For centuries, Catholic churches have rung their bells in the early morning, at noon, and in the evening to remind us to stop our work and remember God's greatest goodness to us by praying the Angelus. It retells the story of today's gospel: the angel Gabriel visits Mary, announces to her God's plan, Mary accepts, and Jesus is conceived.

So much of God and us is contained in this prayer. God is considerate. God does not save us without our consent. And God loves mothers. Jesus is to come into our world in the womb of a young Jewish girl. She would give Jesus his hereditary traits, his character, his flesh, and his first education. God chooses one of us to be the beloved. Mary is God's "highly favored daughter." God yearns for an alliance between us and God's own self—"The power of the Most High will overshadow you." With Mary's "Yes!" God's presence now fills humanity.

Today we celebrate the new alliance between God and us. We are now one family again. Mary is the celebrated patroness of this born-again family. During this Lent take time from your work to listen for the church bells and to pray the Angelus. Remember that through Mary we have become children in the family of God.

Daily Meditations for Lent: Cycle C

Sometimes children have secrets that remind us adults of how life should be. One evening I had dinner with a friend and his family, and after the meal the youngest daughter, who was six years old, seemed to disappear. I asked where Jackie had gone, and they said that she was most likely in her room. Wondering what a little girl of six years old does in her room alone, I went upstairs and peeked in. Little Jackie was bent over a pad of paper, writing and drawing. When I asked her what she was doing, she said that it was too noisy downstairs and that she needed some quiet.

Each of us has a favorite spot to which we escape for privacy, peace, and self-reclamation. You might linger in the woods, surround yourself with soft music, hike up a mountain, or just sit in the kitchen and look out the window. Perhaps this Lent you might consider making the Scripture of the day your place of rest.

It would be important first to find a quiet spot where you will not be disturbed. Once you are settled, open the day's Scripture and read the two readings. Allow the readings to take your mind where they will. Wander with them. After a bit you might wish to read the meditations provided. These reflections are only steppingstones. They offer you a simple thought to ponder and carry with you each day. You might wish to close your session by praying the responsorial psalm.

This Lent, let's quietly climb the stairs to our inner rooms and seek peace in the words and actions of the Lord Jesus Christ.

Ash Wednesday
Joel 2:12–18; 2 Corinthians 5:20–6:2;
Matthew 6:1–6, 16–18

Give me back the joy of your salvation,
and a willing spirit sustain in me.
(Ps 51:14)

Shrove Tuesday (the day before Ash Wednesday) is traditionally a day of relentless partying. Mobs of people crowd the streets. They drink, sing, and yell at the tops of their lungs, acting as if they don't have a care in the world.

Last year, on this same Mardi Gras Tuesday, a woman called me, paralyzed by her burdens. Her daughter was sick; her mother, who had just turned eighty, was lonely and depressed; and her closest personal friend had just ended their relationship.

Both those partying in the streets and this woman shared a common approach to personal growth—there was none! The people who were partying didn't care about growth, and the suffering woman couldn't act.

We read today in Joel and Matthew that one of the tasks of the Christian is to actively pursue change, renewal, and growth. If we find ourselves frozen or not caring, we are invited to kick-start ourselves into a new direction. We do this by changing our hearts (Joel 2:13). Lent is the time to journey in a new direction. To take up the task of personal renewal in earnest. To drop the dead old leaves and open ourselves to new and vibrant growth!

As you begin Lent on this day, let the ashes on your forehead challenge you to seek a new direction for your life. Let the prayer of the psalmist be yours: "A clean heart create for me, O God, / and a steadfast spirit renew within me" (Ps 51:12).

Thursday After Ash Wednesday
Deuteronomy 30:15–20; Luke 9:22–25

I have set before you life and death, the blessing and the curse.
Choose life.
(Deut 30:19)

My very close friend was diagnosed with bone cancer. Over the next three years her active life slowly disappeared, and a hidden life of quiet suffering and small enjoyments appeared. Once she explained how the morning sun filtered through her windows in mysterious and ever-changing patterns. She would thank God for this small gift. Over the many days of her illness, this woman taught me the meaning of suffering. It is possible in the midst of the cross to choose life!

The great mystery of Christ is that he combined suffering with life. Our reading from Deuteronomy challenges us to "choose life," and Jesus challenges us to choose the cross. The task of the Christian is to choose both. We take up our crosses with joy and with a vision that brings life to ourselves and to others! Today, look into your suffering and choose to live joyfully with it. Happy are they who hope in the Lord! (see Ps 1).

Friday After Ash Wednesday
Isaiah 58:1–9; Matthew 9:14–15

This, rather, is the fasting that I wish: releasing those bound unjustly,
untying the thongs of the yoke.
(Isa 58:6)

In our century people have fasted to lose weight, gain spiritual insight, or invoke justice and peace. Mahatma Gandhi once fasted to stop a bloody civil war that was raging between Indian Muslims and Hindus. The conflict became so violent that roving bands were killing even the children. Gandhi declared that he would fast until the rioting ended, and he was close to death when the frenzy finally calmed. Gandhi said: "My greatest weapon is mute prayer!"

Both readings today call for us to rethink our use of fasting. The prophet Isaiah proclaims that fasting should include justice for it to be an acceptable gift to God. Jesus says that fasting must include a sense of celebration, not mourning.

Lent is a good time to invoke a period of fasting. The fast can be a time of personal purification, can be pointed toward social justice, and can have a sense of celebration about it. We can begin our fast by praying with the psalmist, "My sacrifice, O God, is a contrite spirit; / a heart contrite and humbled, O God, you will not spurn" (Ps 51:19).

Saturday After Ash Wednesday
Isaiah 58:9–14; Luke 5:27–32

He will renew your strength, and you shall be like a watered garden.
(Isa 58:11)

I was traveling east to New York. Seated next to me on the plane was an older couple. As we began to talk, they told me that they were on their way to Africa. They had decided to spend the first years of their retirement as Christian missionaries. The idea had always appealed to them, and now was the time to act.

In our first reading, Isaiah clearly tells us that actions directed toward the poor and oppressed will renew our strength and fill us with light. Jesus responds to Isaiah's challenge by calling a tax collector to be one of the first of his followers.

Perhaps today we can take up the prophet's challenge. We can act like Jesus in extending ourselves to those who seem to be less than we are or to have less than we have. If the Lord is right, then we too will be filled with light and grace. We pray with the psalmist, "Teach me, O LORD, your way" (Ps 86:11).

First Sunday of Lent
Deuteronomy 26:4–10; Romans 10:8–13; Luke 4:1–13

Everyone who calls on the name of the LORD will be saved.
(Rom 10:13)

Conversion is probably the most painful of life's processes. Recently I met a widow who, after forty years of being married and raising a family, was attempting to adapt to life as a single woman living alone. Many couples have commented that their first year of marriage was difficult as they attempted to separate from their single lives and form a loving partnership. Perhaps in your life you have also felt the pain and challenge of conversion. You were obliged to accept a new way of living your life and had to let go of the old.

In today's gospel, Jesus models conversion. As a Jew and rabbi, Jesus was accustomed to letting God take care of the Jewish people. After all, God fed them in the desert, set up a powerful line of kings, and made them into the chosen nation. Jesus could have continued to let God do all the work. But Jesus chose a different path. He chose to be converted to a new way of seeing and doing. Jesus would in himself be the Bread of Life, he would be the New Temple, and those who believed in him would be the chosen ones. The temptations in the desert called Jesus to cling to the old and forget the new. Instead, Jesus chose conversion.

Let this first Sunday of Lent draw us to conversion. We toss aside patterns that speak of power, prestige, and manipulation. We put on the new person that is Jesus—a person of service to others, of prayer, and of mercy.

Monday, First Week of Lent
Leviticus 19:1–2, 11–18; Matthew 25:31–46

You shall love your neighbor as yourself. I am the LORD.
(Lev 19:18)

As a young child, I would enter our cavernous parish church on Saturday afternoons to go to confession. A group of older people always seemed to be scattered throughout the church. Their heads were bowed, and their rosaries clinked comfortingly against the pews. I never thought much about what they were praying for, but I embraced the warmth and consolation of their presence.

After I was ordained I asked one of these women about her prayers. She told me that she usually looked around the church and prayed for the people who were there. She knew them all by name and knew their needs. To have someone who will hold you in prayer before the throne of God is truly a gift.

Both readings today give us a vision of how we are to stand before the throne of God. Both suggest that we will stand in holiness before God's throne if we have treated others with kindness and love. As we begin this first week of Lent, pick out someone in your life whom you will hold before the throne of God. Place the image of that person in your mind and surround him or her with prayers of kindness and love. The psalmist says it well: "Let the words of my mouth and the thought of my heart / find favor before you" (Ps 19:15).

Tuesday, First Week of Lent
Isaiah 55:10–11; Matthew 6:7–15

When the just cry out, the LORD hears them,
and from all their distress he rescues them.
(Ps 34:18)

What is the bread of God that will fill you this day? What is the word of God that will fall from heaven into your heart and not leave you? One summer my eyes were opened to new answers to these questions when I was invited to the home of one of my students. He had graduated in the top of his class and was on his way to Harvard to study law. By any measuring rod this man was already a success. At his home I met his mother. She was a single parent, and this young man was her only child. She had quit school early on to devote her life to raising her child. As we sat down for dinner, we prayed the Our Father together. It was a prayer of a humble woman whom God had gifted with a beautiful son.

Today's reading assures us that God does send beauty down from heaven for us. The beauty is encased in God's word and in the person of Jesus. This beauty bursts forth in our daily bread, in our forgiveness, and in our deliverance. The Our Father is the prayer of the humble person who asks God to break open that beauty again this day.

Today let us bow our heads, open our hands, and receive the beauty that will give us life. We pray with the psalmist, "I sought the LORD, and he answered me, / and delivered me from all my fears" (Ps 34:5).

Wednesday, First Week of Lent
Jonah 3:1–10; Luke 11:29–32

For at the preaching of Jonah they reformed,
but you have a greater one than Jonah here.
(Lk 11:32)

In our neighborhood lived an older Irish woman who disliked the Jehovah's Witnesses. When they would climb the front steps to her house and ring her doorbell, she would open the door with broom in hand, swinging and yelling. To her Catholic mind, these people were outsiders who had earned neither her respect nor her time.

In our readings today, both Jonah and Jesus are "outsiders." They carry with them a commission from God and a tremendous message of conversion. Jonah expects to be ignored, but he is accepted. Jesus expects to be accepted, but he is ignored.

These readings challenge us to open our hearts to the mystery of conversion, whether the message comes to us from our traditions or from outsiders. We pray that our hearts are not hardened like the Israelites' but that we will hear God's word, like the Ninevites, and convert. We pray with the psalmist, "A clean heart create for me, O God; / and a steadfast spirit renew within me" (Ps 51:12).

Thursday, First Week of Lent
Esther C:12, 14–16, 23–25; Matthew 7:7–12

The one who seeks, finds. The one who knocks, enters.
(Mt 7:8)

The generation that grew up in the 1950s and 1960s is familiar with the character Richie Rich. He was portrayed in comic books, Saturday morning cartoons, and eventually a Hollywood movie. Richie is a pre-teen who gets everything he wants. His family is wealthy beyond imagination; he needs only to say the word and it is his. Certainly the world of Richie Rich was one that was available only to a privileged few.

Our readings today surprise us with the notion of God's over-abundant providence. We just need to say the word and it is ours! Each of us has access to God. We just need to knock, to ask, to seek, and to believe. Of course, prayer to God can be a bit scary because many times God gives us more than we need, or answers us in a way different from what we requested. God sees much farther and deeper than we. What we receive from God is always from God's depth rather than our shallowness.

Today let us ask, knock, and seek from God those things that we need. Let us pray: Lord, on the day I called for help, you answered me (see Ps 138).

Friday, First Week of Lent
Ezekiel 18:21–28; Matthew 5:20–26

Do I not rather rejoice when he turns from his evil way that he may live?
(Ezek 18:23)

At Christmastime, children can sometimes become fairly greedy. They start grabbing every package, expecting it to be for them. They become impatient when another person takes too much time in opening a present. Sometimes, if children do not like the gift they have received, they toss it aside quickly with a disgusted "ugh!" Parents need great skill and patience to teach children to love and respect every gift and eventually to share their gifts.

Today's readings speak about a change of heart, from grasping and greediness to generosity and respect, and Jesus is the teacher who gives new instructions to Israel. Jesus' ultimate goal is for his new vision of generosity and respect to grow into a sense of sister-hood and brotherhood—a feeling of family.

Lent is a time to return to family. We are to restore a sense of educating our young and ourselves in the practice of generosity and respect. Let our lives echo the psalmist's prayer: "For with the Lord is kindness / and with him is plenteous redemption" (Ps 130:7).

Saturday, First Week of Lent
Deuteronomy 26:16–19; Matthew 5:43–48

> *And today the Lord is making this agreement with you:*
> *you are to be a people peculiarly his own.*
> *(Deut 26:18)*

Recently, a woman proudly displayed her engagement ring for me to see. When I congratulated her, she proceeded to share with me, and everyone else, the story of how her engagement had occurred. Then she went on to explain the proper protocol of whom she told first, second, and third. All the women were nodding in agreement. I thought to myself, *There is a whole environment surrounding the engagement process about which men know nothing.*

In our first reading from Deuteronomy, God tells the Chosen People what their love will be like. We get the feeling from the reading that God knows all about the process of love and that the people are in the dark. God has to teach them the proper protocol of love. Jesus also teaches the people what it means to love in the way that God demands.

Each of us needs to sit quietly before God and learn the way of love. If we open our minds and hearts, the Lord will reveal to us, as he revealed to his people, the contract of love. Lent is certainly a time to renew that covenant of love. Let us do that quietly today in the chambers of our hearts. We pray with the psalmist, "Happy are they who observe [God's] decrees, / who seek [the Lord] with all their heart" (Ps 119:2).

Second Sunday of Lent
Genesis 15:5–12, 17–18; Philippians 3:17–4:1; Luke 9:28–36

But awakening, they saw his glory.
(Lk 9:32)

The surprise of the Transfiguration is found in the expression of Jesus' divinity—"His clothing became dazzlingly white." Not until the Resurrection, not even when Jesus performs some of his most spectacular miracles, is his divinity so expressly revealed. A possible reason for this might be that the apostles need to be strengthened in their belief and in their faith.

The Transfiguration occurs immediately after Jesus predicts his Passion and death. This is the first time that the apostles have heard him speak in this manner. Undoubtedly, this prediction causes some grumbling, a little doubting, and possibly even a hint of uncertainty and confusion among the disciples. So God hands them a vision that would inspire courage!

The voice of God, coming from the clouds, is also an indication of the purpose of the Transfiguration. "This is my Son, my Chosen One. Listen to him." This is a clear exhortation to the apostles to listen to Jesus, and not to the voices of the scribes and Pharisees, those other "voices" that call out for attention.

The power of the witness of the Transfiguration is not limited to the apostles. It is also meant for each of us. If we might be inclined to dismiss the teaching of Jesus, or to listen to the "other voices" that call out to us for our attention, the events of this day are a clear remedy. "This is my Son, my Chosen One. Listen to him."

Monday, Second Week of Lent
Daniel 9:4–10; Luke 6:36–38

Give, and it shall be given to you. Good measure pressed down,
shaken together, and running over.
(Lk 6:38)

Come springtime, many of us become gardeners. There is something wholesome about digging in the earth, planting seedlings, offering loving mixtures of fertilizer and water for their growth. The plants are relying on us totally for their welfare. After all, they can't trim themselves, fertilize themselves, or plant themselves. Once we have accepted responsibility for their growth, they become intimately connected to our compassion.

Our readings today present us with a God who is compassionately connected to our growth. In the first reading from Daniel, we sense that the nation of Israel is like a seedling that needs food. The people have fallen, and they need the compassion of God to raise them up again. Jesus tells us that we also, like the God of Daniel, must be a people of overflowing compassion. Each person a Christian meets is like a seedling. They need our touch, our feeding of them, our care for their growth.

Lent is certainly a time to review our sense of compassion. If it has fallen on hard times, let us bolster ourselves with the courage of the Lord who asks us to have such compassion that it runs over all, filling every fold and crevice. We pray with the psalmist, "May your compassion come quickly to us, / for we are brought very low" (Ps 79:8).

Tuesday, Second Week of Lent
Isaiah 1:10, 16–20; Matthew 23:1–12

Make justice your aim: redress the wronged,
hear the orphan's plea, defend the widow.
(Isa 1:17)

Mother Teresa was fond of saying that we should help those who suffer because it is Jesus who is hidden under the guise of suffering. A very humble woman, Mother Teresa did not place herself above the sick and dying but considered them her equals.

The first step to recognizing Christ in others is to see ourselves as their peers. In the gospel, Jesus says it this way: "Whoever humbles himself shall be exalted" (23:12). Jesus condemns the Pharisees because they are so puffed up with their own clothing, position, and language that they cannot see beyond themselves. In the first reading, Isaiah denounces the towns of Sodom and Gomorrah because they have ceased to care for the wronged, the orphaned, and the widowed.

Today let us look beyond ourselves. Pick out one person who is wronged or poor, orphaned or widowed, sick or imprisoned. Keep him or her in your mind and thoughts throughout this day. Let blessings flow from you to this person. Pray, "Call upon me in time of distress; / I will rescue you, and you shall glorify me" (Ps 50:15).

Wednesday, Second Week of Lent
Jeremiah 18:18–20; Matthew 20:17–28

Whoever wants to rank first among you must serve the needs of all.
(Mt 20:27)

I once overheard a wife and husband quarreling at a store's sunglasses carousel. The husband said that the particular pair of sunglasses his wife had chosen didn't look very good on her. The wife pointed out that she was planning to get her hair cut and buy a new shirt and new boots. Then these glasses would look great. He was talking about one pair of glasses. She was talking a complete make-over.

Most people yearn for something more, something better. In our first reading, Jeremiah wants God to act on his behalf right now to better his situation. In the gospel, the brothers and their mother want Jesus to do more for them. In the response of Jesus we find one of the cornerstones of Christian spirituality: closeness to God is the opposite of having more. In fact, "more" gets in the way of God. Usually, "more" demands our attention and service.

These readings give us a chance to look at all the extra stuff we have and desire. Can we let go and rely on God to give us what we need on this day? Can we push back the encumbrances of desire and allow God's vision of service to lead us? We pray, "My trust is in you, O LORD; / I say, 'You are my God.' / In your hands is my destiny" (Ps 31:15–16).

Thursday, Second Week of Lent
Jeremiah 17:5–10; Luke 16:19–31

Blessed is the man who trusts in the LORD, whose hope is the LORD.
(Jer 17:7)

At an art auction in New York one painting by Pablo Picasso drew more money than any other art piece in history. The irony is that during a large portion of his life Picasso's art was rejected and scorned. Many artists throughout history have shared this experience. During their lives they are despised and poor, and after death they are recognized and their estates are enriched.

The same was true of the prophet Jeremiah. During his life Jeremiah's family abandoned him, and the king gave him up to his enemies in broad daylight. Jeremiah was persecuted and died in a foreign land. Yet his influence on the popular devotion of Israel was greater than that of any other prophet.

In the gospel, Jesus shares with us the story of Lazarus. Lazarus is rejected in life but raised high after death. Both readings today speak to the Christian ideal that inner goodness gives us life and lives on after us. We ask the Lord today for this never-ending water supply that will give us life. Let us pray: Happy are they who hope in the Lord (see Ps 1).

Friday, Second Week of Lent
Genesis 37:3–4, 12–13, 17–28;
Matthew 21:33–43, 45–46

The stone which the builders rejected has become the keystone.
(Mt 21:42)

Dr. Alfred Adler, a famous family therapist, grew up wanting to become a tailor. But in his early life he had a severe eye ailment that prevented him from seeing well enough to pursue the tailoring profession. Instead, he used his eyes to gaze into the minds, spirits, and souls of patients and families and in the process founded a renowned school of psychology.

In today's reading from Genesis, Joseph, a dreamer abandoned by his brothers, uses his dreaming power to bring his people to Egypt and form them into a nation. In the gospel, Jesus is the son who is killed, but in that killing God raises him up to become a vineyard for all people. Today let us not allow our weaknesses to conquer us. Like Jesus we can vanquish our own darkness. We ask the Lord today to raise us up and let our darkness become a great light. Let us pray: Remember the marvels the Lord has done (see Ps 105).

Saturday, Second Week of Lent
Micah 7:14–15, 18–20; Luke 15:1–3, 11–32

Who is there like you, the God who removes guilt and pardons sin?
(Mic 7:18)

I was sitting with a group of people discussing the candidates who were running in the presidential primaries. One person said that he would never vote for a particular candidate because that candidate was born "with a silver spoon in his mouth"—meaning that this candidate from a wealthy family would never have a need for money.

Our readings today remind us that we Christians are also born with silver spoons in our mouths. We are inheritors of a great tradition of wealth. Both Micah and Luke give us examples of this wealth in today's readings. The difficulty is that our wealth is a different kind of wealth and is accessible in a distinctive way. Our Christian wealth is that we are sons and daughters of God and inheritors of God's constant compassion and pardon. We get this wealth by returning to God with a humble, loving attitude. Today open your heart, as the prodigal son did, and allow God's compassion, your inheritance, to flow down upon you. We pray, "Bless the LORD, O my soul; / and forget not all [God's] benefits" (Ps 103:2).

Third Sunday of Lent
Exodus 3:1–8, 13–15; 1 Corinthians 10:1–6, 10–12;
Luke 13:1–9

I am the God of your father, the God of Abraham,
the God of Isaac, the God of Jacob.
(Ex 3:6)

Exodus, chapter three, marks the beginning of God's revealing of the divine presence to us. Obviously, God felt a need to become *personally* involved in the plight of the Jewish people. Having watched them driven into slavery, God intervened to free them by giving Moses the name of God, the authority of God, and then sending Moses to Pharaoh. From this point on God would not be an absentee landlord.

Every so often we believe that God has gone away out of our lives. We don't feel God's presence or see God's power, will, or action in our lives. As one skeptic has said, "God is the laziest person on the block." But the truth of the gospels is just the opposite. God is always present. Sometimes God is hidden behind a burning bush, a quiet morning, a singing lark, or a starlit night, and we are not still enough to hear God speaking. Sometimes God will speak through a lover's embrace, or a small child's beating heart, or a teenager's wail. What does God say to you at these times?

As we read in Luke's Gospel, Jesus calls people to reform. To respond to that call this Lent, let us quiet ourselves so we can listen to the voice of God speaking through the moments of our lives.

Monday, Third Week of Lent
2 Kings 5:1–15; Luke 4:24–30

Now I know that there is no God in all the earth, except in Israel.
(2 Kgs 5:15)

Saint Lawrence was a deacon in the third century. It was a time of persecution, and Deacon Lawrence was informed that the government wished to sell all the treasures of the Christian churches. The governor commissioned Deacon Lawrence to gather all the treasures in one church so that the governor could have his pick before the sale began. When he arrived at the church, he found the sanctuary filled with the weak, the blind, the lame, and the sick. Deacon Lawrence proclaimed to the governor, "These are the treasures of the Church." Deacon Lawrence was martyred for this act of witness.

Our readings today speak to the fact that we are a healing church.

The healing tradition from Elisha in our first reading to Jesus in our gospel is carried on today in our prayers to Jesus, in our prayers to Mary, and in the special intercessions of certain saints. It is our task, as Christians, to believe that in Jesus there is no such thing as an "incurable disease." Healing is a gift from God and is our Christian legacy. Today pray that Jesus will heal you and that the healing power of the Church will extend itself to those you love. Pray with the psalmist, "Athirst is my soul for God, the living God. / When shall I go and behold the face of God?" (Ps 42:3).

Tuesday, Third Week of Lent
Daniel 3:25, 34–43; Matthew 18:21–35

My heavenly Father will treat you in exactly the same way unless each of you forgives his brother from his heart.
(Mt 18:35)

A couple I know struggled for years to conceive a baby. Overcome by their own infertility, they finally sought the path of adoption. They found through one agency that a baby was available from an orphanage in China. It took the wife two weeks to travel to China, go through all the diplomatic channels, and bring the child back to their home. They are now a family. There is a new beginning.

In our first reading from Daniel, Azariah looks at the ruins of his nation and prays to God for forgiveness and a chance to begin anew. In the gospel, Jesus gives his followers the key to beginning again. This key is the gift of forgiveness. Whenever we need to begin again we call for the overwhelming experience of God's kindness and great mercy. Then we turn the key of forgiveness, and the doors will unlock and new life will be ours. Let us pray: "Remember that your compassion, O Lord, / and your kindness are from of old" (Ps 25:6).

Wednesday, Third Week of Lent
Deuteronomy 4:1, 5–9; Matthew 5:17–19

Now, Israel, hear the statutes and decrees
which I am teaching you to observe, that you may live.
(Deut 4:1)

A young girl was explaining to me that her family expected her to strive for very high grades in school, complete college, and eventually enter a prestigious and professional career. I asked her if either of her parents had told her this directly. She said, "No, they never have told me directly, but I know this is what they want." Every family has an unwritten code by which family members live. Even though no one proclaims the code, or even writes it down, every family member knows it.

Both readings today speak about the code by which Jesus and his Jewish nation lived. Parts of the code were written down into laws, other parts every Jewish person just knew. In Jewish life, laws were obeyed not for their own sake but as a way of obeying God. Jesus himself loved the Book of Deuteronomy (Book of the Law) and often quoted from it.

Today would be a good day to look at the laws and beliefs by which you live, some written and others just known. Ask yourself which of your laws are truly ways of obeying God and which are not. We pray with the psalmist, "[God] sends forth his command to the earth; / swiftly runs his word!" (Ps 147:15).

Thursday, Third Week of Lent
Jeremiah 7:23–28; Luke 11:14–23

Listen to my voice; then I will be your God and you shall be my people.
(Jer 7:23)

One summer, I substituted as pastor in a small urban parish. Every day one woman would sit in the second pew from the front for Mass. She always carried her Bible, and during the quiet places in the Mass she would write in the back of it. She appeared holy, even angelic, during these daily appearances. After the first week, I stopped the woman and spoke with her. She told me that during Mass both angels and devils appeared to her; some spoke to her and some didn't. She would write all their names down in the back of the Bible. This quiet, gentle-looking woman was filled with inner conflict and battle.

Both readings today present the battle that is raging beneath the placid exterior. Jeremiah proclaims that the people have become deaf to God and have been won over by "the dark side." Jesus opens the mute man's mouth, and out flies the devil. This provokes Jesus to challenge the evil interior thoughts of those present.

How many times today will we be called to make a choice between the angels and the devils? We ask Jesus to open our mouths to speak the words that are true, holy, and of God. We pray with the psalmist, "Oh, that today you would hear his voice: / 'Harden not your hearts'" (Ps 95:7–8).

Friday, Third Week of Lent
Hosea 14:2–10; Mark 12:28–34

Again they shall dwell in his shade and raise grain;
They shall blossom like the vine.
(Hos 14:8)

Every time he had to do a job that he disliked, a brother in our religious congregation would proclaim to anyone within hearing, "I do this for the Master!" It was his way of dispelling the negative energy around a disagreeable task and giving it over to a higher realm. If you had asked this religious brother what the two greatest laws in all of the world were, he would not have been able to tell you. But his life spoke these laws.

When the religious leaders ask Jesus the two greatest commands in today's gospel, he responds with the laws that rule his heart, his life, his ministry, and his love. Jesus lived them. He certainly didn't need to speak them. The people of Hosea's time had forgotten the inner way of life and the laws that lit that way. They neither lived them nor could speak them.

We ask the Lord today to lead us back to the laws of love that can rule our lives. Laws that we need not speak but can truly live. Let us pray: If only my people would hear me, and Israel walk in my ways, I would feed them with the best of wheat (see Ps 81).

Saturday, Third Week of Lent
Hosea 6:1–6; Luke 18:9–14

For everyone who exalts himself shall be humbled
while he who humbles himself shall be exalted.
(Lk 18:14)

A truck driver came to the rectory to speak to me about prayer. He told me that while he was growing up he had been taught all these formal prayers to say. Now that he was older he had forgotten most of them. When I asked him how he prayed, he told me, "When I drive my truck, I talk to God and God talks to me." I looked at him with a sense of envy, knowing that he had found the secret.

In our readings today, both Hosea and Luke speak to the issue of what is genuine prayer. Each reading gives us clues that can help us find the secret way into the heart of God. Hosea says that prayer is not a magic formula of repeating words to God and then expecting God to act. Hosea condemns this attitude. Luke tells us that prayer is not a sense of self-importance and self-righteous behavior.

For Jesus, the heart of prayer is found in the Jewish tradition surrounding *hesed,* the love that binds family members together. This *hesed* is proclaimed in the obligatory talking that occurs between family members and clans. Genuine prayer is talking to God as a family member and sharing that prayer with other family members.

This day let us renew our commitment to God who is of our family and of our clan. We pray, "A heart contrite and humbled, O God, you will not spurn" (Ps 51:19).

Fourth Sunday of Lent
Joshua 5:9, 10–12; 2 Corinthians 5:17–21;
Luke 15:1–3, 11–32

Let us eat and celebrate because this son of mine was dead and has come back to life.
(Lk 15:23–24)

As Jesus tells the parable in today's gospel, the Father, of course, represents God. The father sees his son afar off and runs out to meet him. The Lord is pointing out that not even sin will keep God from loving us. God can't wait for us to return.

When the artist Rembrandt was an old man, he painted *The Return of the Prodigal Son.* In Rembrandt's painting, however, the father is blind. The father can't run out to meet his son; he has to wait patiently for the son to come to him. Of course, being blind, the father can't see what the son looks like. The father can only sense the son's wanting and needing forgiveness.

Rembrandt was saying that God burns for our return but is powerless to drag us back. In the painting, one hand of the father rests on the returning son's shoulder, the other is raised in blessing. One hand appears very masculine, and the other very feminine. Rembrandt was representing the two faces of God. The one of embracing comfort, the other of righteous forgiveness.

This painting speaks of the love of God who is Father, who is Mother. God's love was present before any rejection was possible and will still be there after all rejections have taken place. This Lent let us, like the prodigal son, return to God and ask for comfort and forgiveness.

Monday, Fourth Week of Lent
Isaiah 65:17–21; John 4:43–54

Return home. Your son will live.
(Jn 4:50)

I recently told a friend that when I am feeling depressed, I paint. Painting seems to lift my spirits. My friend told me that when she is depressed she usually goes and buys herself a new outfit. The "new look" seems to sink into the darker inner chambers and brighten the day. If you looked into yourself, you would probably discover that you have established many different cures to help raise your spirits when you are feeling low.

In today's first reading, Isaiah attempts to lift the spirits of his people by proclaiming to them that the Lord will make all things new for them. They will enjoy good memories, better vineyards, and longer life spans. Jesus does what Isaiah has predicted. Jesus gives to the royal official's son a new and longer life and to the royal official the gift of belief. Now the official has memories of healing and of faith.

Today we can ask for this same gift from God and from Jesus. We ask to be given good memories, a long life, and a deep faith. We pray, "Hear, O LORD, and have pity on me; / O LORD, be my helper. / You changed my mourning into dancing" (Ps 30:11–12).

Tuesday, Fourth Week of Lent
Ezekiel 47:1–9, 12; John 5:1–3, 5–16

Sir, I do not have anyone to plunge me into the pool
once the water has been stirred up.
(Jn 5:7)

West of the city of Denver and across the Continental Divide lies an area of the Rocky Mountains that is surrounded by beautiful deep gullies and running streams. Hot springs bubble from the earth like magic. Native Americans used to hold this place of the hot springs as sacred. It was their belief that the hot springs contained both magical and curative powers. They would travel great distances through the Rockies to pray to the gods and be healed in the curing waters of these springs.

The good news from Ezekiel and John is that we do not have to travel to the Continental Divide to enjoy curative and healing powers. As today's readings tell us, the healing waters are in our midst, flowing continuously from Jesus who is the New Temple and the unending spring. Everything that this water touches becomes a new creation!

We ask the Lord today to lift us up, to be our healing pool, to make us the new creation of his living water. We pray, "The LORD of hosts is with us; / our stronghold is the God of Jacob" (Ps 46:8).

Wednesday, Fourth Week of Lent
Isaiah 49:8–15; John 5:17–30

Can a mother forget her infant,
be without tenderness for the child of her womb?
(Isa 49:15)

A striking picture ran in one of the national magazines. This picture showed a coal miner naked from his waist up, his upper body covered with blackened coal dust, his neck and arm muscles bulging from the long hours of work. In his hands, as large as shovels, he held a sleeping baby. The baby appeared delicate and frail nested in these strong hands. If the coal miner had wanted, he could have closed his hands and crushed the life of that baby, but all the power of the coal miner was focused into tenderness and gentle love for this child.

Jesus is such a loving giant in today's readings. Isaiah proclaims that God's loving hands hold us ever so gently. God is a healing God who would never crush the life out of those held in tender embrace. Jesus is a reflection of this healing God. Even the power of the Sabbath law will not and cannot stop Jesus' healing power.

We also are reflections of Jesus' healing power! Today we look to our family, our friends, our coworkers and ask how we can bring the gentle healing embrace of God to them. We pray with the psalmist, "The LORD is good to all / and compassionate toward all his works" (Ps 145:9).

Thursday, Fourth Week of Lent
Exodus 32:7–14; John 5:31–47

I will make your descendants as numerous as the stars in the sky.
(Ex 32:13)

Whenever my grandmother would come to baby-sit my siblings and me, she would bring a large shopping bag with her. Once my mother

256

and father had left the house, Grandma would reach into her bag and bring out delicious cookies, a teapot with exotic smelling teas, and her large needles and colored yarn. I would watch in amazement as these old hands, wrinkled with time, work, and love, would swing those needles and threads into various colorful patterns. Grandma was a "softy" who loved keeping us fed and amused.

In today's readings, Moses, Abraham, and Jesus know that like Grandma, God also is a "softy." With a few words Moses turns God's anger into compassion. Jesus shows the same compassion as he goes out of his way to explain his ministry to his fellow Jews.

In this tradition of the great prophets, we ask God to let love, patience, and understanding rule us this day. We ask that any anger we have be turned into fond memories and beautiful weavings. We pray with the psalmist, "Remember me, O Lord, as you favor your people" (Ps 106:4).

Friday, Fourth Week of Lent
Wisdom 2:1, 12–22; John 7:1–2, 10, 25–30

And they knew not the hidden counsels of God
nor discern[ed] the innocent souls' reward.
(Wis 2:22)

In *The Color Purple* the main character says, "I think that God would get angry if we walk through a field of flowers and not notice the color purple." Purple is the color that our eye tends to pick up least readily, so we really have to concentrate if we are to find this most delicate color in the vast blooming meadow.

Both readings today present us with evil people who do not look beyond the surface. These "wicked" condemn what they do not see and cannot understand (as the Book of Wisdom says, "their wickedness blinded them" [2:21]). Most of the prophets were at the mercy of these surface-seers, and many prophets died because of them. Jesus

257

knows the history of the prophets, so he challenges the ignorance of these narrow-minded condemners. The way of Jesus is to view each person as a great cathedral full of mystery and depth that would take a lifetime to understand. Or to treat each person as a field of flowers full of an eternity of shades and variances.

It is certainly a challenge to us to recognize the great depth that we have because we are children of God and to respect that beauty in others by loving even their tiniest and most subtle qualities. We pray with the psalmist, "The LORD redeems the lives of his servants; / no one incurs guilt who takes refuge in him" (Ps 34:23).

Saturday, Fourth Week of Lent
Jeremiah 11:18–20; John 7:40–53

But, you, O LORD of hosts, O just Judge, searcher of mind and heart.
(Jer 12:20)

The Catholic press interviewed one of the pilgrims who had come to the Shrine of Our Lady of Lourdes to pray, touch the healing waters, and perhaps be cured. This woman was in a wheelchair. She had been traveling to Lourdes yearly for the past eight years. When the press asked her if she was ever discouraged in coming to Lourdes and in not being cured, she told them that she was cured—she just couldn't walk yet!

Each one of us faces this mystery: only God can help us with some of our problems. All of our human energies and endeavors have come to a dead end. We then beach ourselves on God's shores and pray, Revive me, O Lord.

Jeremiah the prophet is condemned by his own family and friends. In the midst of this darkness he entrusts his cause to the Lord. Jesus also is condemned, taunted, and hunted. Jesus' response is also to remember that he is of God and that God will come to his aid.

To follow Jesus' example, we must learn to face the great mysteries of our life with a sense of trust in God. Like Jeremiah we give our cause to God, and we are confident that God will lead us through mystery into light. Let us pray today with the psalmist, "O LORD, my God, in you I take refuge" (Ps 7:2).

Fifth Sunday of Lent
Isaiah 43:16–21; Philippians 3:8–14; John 8:1–11

Nor do I condemn you. You may go. But from now on, avoid this sin.
(Jn 8:11)

Some years ago there was a national drive to alleviate hunger and give food to the inner-city poor, especially the homeless street people. Most of the millions of dollars that were set aside for this program went into publicity and bureaucracy. In fact, when a homeless person in one of the key cities was asked about the program, she responded, "I am still hungry, and I am still homeless." All the organization in the world means nothing if the one who needs food isn't fed!

Today's gospel shows the woman caught in adultery in such a position. All Jesus' talk about forgiveness and compassion means nothing unless he can forgive the person in front of him who needs his forgiveness! Threatened with exile from his own religion, Jesus chooses love and forgiveness over the law and religious practices. Isaiah also proclaims the greatness of all that God will do for the people. Whole deserts will become gardens, and everyone will eat and drink. These prophecies would have been meaningless had not Jesus shown himself as the Living Water, the Eternal Bread, the Merciful Healer.

The lesson for us concerns choosing. If we follow Christ, we must choose mercy and love over all else. The choice can be difficult, especially if we are people who rely on righteousness and law. But it is the way of Jesus!

Monday, Fifth Week of Lent
Daniel 13:1–9, 15–17, 19–30, 33–62; John 8:1–11

Nor do I condemn you. You may go. But from now on, avoid this sin.
(Jn 8:11)

How many of us, while we were growing up, heard our father or mother tell us that the reason we did things a certain way was because it was our family's tradition. Recently, I was invited to a family's home for dinner. The children, all grown and married, were also invited to this meal. All the plates and food were put before the father, and after prayer he filled each plate and passed it on to us. Obviously, this practice seems odd for a group of adults eating together. But it was that family's tradition.

One of the old traditions in the Jewish law was that of stoning. It was a public way for the community to kill sin when it occurred. Both of today's readings reflect that Jewish tradition. A woman is brought forward who is found to be with sin and condemned. Jesus sets a new precedent, begins a new tradition, and instead of killing the sin through stoning, he kills the sin through forgiveness. Jesus pardons the unpardonable sin.

How many times have we stoned ourselves and those around us, using guilt, shame, or hatred as our rocks? It is time to recommit ourselves to Jesus' tradition, the tradition of forgiveness. We pray, "The Lord is my shepherd; / I shall not want" (Ps 23:1).

Tuesday, Fifth Week of Lent
Numbers 21:4–9; John 8:21–30

When you lift up the Son of Man, you will come to realize that I AM.
(Jn 8:28)

It is amazing how much suffering people can endure and still carry on with their lives. I remember meeting a very professional businesswoman who revealed a history of suffering. She had been abused as a child and gone through a broken marriage as a young woman; in midlife she had faced a bout with alcoholism, and most recently she had transitioned through a period of depression. She told me that she needed to be lifted up a lot!

In our first reading from the Book of Numbers, the Jewish people tell Moses and God that they are sick of suffering! They have had it! At first, God appears pretty unbending and not only refuses to listen to their complaints but sends more suffering into their midst. Finally, God decides that the people need to be lifted up and healed. God sends them a sign of healing. To be healed, all the people have to do is raise their eyes and behold the healing sign.

This tradition of gazing toward the healing sign is carried into today's gospel reading. Jesus has become the healing sign that has been lifted up. When we choose to believe and gaze upon Jesus, we will be healed.

Life's chaos and burdens bite each of us. Today let's each choose to allow the Lord to lift us up. Our faith will be deepened and our wounds healed, and we will live again. Let us pray, "O LORD, hear my prayer; / and let my cry come to you" (Ps 102:2).

Wednesday, Fifth Week of Lent
Daniel 3:14–20, 91–92, 95; John 8:31–42

If the son frees you, you will really be free.
(Jn 8:36)

So many children's stories speak of a transition from being poor, young, ugly, or dumb to being wealthy, older, beautiful, and smart. We can think of *Beauty and the Beast, The Lion King, Thumbelina, The Velveteen Rabbit,* and *The Ugly Duckling.* In each of these stories, the hero is at first downtrodden and enslaved and at the end raised up and set free. Usually, a force from the outside comes and awakens the beauty on the inside.

This is the model presented for a true Christian in our readings today. In the Book of Daniel, the evil king enslaves the young men in the fiery furnace. But God visits them and sets them free to pray, sing, and walk untouched by the fire. In the gospel, Jesus announces to his people that he has come to set them free. He is the outside force that will bring an inner renewal to them. Once renewed they can also pray, sing, and live untouched by the fires of sin and prejudice around them.

Today we bring to the Lord that part of ourselves that feels down-trodden and enslaved. We ask the Lord to be the outside force that will awaken our inner renewal. We pray, Lord, let me see your truth, and let your truth then set me free (based on Jn 8:31).

Thursday, Fifth Week of Lent
Genesis 17:3–9; John 8:51–59

If a man is true to my word he shall never see death.
(Jn 8:51)

A recent TV biography told the story of a woman who had inherited hundreds of millions of dollars from her father. She was a teenager when he died, and she was his only heir. The biography traced her history as she went through a series of broken relationships and sick-nesses until at last she died childless. People continue to fight over her money even to this day. It was a sad and tragic tale: all the money in the world could not give her an heir or a loving life.

Today's readings show us just the opposite story. In Genesis, God promises Abraham that he will have descendants forever. In the gos-pel, Jesus promises his believers that they will have life forever. The only requirement is to "keep my covenant throughout the ages" (Gen 17:9). This covenant is a simple form of generosity. We pour out our love and devotion toward God, and God, in turn, showers love and devotion on us.

Let us look to what can really give us fullness of life. Today is a time to cut ourselves loose from any entanglements that hinder us from loving God or receiving love from God. It is a day to embrace the beauty of being a child of Abraham and a disciple of Jesus. We pray with the psalmist, "[The Lord] remembers forever his covenant, / which he made binding for a thousand generations" (Ps 105:8).

Friday, Fifth Week of Lent
Jeremiah 20:10–13; John 10:31–42

Sing to the Lord, praise the Lord, For he has rescued the life of the poor
from the power of the wicked!
(Jer 20:13)

During the time I was in book publishing, an older man called to tell me the tale of his conversion to Christianity. It was a journey marked with the drama of an escape from Nazi Europe, a return to the Jewish camps in an attempt to save his parents, and emigration to the new world of America. He could pinpoint the very moment of his conversion. It happened as he was passing a Catholic church. God called his name, drew him into the church, and spoke to him. As I listened to him, I pondered how different my own life, that of a cradle Catholic, has been. No dramatic moments but the constant familiarity and comfort of being with the Church.

In today's readings, we have two different calls to conversion. For Jeremiah the call is a very personal one. God calls Jeremiah to a life of being hated by those he is called to serve. But Jeremiah's trust is constant (like that of most of us cradle Catholics), and he knows God will aid him. Jesus, in the gospel, asks his people to be converted by his works. He invites them to open their eyes, see what he is doing, and then convert and believe.

What will bring us to conversion today? Is a dramatic moment of hearing God's voice awaiting us? Will our conversion happen because God's work will shine forth for us to see? Will we rely on the strength of our constant Catholic faith to ignite us? We wait and pray, "I love you, O LORD, my strength, / O LORD, my rock, my fortress, my deliverer" (Ps 18:2–3).

Saturday, Fifth Week of Lent
Ezekiel 37:21–28; John 11:45–57

My dwelling shall be with them; I will be their God,
and they shall be my people.
(Ezek 37:27)

I was reading in a current autobiography about a man who felt absolutely cut off from his parents, his family, and his friends. As he was crying alone one day, a friend heard him and put his arms around him. The friend said, "I will be your family, I will be your friend." The response: "That is all I ever have wanted!" Later in the story the friend went on to steal the man's money and betray his friendship.

In today's reading from Ezekiel, God comes to his people who have been betrayed, cast off, and beaten. God tells them that they will be God's family. They will again be friends of God. In the gospel reading from John, these very people betray God by attacking and plotting against the person of Jesus.

Today we look at our lives. Where have we been befriended? Where have we been betrayed? Can we again go to God and go to Jesus and ask to be his family, ask to be his friend? It is the Christian task to always return to God, who is our family, our friend. We pray with Jeremiah, "I will turn their mourning into joy, / I will console and gladden them after their sorrows" (31:13).

Passion (Palm) Sunday
Luke 19:28–40; Isaiah 50:4–7; Philippians 2:6–11;
Luke 22:14–23, 56

Blessed is he who comes as king in the name of the Lord!
(Lk 19:38)

Mother Teresa said, "Jesus comes to meet us. To welcome him, let us go to meet him. He comes to us in the hungry, the naked, the lonely, the alcoholic, the drug addict, the prostitute, the street beggars. If we reject them, if we do not go out to meet them, we reject Jesus himself." Like Jesus, Mother Teresa triumphed by giving to others.

Today Luke's Passion story presents the image of Jesus, a person who is for the other. Jesus prays, forgives, shows deep concern for the outcast, and asks us to follow him in this holy task. We sing today of Jesus' triumph because of his powerful love for the poor. We praise God in singing Hosanna because the Lord rides in on a donkey, an animal that the poor of his day rode. If we are to triumph like Jesus, we also must ride with the poor. We must triumph in extending ourselves to those who have less, who are sick, who are dying. If we do so, the Lord will sing a Hosanna to us when we pass into heaven, as we do today to the Lord!

Monday of Holy Week
Isaiah 42:1-7; John 12:1–11

I have grasped you by the hand; I formed you,
and set you as a covenant of the people.
(Isa 42:6)

All of us have heard stories of the great meteorites what hit the earth millions of years ago, wiping out the dinosaur population and darkening the skies for some years. There is evidence in recent history of a meteor hitting the forest lands of Siberia and destroying thousands of acres of trees and wildlife. These and other events of our solar system speak of the great power and violence that can change our world.

Jesus, the all-powerful one, begins this week what changes the history of the universe with loving and gentle devotion. Jesus opens himself to be comforted and bathed with perfume, giving us a clue about how Jesus will effect change. He will not be like a great meteor, filled with violence and destruction. Rather, he will change human history by filling the hidden crevices of the human heart with beauty, devotion, and care. It is a call to us that as we begin this week of weeks we are to be calm, gentle, and loving. We open ourselves to Jesus, the gentle one, so that we can be redemptive in his nondestructive way. We pray with the psalmist, "Wait for the LORD with courage; / be stouthearted, and wait for the LORD!" (Ps 27:14).

Tuesday of Holy Week
Isaiah 49:1–6; John 13:21–33, 36–38

I will make you a light to the nations,
hat my salvation may reach to the ends of the earth.
(Isa 49:6)

I was talking to a young couple that I had married a few years back. They were each turning thirty years old and had just given birth to their second child in three years. They wanted to talk to me about their sense of sadness at having their time so limited by their children. All the fun they had had when they were single and newly married was now buried in diapers and middle-of-the-night feedings. It was their task now to commit to a greater and fuller reality—the challenge of being a family, of being parents, of becoming connected to families and parents across the universe. They needed to create the new vision of being family that would carry them through the next phase of their life together.

In our readings today, both Isaiah and Jesus declare that their lives are at a point of new beginning. They both realize that it is time to engage a new reality, a new challenge. For Isaiah the challenge is to be a light that will lead his people through this time of exile. For Jesus the challenge is to depart from his loved disciples and be glorified.

Holy Week is certainly a time of new beginnings. Perhaps we could look into our lives today and see where we need to begin anew. We look at our seedlings of future growth and pray, "For you are my hope, O LORD; / my trust, O God, from my youth" (Ps 71:5).

Wednesday of Holy Week
Isaiah 50:4–9; Matthew 26:14–25

The Lord GOD is my help, therefore I am not disgraced;
I have set my face like flint.
(Isa 50:7)

Most people view betrayal as a great curse. This curse lingers with the betrayer long after his or her death. Think of Benedict Arnold. No matter what great or important things he did in his life, he will always be remembered for his betrayal of the American colonies in the Revolutionary War. In grade school, little kids call another kid a tattletale or a squealer if he or she betrays another. Street gangs also have a code of silence that, if broken, is punishable by death.

Both readings today place us into this dingy dungeon of betrayal. Isaiah, in our first reading, is betrayed by his own people, to whom he came to speak God's word. Jesus, in the gospel, is betrayed by Judas. Both readings reflect the public humiliation, suffering, and agony that accompanies the act of betrayal. Both Isaiah and Jesus rely on the strength of Scripture to see them through this bitter time. By trusting in God they both live to see a better tomorrow. Every one of us who lives long enough will feel the sting of betrayal from someone we love. Some of us might even taste the bile of being the betrayer. Like Jesus and Isaiah, let us turn to the psalms to see us through these moments. Pray, "In your great kindness answer me / with your constant help. Answer me, O LORD, for bounteous is your kindness" (Ps 69:14,17).

Holy Thursday, Easter Triduum
Exodus 12:1–8, 11–14; 1 Corinthians 11:23–26; John 13:1–15

This day shall be a memorial feast for you,
which all your generations shall celebrate.
(Ex 12:14)

One of the miracles of modern communications is that people, long separated, can now search for and usually find one another. Sometime ago during Holy Week there appeared a news story about a woman in America who was searching for her twin sister in Eastern Europe. They had been separated during the Cold War years, and she had given up her sister for dead. But while watching a TV story about food relief in Eastern Europe, she saw a nun who looked like herself. After some weeks of frantic phone calling she found out that this woman was her twin sister. They were finally reunited after a thirty-year separation.

Our readings today bring us the story of God's reuniting with us. No more will we be separated. God's blood runs in our bodies, God's body becomes our flesh. The days of God's "passing over his people" are now ended. In Jesus, God now passes *into* all people. Holy Thursday is a time to celebrate this reunion. Every Eucharist we receive is a remembering that we, once separated, are now together forever. We pray with the psalmist, "But my trust is in you, O LORD; / I say, 'You are my God'" (Ps 31:15).

Good Friday, Easter Triduum
Isaiah 52:13, 53:12; Hebrews 4:14–16; 5:7–9;
John 18:1–19, 42

Through his suffering, my servant shall justify many,
and their guilt he shall bear.
(Isa 53:11)

In the oil-drilling movies of the 1960s and 1970s the climactic moment always comes after weeks of drilling a seemingly empty well. A slight rumbling of the earth begins. The rumbling grows into a deafening roar. Suddenly, the oil shoots from the earth, up the face of the well, soaring high above the rig. The oil men, rejoicing, run under the black rain and become soaked in this primordial fuel.

In today's readings, the cross of Jesus becomes a pipeline into the blackness of our guilt, our destructiveness, our violence, and our sin. The cross of Jesus releases the sin buried under eons of human weakness. Once released, the sin dissipates into the heart of Jesus, and the remaining cavity is filled with Jesus' goodness, peace, and grace.

The drama of this release plays out in the Gospel of John in the interplay between the sorrowing community and the dying Christ. The lesson taught in these Scriptures is that we must learn from Jesus' wounds and death. The lesson is that Christ releases us from sin and death so that his life can become manifest in our bodies and spirits. What the original followers of Jesus saw as a great tragedy, we know today as a great victory. Today we open our souls again and allow the Lord Jesus to pierce the layers of guilt and weakness. We see that darkness spilling from us into the eternal light. We pray with Jesus, "Father, into your hands I commend my spirit" (Lk 23:46).

Holy Saturday, Easter Triduum
Genesis 1:1–2:2; Genesis 22:1–18; Exodus 14:15, 15:1; Isaiah 54:5–14; Isaiah 55:1–11; Baruch 3:9–15, 32—4:4; Ezekiel 36:16–28; Romans 6:3–11; Luke 24:1–12

> *By the word of the Lord the heavens were made;*
> *by the breath of his mouth all their host.*
> *(Ps 33:6)*

When living in the northern regions of the United States, I was amazed that the clearest and most poignantly beautiful days always occurred after huge snowstorms. In fact, it seems to be the rule of nature that the worse the storm, the more brilliant the next day's sun. We see this also in our human lives. People who have survived great personal losses or tragedies seem to become more focused, spiritual, and glowing. The sun seems to shine brighter in their souls.

On this Easter eve we hear evidence that the great reversals of life not only are possible but actually do happen. The darkness of the Easter eve is broken by the Easter fire. The quiet of the surrounding night is driven back by the ringing bells of the Gloria. The seeming death and destruction of Jesus are transformed into vibrant life and growth. These dramatic changes echo the gospel reactions of the people who encounter the Resurrection event. They experience joy, confusion, faith, fear, excitement, peace, and bewilderment. And after all the commotion settles, bursting life that death cannot destroy.

We enter the Easter mystery this Holy Saturday with our hearts in our hands. We know that the whirlwind of Jesus will resurrect these old hearts. We believe that in the mystery of God we will be made new. We have confidence that death is now only a passageway to the deepest chambers of God. We sing with the bells of heaven: Glory to God in the highest!

Easter
Acts 10:34, 37–43; Colossians 3:1–4;
John 20:1–9 (morning Mass);
Luke 24:13–35 (evening Mass)

This is the day the LORD has made; let us be glad and rejoice in it.
(Ps 118:24)

I had the unusual opportunity of spending one Easter in the hospital. My dad was quite weak after a paralyzing stroke, but there was hope as he slowly regained various lost functions. The contrast between the sterile white hospital room and the multicolored richness of the decorated Easter churches played in my mind. It was at this point that a group of hospital nurses entered the room. They had decorated Easter eggs in the early hours of the morning and were passing them out to each patient with jubilant joy and Easter greetings. My dad reached out with a very feeble hand to receive his Easter gift. He held it gently as if it were an ocean of love, and so it was.

The mystery of Easter is that Jesus wanted to fill the world with his love. In his body he was limited to the small area around Galilee that he could travel by foot. Jesus needed to expand into his spirit so that he could fill every chasm and fissure of life.

The small gift of the Easter egg was evidence that the Lord's spirit has indeed spanned earth and time. Jesus has come to live in the hearts and souls of so many. Saint Paul describes these qualities that are Jesus now living: heartfelt mercy, kindness, humility, meekness, and patience (Col 3:13–15). Paul instructs us to robe ourselves in this light. Jesus is our angel of light! Let us rejoice, be glad, and strive to live his light. We pray today, "Christ indeed from death is risen, our new life obtaining" (Easter Sequence).

Feast of the Chair of Peter, Apostle (February 22)
1 Peter 5:1–4; Matthew 16:13–19

God's flock is in your midst; give it a shepherd's care.
(1 Pet 5:2)

During first Communion preparation class, I would bring all the children into the church's sanctuary. I would have each child sit in the presider's chair to see what it is like to be the minister. One boy sat in the big chair and proclaimed to his class, "All my life I've wanted to sit in this chair!" I asked him what he wanted to be when he grew up. He looked up and stated, "I want to be a priest!" I invited him then to tell us what would be the first thing he would do as a priest. He gazed around and declared, "I would get a smaller chair!"

The gift of God's call to each of us is certainly a mystery, and sometimes it is awakened by the tiniest of events. Today in our readings we have the mystery of the call of Peter to be the head of the Church. This certainly wasn't a "chair" in which Peter willingly chose to sit, but he was hoisted into it by the power of Jesus' word and mission. It took many centuries for the Church to come to a true understanding of what this charism of Peter's leadership would mean.

In honoring Peter's vocation today we also honor our vocation. Like Peter we are called to be active members of the Christian community. We are called to be spiritual leaders of our children, our families, our communities. As Peter and his successors are called to be true shepherds of the Church, let us also take up our roles as shepherds of the flocks entrusted to us. We pray with the psalmist, "With your rod and your staff, give me courage" (Ps 23:4).

Solemnity of Joseph, Husband of Mary (March 19)
2 Samuel 7:4–5, 12–14, 16; Romans 4:13, 16–18, 22; Matthew 1:16, 18–21, 24

When Joseph awoke he did as the angel of the LORD had directed him.
(Mt 1:24)

Recently, I overheard a group of women talking about their husbands. One woman said, "My husband is quite a dreamer!" This exclamation reminded me of my own mother's telling me to "get my head out of the clouds." Both of these comments can take on a negative tone when compared with the practicality needed to be successful. The details of raising children, earning money, and building a relationship don't seem to have much to do with dreaming.

It is refreshing, then, to realize that God chose a "dreamer" to be the human father of Jesus and the husband of Mary. Not only did God choose a dreamer, God made a point of communicating important messages to Joseph through the dreaming process.

In today's gospel, Joseph is told about the first step of God's mysterious plan of salvation through a dream. Joseph believes that God truly speaks to him and acts on that belief. If we are to take Joseph as a model for ourselves, then we must say that God will speak to us and reveal God's plan for us in dreams and in other mysterious ways. The task of the Christian is to listen, believe, and then act.

This evening, before you sleep, quiet yourself and ask the Lord to reveal to you, like Joseph, what is the next step in God's providential plan for you. Hopefully in the morning we can pray with the psalmist, "By the LORD this has been done / it is wonderful in our eyes" (Ps 118:23).

Solemnity of the Annunciation of the Lord (March 25)
Isaiah 7:10–14; Hebrews 10:4–10; Luke 1:26–36

Do not fear, Mary. You have found favor with God.
You shall conceive and bear a son and give him the name Jesus.
(Lk 1:30–31)

All famous artists who have painted the Annunciation scene always show Mary alone, in quiet and prayer, being visited by an angel of God. Even though Mary's conception is an earth-changing event, it is portrayed with a delicacy and intimacy that is proper to the moment of conception. Over the centuries the Church has continued to depict Mary as a public figure with a very private intimacy. It is no wonder that people of all ages continue to flock to Mary, the Queen of the Universe, for their most personal needs.

The reading from Luke's Gospel also tells us something about God. God is very considerate toward us human beings. God will not save us without our consent. He will not become flesh without Mary's "yes." God wants to be expected, welcomed, and loved by a mother.

This ancient feast of the Annunciation was a festival in most cultures. The day included great singing, dancing, and partying. It was as if we also wanted to expect, welcome, and love God. Today we take this great sign of heaven meeting earth to be ours. Mary is the first to be evangelized by the gospel of Jesus, and we follow in her great tradition. We invite God into our wombs again this day. We welcome God, we love God. In this we become partners to Mary and can say with Mary, "Let it be done to me as you say" (Lk 1:38).

Glossary of Terms

absolution In the sacrament of penance, absolution is the form (words) prayed by an authorized priest for the forgiveness of sin. The actual words of absolution are, "God, the Father of mercies, through the death and resurrection of His Son, has reconciled the world to himself and sent the Holy Spirit among us for the forgiveness of sin. Through the ministry of the Church may God give your pardon and peace, and I absolve you from your sins in the name of the Father, and of the Son, and of the Holy Spirit."

abstinence In Catholic teaching, abstinence is a penitential practice of doing without (abstaining from) meat or another food or drink. According to the *Code of Canon Law*, "Abstinence from eating meat or another food according to the prescription of the conference of bishops is to be observed on Fridays throughout the year unless they are solemnities," and also on Ash Wednesday and Good Friday (Canon 1251).

actual grace A help of God which enlightens the mind and strengthens the will to do good and avoid evil. Grace is always understood as a free, unearned gift from God.

asceticism Christians under the action of the Spirit have adopted means of self-discipline in order to have greater union with God. True ascesis brings a growth in contemplation and love of God that fosters personal maturity and social responsibility. Asceticism can be exercised internally as discipline applied to the mind, heart, and will, or externally through fasting, bodily mortification, and austerity. Newer forms of asceticism include confrontation of addictions to alcohol, drugs, food, tobacco, television, work, and whatever else holds the heart captive.

ashes These symbols of penance and reconciliation are made by burning the palms blessed on the previous Passion Sunday. These ashes are blessed and then are used to mark the forehead of the people on Ash Wednesday.

Ash Wednesday   The first day of Lent. On this day, ashes from the burning of palms from the previous Passion Sunday are blessed and placed on the foreheads of the faithful as a sign of penance. When the ashes are given to the faithful by the minister a prayer such as, "Remember that you are dust and to dust you shall return," is often prayed.

In the early Church, public penance was performed by people wearing sackcloth, who were then sprinkled with ashes. As public penance gradually died out, about the eleventh century, the custom of receiving ashes on the forehead gradually came into practice.

atonement   The word means "at one." It is an act of reconciliation in which humanity is made one with God through the mediation of Jesus by his Incarnation, life, suffering, and death for the redemption of all.

attrition   Sorrow for sins because they are hateful in themselves or because the person is shamed or fears God's punishment is sometimes referred to as imperfect contrition or attrition. Imperfect contrition is sufficient for the reception of sacramental reconciliation.

baptism   The first of the seven sacraments, baptism is considered the gate to the sacraments and is necessary for salvation, in fact or at least in intention. It is the way by which men and women are reborn as the children of God and welcomed into the Church.

The sacrament is conferred by immersion or the pouring of water on the person to be baptized and the required words (form) is: "I baptize you in the name of the Father, and of the Son, and of the Holy Spirit. Amen."

catechumenate/catechumen   The period of instruction and involvement in the Catholic faith in preparation for the baptism of adults or the reception of baptized non-Catholic Christians into the Catholic Church. The basic elements of the catechumenate are explained in the Rite of Christian Initiation of Adults (RCIA).

Code of Canon Law   The official body of laws for Catholics of the Roman, or Latin, rite. The first code was promlugated in 1917. The present *Code* contains 1,752 codes (laws) and was promulgated in 1983. It contains laws that apply to all members of the church, others that define and govern the hierarchy of the church and members of religious communities and norms for all of the sacraments of the Church. Pope John Paul II, on the occasion of the publication of the *Code* in 1983, reminded all Christians that the code is not to be seen as a substitute for faith or grace but is rather to be viewed as a help and as a necessary discipline.

devotions   Any public or private prayer and/or worship that is not part of the Church's official public worship. Such devotions may include the Stations of the Cross, novenas, a visit to the Blessed Sacrament, and so on.

Easter   A movable feast, celebrated on a Sunday between March 22 and April 25, commemorating the Resurrection of Jesus Christ from the dead (Mk 16:1–7). It is considered the greatest of all Christian feasts and holds a central place in the liturgical year. The celebration of the resurrection continues for a period of fifty days, from Easter to the feast of Pentecost.

Easter duty   A popular term for the obligation that is described in the *Code of Canon Law*: "All the faithful, after they have been initiated into the Most Holy Eucharist, are bound by the obligation of receiving Communion at least once a year." It is understood that this precept must be fulfilled during the Easter season unless it is fulfilled at some other time during the year.

ejaculation   A brief prayer that can be said from memory. Examples are "My Lord and My God" and "Jesus, Son of the living God, have mercy on me, a sinner."

examination of conscience The act of reflecting on one's moral state and its conformance to the will of God; a preliminary to confession.

fasting A traditional form of penance, seen as a way of purifying the spirit or sacrificing some good to the Lord; it consists of one's free choice to limit the kind or quality of food or drink. The gospel emphasizes the motivation for fasting: namely that it be done not for vain display but rather as an expression of interior or religious attitudes (Mt 6:1–18).

Gethsemani A garden at the foot of the Mount of Olives where Jesus suffered the agony in the garden and where he was betrayed.

Good Friday The Friday in Holy Week that commemorates the Passion and death of Jesus Christ. It is the one day of the year on which Mass is not celebrated. The Good Friday liturgy consists of three parts: the reading of the Passion from the Gospel of John, the veneration of the cross, and a communion service. The Eucharist that is consumed on Good Friday was consecrated on Holy Thursday.

guilt A state or condition of mind and soul that follows upon a personal, free, deliberate transgression of God's law; awareness that one has done wrong give rise to what are often referred to as "guilt feelings," that is feelings of spiritual unrest or discomfort. Guilt feelings, in their turn, urge the sinful person to repent and to seek reconciliation, and thus once again to experience inner peace. In contrast to true guilt which follows upon actual sin, false or neurotic guilt seems to arise from a general lack of self-worth or a scrupulous conviction that one is almost always in sin.

heaven The dwelling place of God and the angels and the place of eternal happiness for all those who have been saved; it consists primarily in the face-to-face vision of God and the possession of eternal peace.

hell The dwelling place of Satan (devil) and the evil spirits of all those who die deliberately alienated from God. The primary punishment is the pain of loss; the deprivation of the face-to-face vision of God and eternal happiness and peace. There is also the pain of sense caused by an outside agent, described as fire in the New Testament (Mt 25:41 and Mk 9:43). Hell is the dire destination for one who freely chooses his or her own will against the will of God.

Holy Week   The week before Easter, it is called the "great week" of the Church's liturgical year. It begins with Passion (Palm) Sunday, celebrating Christ's entrance into Jerusalem and also includes Holy Thursday, Good Friday, and the Easter Vigil (Triduum).

INRI   An abbreviation that stands for the Latin words, "Jesus of Nazareth, King of the Jews," which was the phrase Pontius Pilate, the Roman Governor of Judea (Jerusalem), had ordered affixed to the Cross of Jesus.

Last Supper   The traditional name given to the Passover meal which Jesus ate with his apostles in Jerusalem on the night before he died (Mk 14:15, Lk 22:12). According to Catholic teaching, it was on this occasion that Jesus instituted the holy Eucharist and the priesthood. The Church celebrates the Lord's Supper on Holy Thursday evening.

Lent   The penitential season of the Church's year, beginning on Ash Wednesday and ending with the Mass of the Lord's Supper on Holy Thursday. The season of Lent has six Sundays, the sixth of which is called Passion (Palm) Sunday and marks the beginning of Holy Week. The time of Lent is considered penitential throughout the universal Church and is also considered a special time for the practice of prayer, the reception of the sacraments, charity, and almsgiving.

mortal sin   From the Latin word meaning "deadly" the term mortal sin is synonymous in Catholic teaching with "grave" or "serious." A mortal sin is a personal sin involving a fundamental choice against God in a serious way, a free and willing turning away from God's love and law in a grave matter. Traditional Catholic theology has emphasized three conditions for mortal sin: (1) that the matter be grave or

serious; (2) that there be sufficient reflection or advertence or awareness of the seriousness of the choice a person is making; (3) that there
be full consent of the will, that is that one freely chooses to do what
one knows to be seriously wrong even though one could stop from
doing it.

mortification   From the Latin word which means "death," the Christian ideal of dying to self through the deliberate restraint of passions
and appetites; the struggle against one's evil inclination so as to bring
them into conformity with the will of God. Spiritual writers often distinguish between external mortification (the discipline of the senses
by way of fasting, abstinence, control of the tongue) and internal mortification (control over errant passions, emotions, and feelings).

novena   A word signifying "nine" and referring to a public or private
devotion that extends for nine consecutive days or, in less common
usage, for nine consecutive weeks, with the devotion being held on a
particular day for those nine weeks. The Church approves of such devotional practices, provided that there is no superstition connected
with the number nine and that such externals are used as a help to
prayer.

palms, blessed   Palm or other branches blessed and distributed to the
faithful on Passion (Palm) Sunday, the sixth Sunday of Lent. The blessed
palms are carried in procession to commemorate the triumphant entrance of Jesus into Jerusalem (Mt 21:1–9) shortly before he died.

penance   Prayers, alms, good works, acts of denial, service to one's
neighbor, and so forth, that are performed in satisfaction for personal
sins or the sins of others.

Precepts of the Church   Obligations imposed on Catholics by the law
of the Church; traditionally six are listed: (1) to participate in Mass on
Sundays and holy days of obligation; (2) to fast and abstain on days
designated by the Church; (3) to confess one's sins once a year; (4) to

receive holy Communion during the Easter season; (5) to contribute to the support of the Church; (6) to observe the laws of Church governing marriage.

reconciliation   The act of reestablishing a damaged or destroyed relationship between two parties. Reconciling humankind to God was the primary work of Jesus Christ and is an essential part of the Good News (2 Cor 4:17–19). According to Catholic teaching, reconciliation with God after one has gravely sinned against him and reconciliation with the Church which is wounded by sin, are basic results of the sacrament of penance.

sacraments of initiation   Baptism, Confirmation, and Eucharist are considered to be the sacraments of initiation. When a person has received all three sacraments they are considered to be full participating members of the Church.

sanctifying grace   Created or sanctifying grace is a created sharing or participation in the life of God, given to human beings through the merits of Jesus Christ. Grace is always understood as a free, unearned gift from God.

Seven Last Words of Christ   Words spoken by Jesus on the Cross: (1) "Father, forgive them; for they know not what they do"; (2) to the repentant thief, "Truly I say to you, today you will be with me in paradise"; (3) to the Blessed Mother and the apostle John, "Women, behold your son...Behold your mother"; (4) "My God, my God, why have you forsaken me?"; (5) "I thirst"; (6) "It is finished"; (7) "Father, into your hands I commend my spirit."

Stations of the Cross   A popular devotion (also called Way of the Cross) in honor of the Passion and death of Christ; it consists of meditating on fourteen "stations" or "stages" in the Passion of Christ, such as his condemnation by Pilate, his scourging, his journey to Calvary, and the tomb. The stations are wooden crosses, often inserted in paintings or sculptures, and may be attached to the walls of a church or oratory or erected outdoors.

Ten Commandments   Commandments given by God to Moses on Mount Sinai as found in Exodus 20:1–21 and Deuteronomy 5:2–33 and interpreted by Jesus (Mt 5:17–48).

As given in the Book of Exodus, the Ten Commandments are as follows: (1) I am the Lord your God and you shall have no other gods before me; (2) You shall not take the name of the Lord your God in vain; (3) Remember to keep holy the sabbath; (4) Honor your father and your mother; (5) You shall not kill; (6) You shall not commit adultery; (7) You shall not steal; (8) You shall not bear false witness against your neighbor; (9) You shall not covet your neighbor's house; (10) You shall not cover your neighbor's wife.

Triduum   The Easter Triduum consists of Holy Thursday (commemorating the institution of the holy Eucharist and the priesthood), Good Friday (commemorating the Passion and death of Jesus Christ), and the Easter Vigil on Holy Saturday (commemorating the Resurrection of Jesus).

venial sin   In contrast to mortal sin, a venial sin may be described as a less serious rejection of God's love, not a fundamental choice against God, not a complete turning away from God. It is a failure to love God and others as much as we should, a transient neglect of God and God's law.

Vulgate   The Latin version of the Bible translated by Saint Jerome from the Greek and the Hebrew in the fourth century. This version of the Bible is the one commonly used in the Catholic Church and was declared authentic by the Council of Trent in 1546.

ways of the spiritual life   There are three stages of the spiritual journey of the Christian. Traditionally, the three phases were described as the purgative, the illuminative, and the unitive way. The purgative involved conversion from sin and disengagement from the senses or material things. The illuminative phase entailed a deepening of one's knowledge and love of God through contemplation. In the unitive phase, desire is overshadowed by the love of God and prayer consisting of loving attentiveness in which the person experiences an intense union with God.

These phases are not rigid, distinct, or successive and are governed by the uniqueness of the person and the ability to respond to God's grace. As persons mature in their spiritual journey they may be at different points in their prayer life and have distinctive needs. It is helpful for a spiritual director to be familiar with the process of prayer so that the directee might be properly companioned.

Wounds, the Five Sacred   During the Passion and the Crucifixion, Jesus incurred the four nail marks in his hands and feet and the wound in his side from the soldiers spear (Jn 19:34). Devotion to the Five Wounds has entailed explicit emphasis on Jesus' endurance of the pain of the Cross and on the symbolic implications of the blood and water pouring from his side.

Sources

Litany of Forgiveness, abridged from *From My Youth: Prayers As I Grow Old* by William Rabior, ACSW, Liguori, MO: Liguori Publications, 1994.

Prayer Before Confession, from *Making a Better Confession* by Con O'Connell, O.F.M., Liguori, MO: Liguori Publications, 1989.

Some traditional payers and devotions, from *The Raccolta*, Milwaukee, WI: Benziger Brothers, Inc, 1944.

Prayer of Openness to Healing and Transformation, from *Praying With a Passionate Heart* by Bridget Mary Meehan and Regina Madonna Oliver, Liguori, MO: Liguori Publications, 1999.

Traditional Examination of Conscience, from *The Mission Book of the Redemptorists*, compiled by V. Rev. F. Girardey, C.Ss.R., St. Louis, MO: Herder Book Company, 1947.

Canticle III: Joyful Paradox, from *God-Birthing* by Michael Dwinell, Liguori, MO: Liguori/Triumph, 1994.

Prayer to the Heart of Jesus, from *The Sacred Heart of Jesus: Yesterday, Today, and Forever* by Bernard Häring, C.Ss.R., Liguori, MO: Liguori Publications, 1999.

Daily Meditations for Lent, from *Lenten Daybreaks, Cycle A, B, and C* by Paul Coury, C.Ss.R., Liguori, MO: Liguori Publications, 1996, 1998.

Traditional Way of the Cross, from *Way of the Cross, Saint Alphonsus Liguori*, revised by Thomas M. Santa, C.Ss.R., Liguori, MO: Liguori Publications, 1994.

Lenten Family Graces, from *Lenten Family Graces* by Thomas M. Santa, C.Ss.R., Liguori, MO: Liguori Publications, 1998.

A Family-Centered Way of the Cross, from *Lenten Family Prayers* by Paul Coury, C.Ss.R., Liguori, MO: Liguori Publications, 1998.

Lenten Reconciliation Service, from *Lenten Reconciliation Service* by Daniel Korn, C.Ss.R., Liguori, MO: Liguori Publications, 1998.

Rule of Life, from *How to Live a Holy Life,* by Saint Alphonsus Liguori, revised by Thomas M. Santa, C.Ss.R., Liguori, MO: Liguori Publications, 1999.

Lenten Meditations, from *Meditations for Lent* by Saint Alphonsus Liguori, edited by Thomas M. Santa, C.Ss.R., Liguori, MO: Liguori Publications, 1999.

Visit to the Blessed Sacrament, from *Visits to the Blessed Sacrament* by Saint Alphonsus Liguori, Liguori, MO: Liguori Publications, 1994.

Steps of the Passion and Little Chaplet of the Five Wounds, from *The Passion and Death of Jesus Christ* by Saint Alphonsus Liguori, edited by Thomas M. Santa, C.Ss.R., from *The Ascetical Works*, volume V, edited by Rev. Eugene Grimm, 1927, The Redemptorist Fathers.

A Lenten Prayer, version used as the basis for the Lenten Prayer as it appears in this volume, is reprinted with permission of Claretian Publications, 205 West Monroe Street, Chicago, Illinois, 60606. Used with permission.

Psalms quoted are from *The Christian Community Bible*, Catholic Pastoral Edition, 1995, Claretian Publications and Liguori Publications.